Building ERP Solutions with Microsoft Dynamics NAV

Create real-world enterprise solutions with NAV, Cloud, and the Microsoft stack

Stefano Demiliani

BIRMINGHAM - MUMBAI

Building ERP Solutions with Microsoft Dynamics NAV

First published: March 2017

Production reference: 1170317

Published by Packt Publishing Ltd.
Livery Place
35 Livery Street
Birmingham
B3 2PB, UK.
ISBN 978-1-78712-308-3

www.packtpub.com

Credits

Author
Stefano Demiliani

Reviewer
Duilio Tacconi

Commissioning Editor
Aaron Lazar

Acquisition Editor
Rahul Nair

Content Development Editor
Rohit Kumar Singh

Technical Editors
Parag Topre
Vibhuti Gawde

Copy Editor
Safis Editing

Project Coordinator
Vaidehi Sawant

Proofreader
Safis Editing

Indexer
Mariammal Chettiyar

Graphics
Jason Monteiro

Production Coordinator
Shantanu Zagade

About the Author

Stefano Demiliani is a Microsoft Certified Solution Developer (MCSD), MCSA, MCAD, MCTS on Microsoft Dynamics NAV, MCTS on Sharepoint, MCTS on SQL Server, and an expert on other Microsoft-related technologies.

He has a master's degree in computer engineering from Politecnico of Turin. He works as a senior project manager and Solution Developer for EID (`http://www.eid.it`), a company that is part of the Navlab group (`http://www.navlab.it`), one of the biggest Microsoft Dynamics groups in Italy (where he's also the chief technical officer).

He has a lot of experience in Microsoft Dynamics NAV (from the first versions of the ERP). His main activity is architecting and developing enterprise solutions based on the entire stack of Microsoft technologies (Microsoft Dynamics NAV, Microsoft Sharepoint, Azure, Cloud apps, and .NET applications in general and OLAP and BI solutions for data analysis) and he's often focused on engineering distributed service-based applications.

He works as a full-time NAV consultant (with over 15 years of experience in handling international NAV projects) and is available for architecting solutions based on Microsoft's ERP as well as for NAV database tuning and optimization (performance and locking management) and for architecting cloud solutions and applications.

He's the author of various Microsoft Certified NAV add-ons (for example, the first cost accounting NAV add-on). He has written many articles and blogs on various Microsoft-related topics, and he's frequently involved in consulting and teaching. He has worked with Packt Publishing for many books on Microsoft Dynamics NAV.

You can find out more about Stefano and get in touch with him by visiting `http://www.demiliani.com` or via Twitter (`@demiliani`) or LinkedIn.

This book is the result of months of work and it's a dream that comes true. Thanks to all the wonderful staff that has worked with me in these months (Rohit, Aaron, Rahul, Duilio): your support was unbelievable.

I would like to dedicate this book to my little daughter Sara: I love you, maybe a day you will be proud of me also for this!

About the Reviewer

Duilio Tacconi is a senior Microsoft Dynamics NAV support engineer at Microsoft EMEA Customer Support and Services (CSS). He joined Microsoft in 2008 after working customer support with a focus primarily on the technical side of Microsoft Dynamics NAV. He was attracted to Microsoft Dynamics NAV starting from Microsoft Business Solution Navision 3.70 A and User Portal in 2004. Despite graduating with the highest score in Agricultural science, he is in the ERP circuit since 1998 as developer for several companies with Microsoft and non-Microsoft technologies. Currently, he is a subject matter expert in the EMEA region for RDLC reports and Microsoft EMEA CSS senior reference for Managed Service for Partner (NAV PAAS). Three times IronMan competition finisher, Duilio lives in Cernusco Sul Naviglio, Italy, with his beloved wife, Laura, and his new born son, Leonardo.

www.PacktPub.com

For support files and downloads related to your book, please visit `www.PacktPub.com`.

Did you know that Packt offers eBook versions of every book published, with PDF and ePub files available? You can upgrade to the eBook version at `www.PacktPub.com` and as a print book customer, you are entitled to a discount on the eBook copy. Get in touch with us at `service@packtpub.com` for more details.

At `www.PacktPub.com`, you can also read a collection of free technical articles, sign up for a range of free newsletters and receive exclusive discounts and offers on Packt books and eBooks.

`https://www.packtpub.com/mapt`

Get the most in-demand software skills with Mapt. Mapt gives you full access to all Packt books and video courses, as well as industry-leading tools to help you plan your personal development and advance your career.

Why subscribe?

- Fully searchable across every book published by Packt
- Copy and paste, print, and bookmark content
- On demand and accessible via a web browser

Customer Feedback

Thanks for purchasing this Packt book. At Packt, quality is at the heart of our editorial process. To help us improve, please leave us an honest review on this book's Amazon page at https://www.amazon.com/dp/1787123081.

If you'd like to join our team of regular reviewers, you can e-mail us at customerreviews@packtpub.com. We award our regular reviewers with free eBooks and videos in exchange for their valuable feedback. Help us be relentless in improving our products!

Table of Contents

Preface

I started my professional career in the IT world many years ago as a pure developer, and I've spent many years of my life developing custom applications from scratch with Microsoft technologies.

When more than 12 years ago I also started working in the ERP field (and, in particular, with Microsoft Dynamics NAV), I learned that when implementing an ERP solution, there are some business tasks that you can efficiently solve using the internal ERP programming language (C/AL for Microsoft Dynamics NAV), but there are also many tasks that require the usage of other technologies to be solved in a brilliant way.

During these years, I had the chance to be involved (directly or indirectly) in many different ERP projects in different functional areas, and I've always seen what I call a "bad habit": the standard ERP developer (or Microsoft Dynamics NAV developer in this case) tries to solve all development tasks using what he knows best: the C/AL programming language! He forgets that outside the ERP box, there's a world of technologies that permit you to have a final solution that rocks, and many times, I see solutions (especially when integrating Microsoft Dynamics NAV with other applications) that are solved using old technologies or in a bad way.

A typical example is integrating Microsoft Dynamics NAV with an external application: I see very often that the NAV developer proposes to create integrations via file exchange (CSV) too if the external application supports APIs based on web services, and only because he only knows C/AL.

The main goal of this book is to open the mind of the ERP developer and help him understand how to solve integration tasks in a modern (and efficient) way.

This is my mantra: *not all tasks must be solved using C/AL. Leave C/AL for the internal ERP business logic!*

In this book, we'll cover many business scenarios that you can find when implementing an ERP solution (all of them come from the real world), and we'll see how to solve them in a modern way using "service-oriented" solutions and cloud services.

What this book covers

Chapter 1, *Introducing Microsoft Dynamics NAV Architectures*, introduces you to Microsoft Dynamics NAV. This covers the history and the evolution of this ERP solution and helps you explore the different architectures that you can have when implementing a Microsoft Dynamics NAV ERP solution.

Chapter 2, *Configuring Microsoft Dynamics NAV Web Services*, introduces you to what Microsoft Dynamics NAV web services are and how you can publish the internal business logic to external applications using SOAP and OData web services.

Chapter 3, *Creating an Application Using NAV Web Services*, shows you how to implement an external application using .NET and Visual Studio, which interact with the Microsoft Dynamics NAV business logic using web services.

Chapter 4, *Using NAV Web Services with Power BI*, explains how you can expose the ERP data by using OData web services on the Power BI platform for data analysis and reporting.

Chapter 5, *Integrating NAV Web Services and External Applications*, shows how you can implement a real-world interface between Microsoft Dynamics NAV and an external application (a B2B web site). In this chapter, you will learn how you can publish the ERP business logic you need, how you can create an integration layer with open communication standards such as XML or JSON, and how you can expose a RESTful service to the external application that connects it with the ERP.

Chapter 6, *Extending NAV Pages with Control Add-ins*, demonstrates how you can extend the ERP user interface by using custom control add-ins.

Chapter 7, *Programming Universal Windows Apps with NAV and Devices*, shows you how you can create a RESTful integration service (by using ASP.NET Web API) that connects your Microsoft Dynamics NAV with custom application developed using the Universal Windows Platform. We'll see how you can implement a solution for device tracking and monitoring health data.

Chapter 8, *Exploring Microsoft Azure and its Services*, introduces you to the Microsoft Azure cloud platform and its services. You'll get an overview of the Azure platform and learn about the main Azure concepts. You will also get an overview of the main cloud services offered by Azure that could be helpful when implementing distributed architectures based on Microsoft Dynamics NAV.

Chapter 9, *Working with Azure App Service and NAV*, covers how you can take advantage of cloud services in order to implement a distributed and totally scalable architecture that integrates the Microsoft Dynamics NAV ERP to external systems.

Chapter 10, *Implementing a Message-Based Architecture with Azure Service Bus and NAV*, covers how you can use another interesting cloud service offered by the Azure platform (the Azure Service Bus) in order to implement a reliable message-based solution (order exchange from distributed locations) with Microsoft Dynamics NAV.

What you need for this book

To successfully follow the examples described in this book, you will need the following software:

- A Microsoft Dynamics NAV 2017 product DVD with a valid developer license to install the application on your own server
- Microsoft Visual Studio 2015 Professional or at least the free Microsoft Visual Studio Community Edition version
- An active Microsoft Azure subscription

Who this book is for

The audience of this book is essentially the following:

- NAV consultants and developers
- IT solution architects (mainly involved in implementing ERP solutions)
- Designers of business applications

This book assumes that you have a working knowledge of Microsoft Dynamics NAV (mainly in the developer field) and a basic knowledge of C#, Visual Studio, and web services.

Conventions

In this book, you will find a number of text styles that distinguish between different kinds of information. Here are some examples of these styles and an explanation of their meaning.

Code words in text, database table names, folder names, filenames, file extensions, pathnames, dummy URLs, user input, and Twitter handles are shown as follows: "This will be done by calling a method in a proper `Data Access Layer` class."

A block of code is set as follows:

```
public Dictionary<string,Boolean> GetItems()
{
    Dictionary<string, Boolean> dict = new Dictionary<string,
    Boolean>();
    LoadProductionOrders(ref dict);
    return dict;
}
```

Any command-line input or output is written as follows:

```
SN.exe -T <NameOfYourDLLAddinFile>
```

New terms and **important words** are shown in bold. Words that you see on the screen, for example, in menus or dialog boxes, appear in the text like this: "Right-click on the solution and navigate to **Add** | **Class....**"

 Warnings or important notes appear in a box like this.

 Tips and tricks appear like this.

Reader feedback

Feedback from our readers is always welcome. Let us know what you think about this book-what you liked or disliked. Reader feedback is important for us as it helps us develop titles that you will really get the most out of. To send us general feedback, simply e-mail feedback@packtpub.com, and mention the book's title in the subject of your message. If there is a topic that you have expertise in and you are interested in either writing or contributing to a book, see our author guide at www.packtpub.com/authors.

Customer support

Now that you are the proud owner of a Packt book, we have a number of things to help you to get the most from your purchase.

Downloading the example code

You can download the example code files for this book from your account at `http://www.p acktpub.com`. If you purchased this book elsewhere, you can visit `http://www.packtpub.c om/support` and register to have the files e-mailed directly to you.

You can download the code files by following these steps:

1. Log in or register to our website using your e-mail address and password.
2. Hover the mouse pointer on the **SUPPORT** tab at the top.
3. Click on **Code Downloads & Errata**.
4. Enter the name of the book in the **Search** box.
5. Select the book for which you're looking to download the code files.
6. Choose from the drop-down menu where you purchased this book from.
7. Click on **Code Download**.

Once the file is downloaded, please make sure that you unzip or extract the folder using the latest version of:

- WinRAR / 7-Zip for Windows
- Zipeg / iZip / UnRarX for Mac
- 7-Zip / PeaZip for Linux

The code bundle for the book is also hosted on GitHub at `https://github.com/PacktPubl ishing/Building-ERP-Solutions-with-Microsoft-Dynamics-NAV`. We also have other code bundles from our rich catalog of books and videos available at `https://github.com/P acktPublishing/`. Check them out!

Downloading the color images of this book

We also provide you with a PDF file that has color images of the screenshots/diagrams used in this book. The color images will help you better understand the changes in the output. You can download this file from `http://www.packtpub.com/sites/default/files/downl oads/BuildingERPSolutionswithMicrosoftDynamicsNAV_ColorImages.pdf`.

Errata

Although we have taken every care to ensure the accuracy of our content, mistakes do happen. If you find a mistake in one of our books-maybe a mistake in the text or the code-we would be grateful if you could report this to us. By doing so, you can save other readers from frustration and help us improve subsequent versions of this book. If you find any errata, please report them by visiting http://www.packtpub.com/submit-errata, selecting your book, clicking on the **Errata Submission Form** link, and entering the details of your errata. Once your errata are verified, your submission will be accepted and the errata will be uploaded to our website or added to any list of existing errata under the Errata section of that title.

To view the previously submitted errata, go to https://www.packtpub.com/books/content/support and enter the name of the book in the search field. The required information will appear under the **Errata** section.

Piracy

Piracy of copyrighted material on the Internet is an ongoing problem across all media. At Packt, we take the protection of our copyright and licenses very seriously. If you come across any illegal copies of our works in any form on the Internet, please provide us with the location address or website name immediately so that we can pursue a remedy.

Please contact us at copyright@packtpub.com with a link to the suspected pirated material.

We appreciate your help in protecting our authors and our ability to bring you valuable content.

Questions

If you have a problem with any aspect of this book, you can contact us at questions@packtpub.com, and we will do our best to address the problem.

1
Introduction to Microsoft Dynamics NAV Architectures

Microsoft Dynamics NAV is an **Enterprise resource planning** (ERP) software and it is part of the Microsoft Dynamics product's family.

In this chapter, we will cover the following topics:

- Microsoft Dynamics NAV and its functional areas
- History of Microsoft Dynamics NAV
- An overview of Microsoft Dynamics NAV architectures and components
- NAV deployment's solutions and the differences between them

Introducing Microsoft Dynamics NAV

Microsoft Dynamics NAV delivers integrated functionality to provide support for the following aspects:

- Financial management
- Supply chain management
- Manufacturing
- Distribution
- Customer relationship management
- Sales and marketing
- Service management
- Human resource management

- Project and resource management
- Warehouse management

Microsoft Dynamics NAV is considered to be one of the most versatile and agile ERPs on the market. It's very quick and affordable to customize and it has the power to be able to grow with your business needs.

With NAV you can customize every aspect of the application (from fields to business logic) and you can build new modules from scratch. You have complete access to the source code of the application and you have an integrated environment that helps you to make customizations and implementations.

Microsoft Dynamics NAV history

Microsoft Dynamics NAV was born from **Navision**, a suite of accounting applications which Microsoft acquired in 2002.

Navision was created at **Personal Computing and Consulting (PC&C A/S)**, a company founded in Denmark in 1983 by three college students. This company released its first accounting package, **PC Plus**, in 1984 (a single-user character-based application) and then in 1987 they released the first version of Navision, a character-based client/server accounting application that works over a LAN and with more simultaneous users:

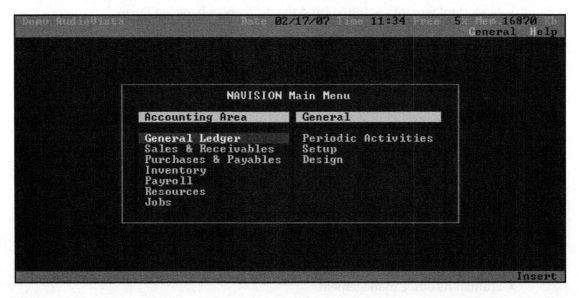

In 1990, Navision 3.0 was launched. This version introduced AL, an internal application language similar to the actual **Client/server Application Language (C/AL)**. This was a killer feature: the new application language made it possible to customize every part of the application and this was unique on the market at that time.

The product grew and in 1995 Navision Financials 1.0 was launched based on the Microsoft Windows 32-bit client/server platform:

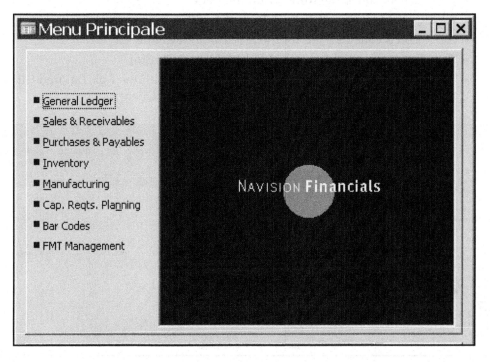

The product was improved in the following years by adding more features as follows:

- Integration of e-commerce applications such as Commerce Gateway, Commerce Portal
- User portal, browser-based access
- Supply chain collaboration functionality including manufacturing and distribution
- Extended financial management functionality
- Extended and new functionality within customer relationship management
- Multicurrency
- Multilanguage

On July 11, 2002, Navision was acquired by Microsoft and Microsoft created the *Microsoft Business Solutions* division. In September, 2005 Microsoft re-branded the product as *Microsoft Dynamics NAV*.

In November 2008, Microsoft announced **Microsoft Dynamics NAV 2009**, with a totally new architecture, as follows:

- A new client called the **RoleTailored Client**
- An old client (renamed as the **Classic Client**)
- New objects called `Pages` for the RoleTailored Client
- A new report architecture (**RDLC with Visual Studio**)
- The possibility to have a three-tier architecture (with the RoleTailored Client) and the old client/server architecture (with the Classic Client):

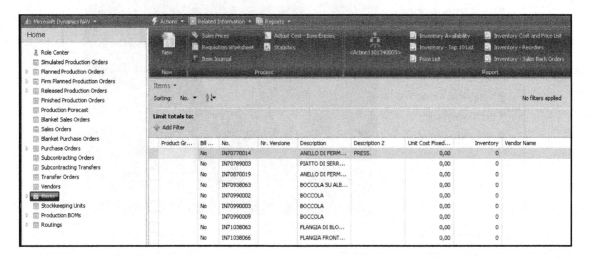

Microsoft Dynamics NAV has had continuous improvements over the years on every aspect of its technical and functional side.

Microsoft Dynamics NAV 2013 introduced the following new features:

- A totally new Web client with rich experience
- A **SharePoint** client
- Internal encoding is now **Unicode** (no longer **ASCII**)

The next main release, **Microsoft Dynamics NAV 2013 R2**, introduced the following new features:

- **Multitenancy (optional)**: The multitenancy architecture in NAV 2013 R2 consists of a single application database (containing tables common to all databases and objects) and multiple data databases (customer data and login tables). One NAV service tier can serve one application database and multiple tenant databases (and can also sit on different SQL server instances).
- **Provisioning tools**: These tools are used for fully automating the deployment of NAV in Azure virtual machines (as IaaS). The provisioning tools include a set of Windows PowerShell cmdlets and scripts that install and configure Microsoft Dynamics NAV components, including Microsoft Dynamics NAV web server components, Microsoft Dynamics NAV Server, and SQL database components.

With **Microsoft Dynamics NAV 2015**, we saw the introduction of the following topics:

- **RapidStart Services**: This is a set of tools and services to automate and speed up the setup and initialization phase of a NAV installation
- **New Tablet client**: This is a new client for touch-optimized devices that enables you to access your NAV data regardless of location or what device you are using
- **Web client:** The Web client is much improved and faster
- **Office 365 integration**: This is simplified e-mail messaging via SMTP including Office 365, signing in to the Windows client using an Office 365 account
- **Document reporting with Microsoft Word:** With this release, Microsoft has introduced the possibility to make document reporting by using Word with NAV

With the next release, **Microsoft Dynamics NAV 2016**, Microsoft introduced the following services:

- **NAV Universal App**: By using the Universal Windows Platform, now we have one single app for all devices (it works as a tablet application or as a phone application according to the device you're using).
- **Eventing**: Now we have events triggered on code like standard object oriented programming. A publisher raises an event when something happens and a subscriber can listen to this triggered event and make actions.

- **Code editor**: We have a new code editor with code completion and IntelliSense.
- **Workflows**: Based on eventing, you are now able to create your own business workflows with conditions and responses.
- **Microsoft Dynamics NAV support in Power BI**: When you enter your Power BI account, now you have a new service called **Microsoft Dynamics NAV** that permits you to integrate your data to **Power BI**.
- **Integration with CRM**: Integration with CRM is now native (coded in C/AL), so no more need to use the old CRM **External Connector** for handling integration tasks.
- **Microsoft Dynamics NAV managed service for partners**: A significant new option for Microsoft partners interested in providing multitenant **Software as a Service (SaaS)** solutions built on Microsoft Dynamics NAV and deployed in the cloud on Microsoft Azure.

The latest release (**Microsoft Dynamics NAV 2017**) introduced the following new features:

- Assisted setup
- Smart notifications
- Cash flow forecast with Cortana Intelligence
- Design mode in the Web client
- Improved integration with Office 365 and a new Outlook add-in
- Embedded Power BI reports in the NAV RoleTailored Client
- Improved extensions (new ways to develope customizations)
- Dynamics 365 for Financials (NAV as SaaS)

Now we have a complete and full-featured enterprise platform that is appreciated all over the world, able to work on-premise and on-cloud, and on many devices as shown in the following screenshot:

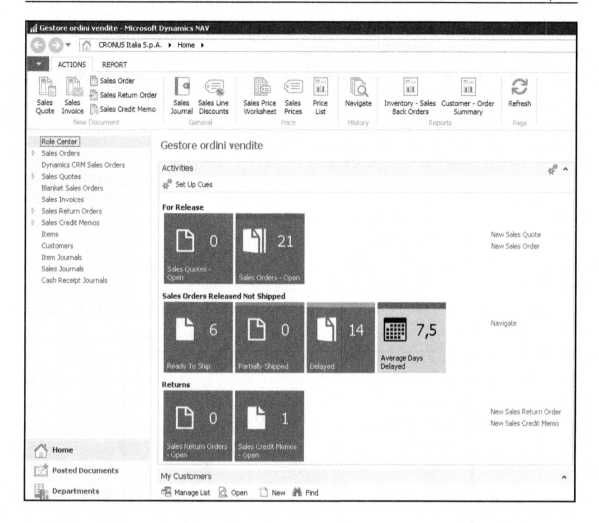

Microsoft Dynamics NAV architecture

Before version 2009, Microsoft Dynamics NAV had a two-tier architecture.

In two-tier architectures (client/server data model), the data layers reside on the server and the application logic, presentation logic, and presentation layers reside on the client.

Starting from version 2009, Microsoft Dynamics NAV is composed of three major components (three-tier architecture), as follows:

- **Data tier**: A database (database server) where the data are stored. Actually Microsoft Dynamics NAV supports only Microsoft SQL Server as the database server.
- **Middle or service tier**: This is an application server. A NAV service that controls all the NAV business logic and operations.
- **Client tier**: This represents NAV clients and is the layer that handles the real user interface for the application (presentation logic). NAV can have different types of client as follows:
  - Windows client
  - Web client
  - Tablet client
  - Phone client

In a production environment, you can obviously have multiple instances of each of the core NAV components:

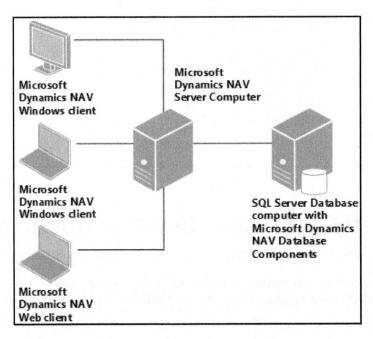

The most common NAV architecture configurations that you can have in a real-world installation are as follows:

- All three tiers are on the same computer, useful only for a demo or a developer dedicated environment.
- The RoleTailored client and Microsoft Dynamics NAV Server are on the same computer, the data tier is on a separate computer.
- The data tier and Microsoft Dynamics NAV Server are on the same computer. The RoleTailored client is on a separate computer (one of the most common scenarios).
- Each of the three tiers is on a separate computer. This is the suggested configuration for a production environment.

In addition to these three core components, there are other additional components that you can have on a NAV installation:

Component	Purpose
Microsoft Dynamics NAV Help Server	A website with the Help content for Microsoft Dynamics NAV in the languages that your version of Microsoft Dynamics NAV includes. You can deploy a single Help Server for all users, or customer-specific Help Servers, depending on your requirements.
Web Server Components	The components that are needed to enable Microsoft Dynamics NAV Web clients to connect with a browser.
Microsoft Dynamics NAV Server Administration Tool	A tool for configuring and managing the Microsoft Dynamics NAV Server and Microsoft Dynamics NAV sites. It has a GUI that permits an easy way to manage all the server's features.
Development Environment (C/SIDE)	The Development Environment for creating and modifying Microsoft Dynamics NAV applications (business logic) in C/AL.
Microsoft Office Outlook Add-In and Business Inbox	A set of components for synchronizing data, such as to-dos, contacts, and tasks, between Microsoft Dynamics NAV and Outlook and using Dynamics NAV as your business **Inbox** in Outlook.
Automated Data Capture System	A Microsoft Dynamics NAV tool for accurately capturing data for inbound, outbound, and internal documents, primarily in connection with warehouse activities. With **Automated Data Capture System** (**ADCS**), company employees use handheld devices and radio frequency technology to continuously validate warehouse inventories.

ClickOnce Installer Tools	A set of tools designed to create ClickOnce deployments for applications for the Microsoft Dynamics NAV Windows client.

When using the NAV Web client, all NAV web server components are installed as a website on the **Internet Information Server (IIS)**, so you need to install and properly configure it:

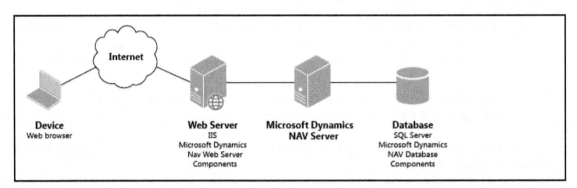

You can deploy the web server components on one computer or on separate computers (for example, Microsoft Dynamics NAV web server components installed on a server and Microsoft Dynamics NAV Server and SQL Server installed on another server). When you install Microsoft Dynamics NAV web server components, the setup adds a web server instance (virtual directory and application) on IIS for the Microsoft Dynamics NAV Web client.

Microsoft Dynamics NAV supports four methods for authenticating users who access the Microsoft Dynamics NAV Web client: `Windows`, `UserName`, `NavUserPassword`, and `AccessControlService`. Windows authentication is configured by default.

When installing the Microsoft Dynamics NAV web server components (or after installation), you can also enable **Secure Sockets Layer (SSL)** on the connection to the Microsoft Dynamics NAV Web client to increase security.

The following table describes the required components when using the Web client:

Tier	Description
Device	A computer or device that has access to the Internet with a browser.
Web Server	A computer that is running IIS. Microsoft Dynamics NAV web server components are installed on a website on IIS.
Microsoft Dynamics NAV Server (Service Tier)	A Microsoft .NET Framework-based Windows service that manages communications and provides a security layer between clients and Microsoft Dynamics NAV databases in SQL Server.

When activated, the NAV Web client appears as shown in the following screenshot:

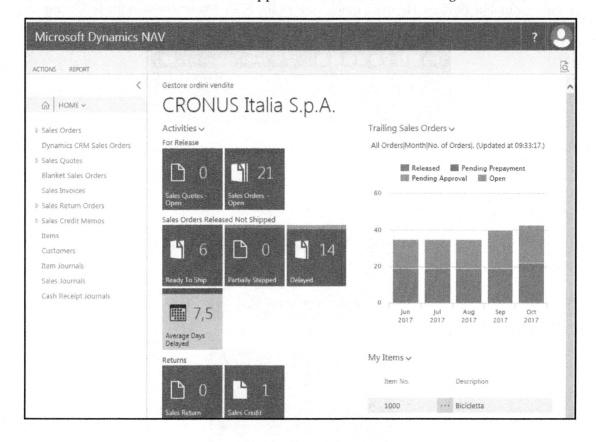

As previously described, starting from Microsoft Dynamics NAV 2016, we have also native clients for mobile devices. Here is a quick view of the NAV Phone client in the following screenshot:

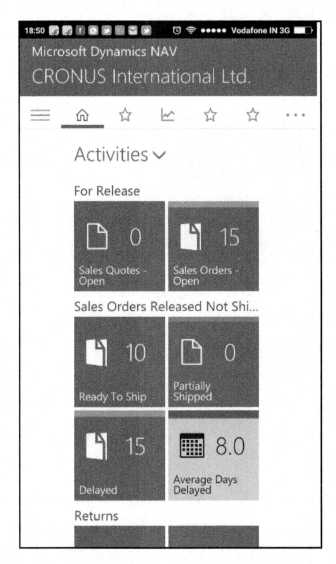

You can now download a native Microsoft Dynamics NAV application from the store of your mobile platform (iOS, Android, Windows):

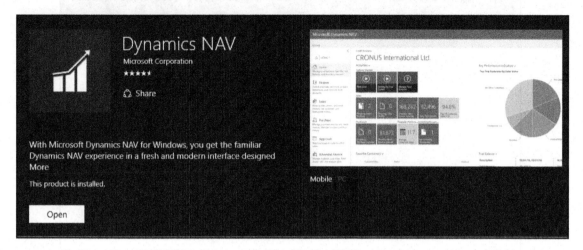

After downloading the app from the store, you can start using Microsoft Dynamics NAV from your mobile device. You can also work with your NAV data directly from Outlook:

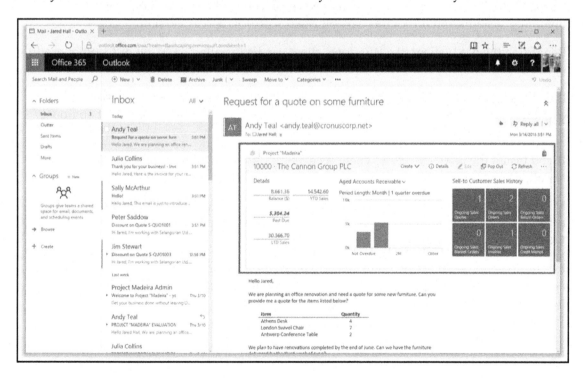

In Outlook, you can now also create new **NAV** documents:

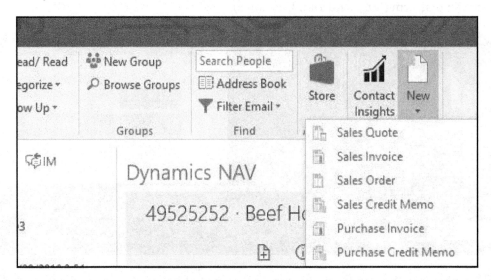

The new three-tier architecture is multithreaded and it can handle more than one process at a time. Actually, the Microsoft Dynamics NAV server can be installed only on 64-bit operating systems and it requires a 64-bit Microsoft SQL Server version.

Regarding the NAV client, the Windows client can be installed on 32-bit or 64-bit operating systems.

If you install the NAV Windows client on a 64-bit OS, you will have two version of the client installed (32-bit and 64-bit). The default is the 64-bit Windows client, but obviously you can change it.

If you install the NAV Windows client on a 32-bit OS, you will have only the 32-bit client installed.

Microsoft Dynamics NAV also supports deployments where several different companies access a centrally maintained Microsoft Dynamics NAV application. This is called a **multitenant architecture**.

In a multitenant architecture, information about the Microsoft Dynamics NAV application is stored in a separate application database while data is stored in separate business databases, each of which is a tenant in your deployment.

By separating the application from the data, you can deploy the same solution to many customers with centralized maintenance of the application and isolation of each tenant.

The application database contains the tables that define an application and other NAV system tables.

Microsoft Dynamics NAV now includes Windows PowerShell cmdlets that create an application database, and other cmdlets that enable you to create and administer tenant-specific databases. You can find a complete overview of every cmdlets at `https://msdn.microsoft.com/en-us/library/jj672916(v=nav.90).aspx`.

The `Export-NAVApplication` cmdlet is the one used to extract application tables in a Microsoft Dynamics NAV database to a separate database. The new application database is created on the same SQL Server instance as the original database.

The following table describes which system tables are moved to the application database when you run this cmdlet and which tables remain in the business data database:

Application database	Business data database
Chart	Access Control
Client Add-in	Active Session
Client Add-in Resources	Company
Debugger Breakpoint	Device
Debugger Watch	Document Service
Object	Integration Page
Object Metadata	Object Metadata Snapshot
Object Tracking	Object Translation
Permission	Page Data Personalization
Permission Set	Printer Selection
Profile	Record Link
Profile Metadata	Report List Translation
Send-To Program	Session Event
Server Instance	User
Style Sheet	User Default Style Sheet

Web Service	User Metadata
	User Personalization
	User Property

 For more information and details about NAV installation, you can check the *Installation and Configuration Walkthroughs* section at `https://msdn.microsoft.com/en-us/library/dd301193(v=nav.90).aspx`.

Microsoft Dynamics NAV deployments

A NAV deployment can essentially be as follows:

- On-premise
- On-cloud (IaaS or PaaS)
- SaaS

With an **on-premise** deployment, Microsoft Dynamics ERP software is hosted at your own location on your own servers.

This type of architecture guarantees predictable performance (not subject to Internet connection related fluctuations in performance or availability), you can use the hardware and software infrastructure you already own, you can easily connect NAV with external systems that you can have inside your company, and obviously you have to guarantee data security (backup and so on) by yourself.

With **on-cloud** deployment, you can choose to deploy your NAV installation on the cloud by choosing from an **Infrastructure as a Service** (**IaaS**) architecture or a PaaS architecture. The Windows Azure platform permits you to have a complete NAV environment (virtual machine) totally scalable. Security is guaranteed by the Azure platform (redundancy, scalability, and so on).

Azure is the fastest and recommended way to implement a totally on-cloud NAV deployment.

The on-cloud deployment permits you to minimize your initial IT investments (no hardware costs, no IT staff for maintenance) and it supports your business as it grows (costs can scale with the actual use and needs of your solutions).

In an on-cloud deployment, you can choose to have the Microsoft SQL Server installed on a dedicated instance on an Azure virtual machine or you can use the Azure SQL database, a cloud service that permits you to have the SQL Server as a service, with reduced costs and no investments in database management tasks. With Azure SQL, you could also have a **mixed deployment**, where only the database tier is on the cloud.

There's also a very new option available on the market now: **Microsoft Dynamics 365 for Financials** (also known as **Project Madeira**).

Microsoft Dynamics 365 is a **Software as a Service (SaaS)** business proposition by Microsoft that aims to bring together the best of their CRM and ERP cloud offerings into one cloud service with specific, purpose built apps for each of your key business processes.

Microsoft Dynamics 365 for Financials is available on a simplified subscription model similar to the actual Office 365 offering and it guarantees a rapid ERP implementation (nothing to install or configure for the startup, no IT staff needed) and a familiar usage and user interface. You can work with Dynamics 365 from within Office 365 (no separate login to connect to the ERP) and you can do all your business from your familiar applications, for example, without having to leave Outlook (Dynamics 365 recognizes content such as invoice numbers inside an Outlook message and it suggests to you all the tools you need to process the document and complete your business process).

The interesting feature of this new SaaS ERP platform is that Dynamics 365 shares a **Common Data Model (CDM)** with Office 365. According to Microsoft's definition: *it is a database of entities that are common across industry domains.*

This new CMD provides all the standard business entities and it allows you to extend them and create new entities that suit your business. The CDM uses Azure technologies such as **Service Fabric** and **Elastic SQL** and it guarantees security, scalability, and consistency across applications.

The following screenshot shows an overview of the Dynamics 365 platform's architecture:

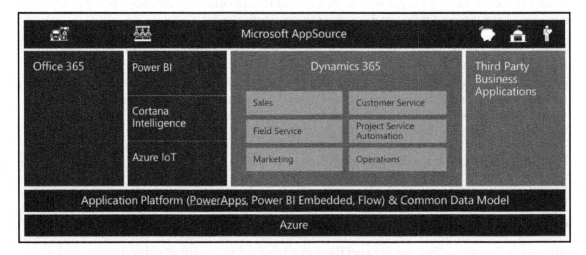

Dynamics 365 is available in the following two editions:

- **Business** (a cloud-based solution based on NAV core)
- **Enterprise** (AX and CRM core)

Dynamics 365 is licensed by the following three features:

- **License by App**: It will be licensed by **app** (you can activate a specific functionality you need).
- **License by Role (or by Plan)**: It will be licensed based on the role of your employees. Licensing by Role/Plan is a package of apps for companies that need to access multiple functions (for example when an employee works on **Operations** and **Finance** at the same time)
- **License for team members**: It will be licensed by **team members** (something like a light user):

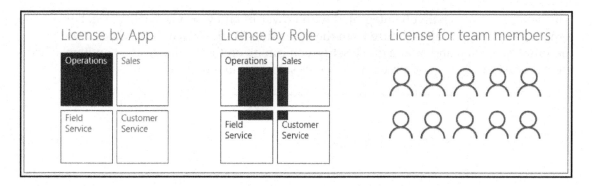

A big new feature of Dynamics 365 will be the **app** concept. Users will be able to go to Microsoft's dedicated marketplace called **AppSource** and download a range of applications to suit their specific needs. You can reach the **AppSource** website at `https://appsource.mi crosoft.com`:

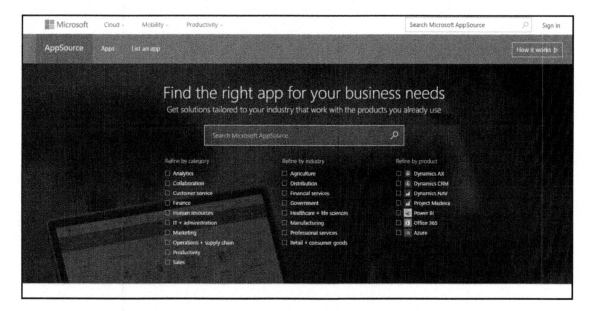

The new **apps** are built as extensions to the ERP core and they can be easily and independently deployed (you can pay for what you really need and use).

The new platform is natively integrated with Power BI and Cortana Intelligence. For example, you can install a feature from the **Extension MarketPlace** called **Sales and Inventory Forecast** and after a quick setup you can go on the item list, select an item, click the **Forecast** FactBox, and immediately see its sales and inventory forecast:

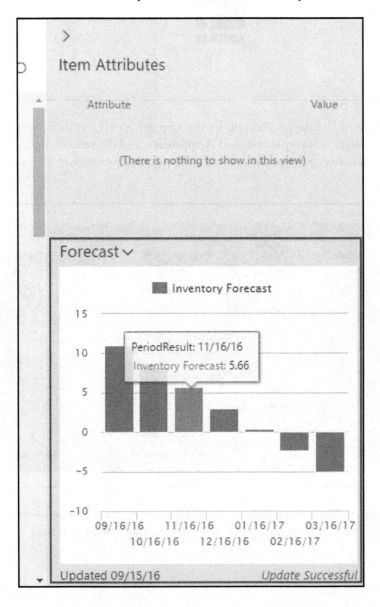

The connection with **Cortana Intelligence** is given natively by the platform (no configuration needed), as shown in the following screenshot:

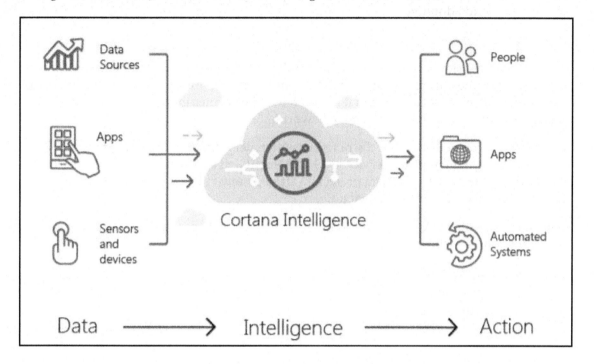

Dynamics 365 is an ongoing project, and more and more features will be added in the coming months and years.

Differences between NAV deployments

Choosing the best NAV installation architecture is not always an easy task.

The first question that an IT staff has to decide is: should I go on-premise or should I want to embrace the cloud?

Normally, the ERP is a core software component for a company and this decision can affect your business a lot.

Statistically, about 49% of IT decision makers said that they are worried about the security implications of cloud services. Data protection, privacy, and availability are the main obstacles to cloud adoption.

But is this true?

When a company stores all its core data internally, it has more or less complete control over who can access the data and data availability. An IT decision maker normally considers the company's data more secured when it is stored in a data center that he/she can completely manage and protect from the devil outside world.

This could be true in theory, but the practice is often very different. Actually, there's no company that can guarantee a service level agreement and a security policy like the cloud. Obviously, a safe backup and data protection strategy must always be guaranteed, no matter if you go on-premise or on-cloud.

There are many other aspects to consider when choosing between on-premise or cloud-based solutions, as follows:

- Infrastructure costs
- Performance
- Growth of solutions
- Upgrades

Infrastructure costs

On-premise architectures require an initial investment in order to buy the required hardware and software and to have experienced IT staff to manage the system. Once the system is fully functional, you will also require costs and time for periodically maintaining and upgrading the entire hardware and software solutions.

In a cloud-based architecture, normally you have a much lower initial cost (pay-as-you-go) and you don't have to take care of hardware maintenance. The cloud platform gives you these services.

Performance

The main obstacle in this field is certainly the latency of Internet connection. When you're on-premise, everything is on your LAN and performance is managed by the internals.

On a cloud-based solution, Internet connection and bandwidth are a requirement that can affect your business a lot. If the Internet connection is missing, your business could be blocked. If the bandwidth is poor and network latency is high (too much delay in data communication over the network), your working experience could be a pain. You need stable and high speed Internet connectivity to go on-cloud.

Growth of solutions

When you start a project, normally you analyze all the requirements and at the final stage you arrive at a final hardware size structure that satisfies your needs and maybe your predictable growth:

- In an **on-premise solution**, you have your hardware infrastructure that satisfies your actual needs. If one day you have to increase the growth of your architecture, you have to review your hardware and invest money for on infrastructure upgrades.
- In a **cloud-based solution**, if your business has big growth or during peak periods, you can easily expand your solutions by increasing the calculation performance or expand your infrastructure in new regions, all in an easy, quick, and transparent way (scaling).

Upgrades

With an **on-premise architecture**, you have complete control over your infrastructure's upgrades (hardware and software) and you can decide what type of upgrade to apply and when to apply it.

In an **on-cloud architecture**, you could have some aspects of the infrastructure where upgrades are not completely under your control but they can be deployed globally from the solution provider.

Here's a comparison between the different types of Microsoft Dynamics NAV installation previously discussed (pros and cons):

On-premise	On-cloud with Azure VM	On-cloud with Azure SQL	SaaS (Dynamics 365)
Physical hardware is required.	No hardware is required.	No hardware is required.	No hardware is required.
IT staff (internal or partners) is required for infrastructure maintenance and SLA.	Infrastructure SLA comes from the Azure platform. IT tasks are reduced.	Infrastructure **service level agreements (SLAs)** come from the Azure platform. IT tasks are reduced.	No IT staff is required
Software installation is required (server + NAV + clients).	Server installation is deployed via the Azure portal.	Server installation is deployed via the Azure portal.	No installation is required.
Predictable performances, but is difficult to scale.	It is easy to scale as needed.	It is easy to scale as needed.	There is no control on scaling.
It is not dependent on Internet connection.	It is dependent on Internet connection.	It is dependent on Internet connection.	It is dependent on Internet connection.
It involves high startup costs.	It invovles medium startup costs.	It involves medium startup costs.	It involves low startup costs.
There are no costs per usage.	There are costs per usage (Azure VM).	There are costs per usage, based on database throughput units (DTUs) consumed.	There are costs per usage.
SQL Server license is required.	SQL Server license is required.	No SQL Server license is required (Azure SQL has different pricing).	No SQL Server license is required.
Maximum DB size is based on SQL Server license.	Maximum DB size is 16 terabytes (due to Azure VM disk restrictions).	Maximum DB size is actually 1 terabyte (via the P11 offering).	

Actually, we have also a new value proposition by Microsoft: **Microsoft Dynamics NAV Managed Services for Partners**. With this PAAS proposition, Microsoft hosts your NAV database to the cloud and you build and sell your NAV solution to your customers.

This proposition could be interesting if your business model is repeatable, volume-oriented, and with a low cost of sale. The solution must be multitenant.

As a final consideration, we can say that nowadays a cloud-based solution has more benefits than risks. The only real limit to this choice is availability: if your cloud service shuts down or your Internet connection is down, your business could be at a huge risk.

If you decide to embrace the cloud for the deployment of a Microsoft Dynamics NAV architecture, you have to carefully check your Internet connectivity and bandwidth and you have to carefully choose your cloud provider. It has to guarantee a big uptime (SLA) over time.

 For the Microsoft Azure SLA, you can check out
`https://azure.microsoft.com/en-us/support/legal/sla/`.

Performance and installation tips

For a successful NAV implementation, performance is an important aspect to consider and to carefully monitor.

The following are the main NAV points to check in order to have better performance:

- Data tier (SQL Server Database)
- Service tier
- C/AL code

Data tier (SQL Server Database)

Microsoft Dynamics NAV relies on Microsoft SQL Server as its database, so recommendations on optimizing SQL Server performance for NAV are much the same as other types of data-intensive applications:

1. Split the database into more data files and locate them on different disks.
2. Every time a record is added, modified, or deleted from any table in the database, SQL Server updates all the indexes that are related to those tables. Check the indexes and re-build them periodically by using *SQL Server Maintenance Plans*. By rebuilding the indexes, you avoid fragmentation.
3. Rebuild the indexes and recalculate the statistics (this is automatically done when you rebuild an index).
4. Check your database *Recovery Model* and periodically shrink your transaction log.

SQL Server indexes are created on a column level in tables and views and they provide a quick way to retrieve data based on the values within the indexed columns. After frequent database operations (`insert`, `update`, `delete`) indexes can have pages where logical ordering (based on the key value) differs from the physical ordering inside the data file. This means that there is a high percentage of free space on index pages, and that SQL Server has to read higher number of pages when scanning each index. As a result, performances will suffer.

You can use this script to manually rebuild indexes on your NAV database:

```
DECLARE @TableName varchar(255)

DECLARE TableCursor CURSOR FOR
SELECT table_name FROM information_schema.tables
WHERE table_type = 'base table'

OPEN TableCursor

FETCH NEXT FROM TableCursor INTO @TableName
WHILE @@FETCH_STATUS = 0
BEGIN
DBCC DBREINDEX(@TableName,' ',90)
FETCH NEXT FROM TableCursor INTO @TableName
END

CLOSE TableCursor

DEALLOCATE TableCursor
```

For more information, check the MSDN site at
`https://msdn.microsoft.com/en-us/library/hh169233(v=nav.90).aspx`
.

Service tier

Here is a summary of the most important things to check.

Number of Microsoft Dynamics NAV service tiers

If you have many users, you have to consider creating more than one NAV service tier and *balance* the user's connection between the different services. In my experience, the number of users for the service tier without impacting on performance is about 40. If the number of your users is more than 40, you should start thinking about using more than one service tier.

Server memory

Each Microsoft Dynamics NAV service tier needs about 500 MB of memory to run and a certain amount of memory for every active session (even if idle). The standard amount of memory to count is about 10 MB per session, but obviously the more pages a user opens, the more memory usage increases.

Server CPU – cores and speed

This could be obvious, but if you have a fast CPU you will have better performance. The more cores you have, the more things in parallel you can do (the NAV service tier is 64-bit and multicore enabled). Idle sessions on the Microsoft Dynamics NAV service tier don't use any CPU power.

Data cache size

This is a Microsoft Dynamics NAV server setting, which is located in the `CustomSettings.config` file:

```
<add key="DataCacheSize" value="9" />
```

The number specified in the `DataCacheSize` setting determines how much memory is used for caching the data:

Value	Memory
9 (default)	512 MB
10	1 GB
11	2 GB
12	4 GB
13	8 GB
14	16 GB
15	32 GB

When running a single tenant system (classic installation) the default value of 9 is probably good but on a multitenant installation (where the cache is shared between tenants) this value could be increased.

Metadata provider cache size

This is a Microsoft Dynamics NAV server setting, which is located in the `CustomSettings.config` file. It sets the **metadata provider** cache size (the number of objects cached). A value of 0 means the cache is disabled:

```
<add key="MetadataProviderCacheSize" value="150" />
```

In the three-tier environment, objects are cached in the service tier. The value of 150 is default one but in my experience this value is too low. You can try to up this parameter and monitor memory load on the server.

Maximum concurrent calls

This is a Microsoft Dynamics NAV server setting, located in the `CustomSettings.config` file, and it's the maximum number of concurrent client calls that can be active on the Microsoft Dynamics NAV server.

To disable this setting, set the value to `MaxValue`:

```
<add key="MaxConcurrentCalls" value="40" />
```

The more cores in your server, the higher this value can be.

Maximum concurrent connections

This is a Microsoft Dynamics NAV server setting, which is located in the `CustomSettings.config` file, and it's the maximum number of concurrent client connections that the service tier will accept. To disable this setting, set the value to `MaxValue`:

```
<add key="ClientServicesMaxConcurrentConnections" value="150" />
```

 For more information about monitoring the Microsoft Dynamics NAV Server using performance counters, check the MSDN site at `https://msdn.microsoft.com/en-us/library/dn414713(v=nav.90).aspx`.

C/AL performance

Obviously, the way you write code on NAV can seriously affect performance.

C/AL (the NAV native language) has a set of commands optimized for SQL Server data access and your code should consider these new instructions. Here are a few basic things to remember:

- Never use `FIND('-')` or `FIND('+')` but use `FINDFIRST` or `FINDLAST` instead (these are optimized for finding the single first or last record in the specified filter and range).
- Use `GET` when you have to retrieve a record via a primary key.

- When you want to retrieve a set of data or loop through it, use `FINDSET`. This function is optimized for finding and modifying sets of data, without creating cursors (and without using the `FETCH` commands called on SQL Server). However, this is only valid for the first 500 records (this number can be changed in the NAV database properties and can be increased if needed). After the default 500 records, the loop will still create a cursor, like in the old NAV versions. These are the general rules when using `FINDSET`:
  - `FINDSET(FALSE,FALSE)`: This is a read-only command and uses no server cursors, and the record set is read with a single server call.
  - `FINDSET(TRUE,FALSE)`: This is used to update non-key fields. This uses a cursor with a fetch buffer (similar to `FIND('-')`).
  - `FINDSET(TRUE,TRUE)`: This is used to update key fields.
- To check if a set of records contains data after filters have been applied, use the `ISEMPTY` function.
- Avoid too many FlowFields on tables and pages.
- Use `SETAUTOCALCFIELDS` when you have to retrieve data and request a calculation of associated FlowFields.
- When you have to apply filters to a set of records, use the right index by using `SETCURRENTKEY`.

  - For more information, check the MSDN site at `https://msdn.microsoft.com/en-us/library/dd355237(v=nav.90).aspx`.

- It is recommended to check also the C/AL Coding Guidelines published by the **NAV Design Pattern Team** at `https://community.dynamics.com/nav/w/designpatterns/156.cal-coding-guidelines`.
- You can perform C/AL performance testing by using tools such as the Microsoft Dynamics NAV performance testing repository in GitHub at `https://github.com/NAVPERF`. This is out of the scope of this book but it could be useful to bookmark the link.

Summary

In this chapter, we have covered the NAV architecture and we took an overview of the different NAV installations (on-premise, on-cloud, SaaS), discussing the pros and cons of each.

In the second part of the chapter, we analyzed the performance problems you can have in your NAV architecture and provided tips to help you rectify them.

In the next chapter, we'll see how to open a Microsoft Dynamics NAV implementation to the outside world by using the web services native functionalities of NAV.

2
Configuring Microsoft Dynamics NAV Web Services

Starting from version 2009, Microsoft Dynamics NAV supports the creating and publishing Microsoft Dynamics NAV objects and functionalities as web services.

Web services permit an easy, open, and flexible way to integrate NAV with the external systems and applications.

In this chapter, we'll learn about the following topics:

- Types of web service you can have in NAV
- Activating NAV web services
- Publishing NAV objects as web services

Microsoft Dynamics NAV web service protocols

From NAV objects, you can publish two types of web service:

- SOAP web services
- OData web services

Simple Object Access Protocol (SOAP) is an XML-based, platform-independent, and language-independent messaging protocol for exchanging information via the Internet. SOAP enables client applications to easily connect to remote services and invoke remote methods.

The most common type of messaging pattern in SOAP is the **Remote Procedure Call** (RPC), where one network node (the client) sends a request message to another node (the server), and the server sends a response message back to the client.

Open Data Protocol (OData) is a web protocol that is designed for querying tabular data. The protocol enables the creation and consumption of **Representational State Transfer (REST)** APIs using normal HTTP messages.

The OData standard is good for web service applications that require a uniform, flexible, general purpose interface for exposing **Create, Retrieve, Update, Delete** (CRUD) operations on a tabular data model to clients.

As described in the official protocol definition, it supports **Representational State Transfer (REST)** based data services, which enable resources, identified using **Uniform Resource Identifiers** (URIs), and defined in an **Abstract Data Model** (**Entity Data Model**), to be published and edited by Web clients within corporate networks and across the Internet using simple HTTP messages.

Whereas SOAP web service expose a WSDL document, OData web service expose an EDMX document containing metadata for all published web services (useful when you need to create a proxy code for an application that uses the OData services).

You can reach this metadata by using the OData URL at
`http://yourserver:port/OData/$metadata`.

Microsoft Dynamics NAV web service types

The NAV objects that can be exposed as web services are:

- `Page` web services
- `Codeunit` web services
- `Query` web services

To use NAV web services, a client must be properly authenticated on NAV. After a successful authentication, it can read and write data using SOAP over the HTTP protocol.

Page web services

A NAV page published as a web service permits you to have **CRUD** operations (**Create, Read, Update, Delete**) on the entity linked to the `Page` object.

When you expose a page as an OData web service, you can query that data to return a service metadata **Entity Data Model Extension (EDMX)** document, an AtomPub document, or a **JavaScript Object Notation (JSON)** document. If the exposed page has write permissions, you can also insert data on NAV.

In a page web service, each operation is executed on a single transaction with optimistic concurrency. These are the functions exposed on a page web service by default:

Operation	Description and signature
`Create`	Creates a single record: `void Create(ref Entity entity)`
`CreateMultiple`	Creates a set of records: `void CreateMultiple(ref Entity[] entity)`
`Read`	Reads a single record: `Entity Read(string no)`
`ReadMultiple`	Reads a filtered set of records (using pagination): `Entity [] ReadMultiple(Entity_Filter[] filterArray, string bookmarkKey, int setSize)`
`ReadByRecId`	Reads the record that is identified by `RecId`. You can use `GetRecIdFromKey` to obtain a record ID. If the record is not found, then the operation returns null: `Entity ReadByRecId(string formattedRecId)`
`GetRecIdFromKey`	Converts a key, which is always part of the page result, to a record ID: `string GetRecIdFromKey(string key)`
`Update`	Updates a single record: `void Update(ref Entity entity)`
`UpdateMultiple`	Updates a set of records: `void UpdateMultiple(ref Entity[] entity)`
`Delete`	Deletes a single record: `bool Delete(string key)`

| IsUpdated | Checks if an object has been updated since the key was obtained:
`bool IsUpdated(string key)` |
| Delete_<part> | Deletes a subpage of the current page:
`bool Delete_<part>(string key)` |

The term `entity` used in operation signatures describes the data type that is used (the NAV table linked to the `Page` object).

Codeunit web services

NAV codeunits can be exposed only as SOAP web services. When a `codeunit` is exposed as a web service, all functions defined in the `codeunit` web service and marked as `Local = No` are exposed as operations to the client application.

To target a function defined in a `codeunit` as `public`, navigate to **Functions** | **Properties** and select `Local = No`:

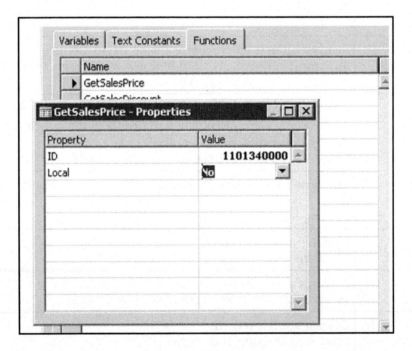

Query web services

A NAV Query object can be exposed only as an OData web service.

Query objects can return the desired maximum number of rows as a result and you can specify this number via the TopNumberOfRows property in the NAV Query object:

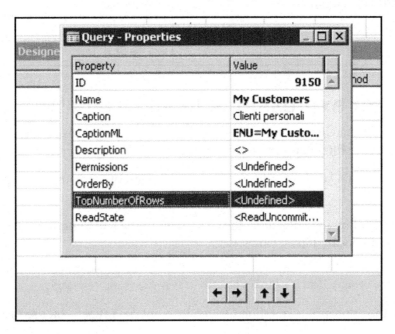

In the service tier configuration (CustomSettings.config file), the ODataServicesPageMaxSize setting contains the maximum number of entities returned per page of OData results. The default value is 1000 but often you need to change this value in order to retrieve the correct result set. It's extremely important that you check this value or you may not have a correct result set returned.

When exposing Microsoft Dynamics NAV objects as web services, a developer has to decide which type of web service is better suited to their needs. Actually, the NAV platform offers these limitations:

- It is not currently possible to access Microsoft Dynamics NAV Query objects with SOAP web services
- It is not currently possible to access codeunits with OData web services

The following table summarizes the types of web service applications that you can create with NAV:

	SOAP web services	OData web services
Pages	Yes: Create, Read, Update, Delete (CRUD) operations	Yes: Create, Read, Update, Delete (CRUD) operations
Codeunits	Yes	No
Queries	No	Yes, read-only

Using filter expressions in an OData URI

When using an OData URI (for example by calling a `Query` object exposed as a web service), you can use filter expressions directly in the URL.

To add a filter to an OData URI, add `$filter=` at the end of the name of the published web service.

For example, the following URI filters the `City` field in the **Customer** page to return all customers who are located in `Milan`:

```
http://localhost:7048/DynamicsNAV/OData/Company('CRONUS
International Ltd.')/Customer?$filter=City eq 'Milan'
```

You must use the appropriate notation for the different data types you use in a filter expression:

- String values must be delimited by single quotation marks
- Numeric values require no delimiters
- `DateTime` values must be delimited by single quotation marks and preceded by the word `datetime`, such as `datetime'2016-06-10T23:59:30.1432453Z'`

The following table shows the most used filters that are supported in Microsoft Dynamics NAV OData web services and the equivalent C/AL filter expressions. Samples come from the publication of `Page 21` (`Customer Card`, `Customer` as the service name) and `Page 20` (General Ledger Entry, GLEntry as the service name), as explained on the MSDN site:

Definition	Example and explanation	Equivalent C/AL expression
Select a range of values	`filter=Entry_No gt 300 and Entry_No lt 500` Query on GLEntry service returns entry numbers 301 through 499.	`..`
And	`filter=City eq 'London' and Payment_Terms_Code eq '14 DAYS'` Query on Customer service returns customers where City is `London` and `Payment_Terms_Code=14 DAYS`.	`&`
Or	`filter= Country_Region_Code eq 'IT' or Country_Region_Code eq 'US'` Query on Customer service returns customers where Country Region Code is Italy and United States. You cannot use the OR operator to apply filters on two different fields.	`|`
Less than	`filter=Entry_No lt 300` Query on GLEntry service returns entry numbers that are less than `300`.	`<`
Greater than	`filter= Entry_No gt 500` Query on GLEntry service returns entry numbers higher than `500`.	`>`
Greater than or equal to	`filter=Entry_No ge 500` Query on GLEntry service returns entry numbers `500` and higher.	`>=`
Less than or equal to	`filter=Entry_No le 500` Query on GLEntry service returns entry numbers up to and including `500`.	`<=`
Different from (not equal)	`filter=VAT_Bus_Posting_Group ne 'EXPORT'` Query on Customer service returns all customers with `VAT_Bus_Posting_Group` not equal to `EXPORT`.	`<>`

endswith	`filter=endswith(VAT_Bus_Posting_Group,'RT')` Query on Customer service returns all customers with `VAT_Bus_Posting_Group` values that end in `RT`.	*
startswith	`filter=startswith(Name, 'S')` Query on Customer service returns all customer names beginning with `S`.	
substringof	`filter=substringof(Name, 'xxx')` Query on Customer service returns customer records for customers with names containing the string `xxx`.	
length	`filter=length(Name) gt 20` Query on Customer service returns customer records for customers with names longer than 20 characters.	
indexof	`filter=indexof(Location_Code, 'BLUE') eq 0` Query on Customer service returns customer records for customers having a location code beginning with the string `BLUE`.	

NAV web services configuration

When you install the Microsoft Dynamics NAV server, you can provide configuration information for web services directly in the setup phase or after that via the Microsoft Dynamics NAV Server `Administration` tool application.

All these settings can also be manually managed by editing the `CustomSettings.config` file on the server (this file is located by default in the `C:Program FilesMicrosoft Dynamics NAV<versionNumber>Service` folder), where `<versionNumber>` is the number that corresponds to the NAV version (for example 90 for NAV 2016).

If you open the Microsoft Dynamics NAV Server Administration tool and connect to your server instance, you can find these two settings tabs:

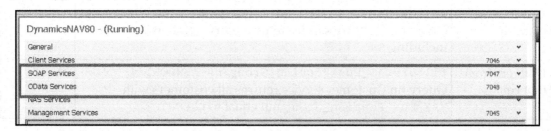

SOAP Services tab settings

Take a look at the fields in the **SOAP Services** tab in the Microsoft Dynamics NAV Server **Administration** tool in the following screenshot:

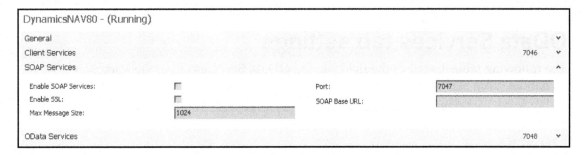

The following table depicts the fields in the **SOAP Services** tab as shown in the preceding screenshot:

Setting	Description
Enable SOAP Services	Specifies whether SOAP web services are enabled for this Microsoft Dynamics NAV server instance. **Default:** Enabled
Enable SSL	Specifies whether SSL (HTTPS) is enabled for the SOAP web service port. **Default:** Not enabled
Max Message Size	The maximum permitted size of a SOAP web services request, in kilobytes. This setting also pertains to OData web services. **Default:** 1024
Port	The listening HTTP port for Microsoft Dynamics NAV SOAP web services. **Default:** 7047 **Valid range:** 1 – 65535
SOAP Base URL	Specifies the root of the URLs that are used to access SOAP web services. For example, you can change the value if you want to change the externally facing endpoint. The base URL must have the following syntax: `http[s]://hostname:port/instance/WS/` This field maps to the `PublicSOAPBaseUrl` setting in the `CustomSettings.config` file for the Microsoft Dynamics NAV server instance.

The maximum permitted size of an OData web service request is specified by the **Max Message Size** option in the **SOAP Services** tab as previously described.

OData Services tab settings

The following table describes the fields on the **OData Services** tab in the Microsoft Dynamics NAV Server Administration tool:

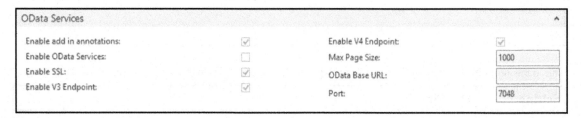

Setting	Description
Enable add in annotations	Specifies whether Excel add-in annotations should be provided in OData metadata.
Enable OData Services	Specifies whether OData web services are enabled for this Microsoft Dynamics NAV server instance: **Default**: Enabled
Enable SSL	Specifies whether SSL (HTTPS) is enabled for the OData web service port: **Default**: Not enabled
Enable V3 Endpoint	Specifies whether the OData Version 3 service endpoint will be enabled.
Enable V4 Endpoint	Specifies whether the OData Version 4 service endpoint will be enabled (OData version 4 is the current recommended version of OData).
Max Page Size	Specifies the maximum number of entities returned per page of OData results: **Default**: 1000

ODatabase URL	Specifies the root of the URLs that are used to access OData web services. For example, you can change the value if you want to change the externally facing endpoint. The base URL must have the following syntax: `http[s]://hostname:port/instance/OData/` This field maps to the `PublicODataBaseUrl` setting in the `CustomSettings.config` file for the Microsoft Dynamics NAV server instance.
Port	The listening HTTP port for Microsoft Dynamics NAV OData web services: **Default**: 7048 **Valid range**: 1 – 65535

Publishing NAV web services

Web services can be set up in the Microsoft Dynamics NAV Windows client (RoleTailored Client) or in the Microsoft Dynamics NAV Web client. You must then publish the web service in order to have it available to the client applications.

Users can discover web services by pointing a browser at the computer that is running the Microsoft Dynamics NAV Server and requesting a list of available services.

When you publish a web service, it is immediately available over the network for authenticated users (only users with the correct NAV permissions can access and use published web services).

Creating and publishing NAV web services

To create and then publish a NAV object as a web service, follow these steps:

1. Open the Microsoft Dynamics NAV Windows client or the Microsoft Dynamics NAV Web client and, in the **Search** box, enter `web services` as the keyword and choose the related link:

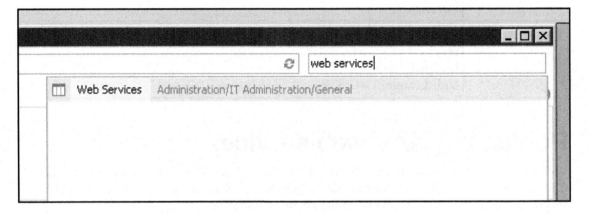

2. In the **Web Services** page, click on **New**:

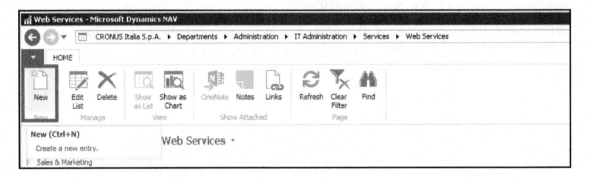

3. Insert a new record in the table:

- **Object Type**: Choose the object you want to publish (`Codeunit`, `Page`, or `Query`).
- **Object ID**: Select the object ID of the NAV object that you want to expose.

- **Service Name**: Assign a name for the web service. Please avoid spaces and special characters.
- **Published**: Click to activate the web service.

4. When you publish the web service, in the **OData URL** and **SOAP URL** fields, you can see the URLs that are generated for the web service.

5. For example, to publish the `Customer Card (Page 21)` object as a web service:

6. After publishing, NAV gives you the OData URL and SOAP URL for the service.

7. If you publish a `Query` object, for example the `Item Sales by Customer` query, you have only the **OData URL**:

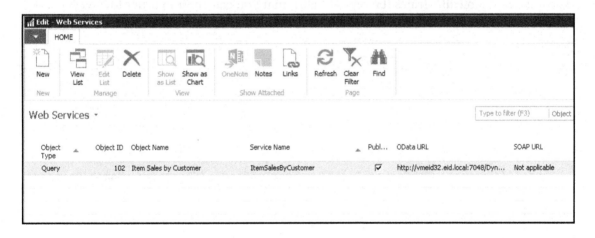

8. If you publish a `Codeunit` object, for example the `Cost Account Mgt` codeunit:

9. You have only the **SOAP URL**.

Checking NAV web services

You can verify the availability of a web service by using a browser and entering the relevant URL, or you can choose the link in the **OData URL** and **SOAP URL** fields that you can see in the **Web Services** page in NAV.

The following table illustrates the types of URL that you can enter in order to have a list of available web services on a NAV instance:

Web service type	Syntax	Example
SOAP	`https://Server:SOAPWebServicePort/ServerInstance/WS/CompanyName/services/`	`https://localhost:7047/DynamicsNAV90/WS/CRONUS International Ltd./services/`
OData	`https://Server:ODataWebServicePort/ServerInstance/OData/Company('CompanyName')`	`https://localhost:7048/DynamicsNAV90/OData/Company('CRONUS International Ltd.')`

The URL for accessing a page published as a web service has the following syntax:

```
http://<Server>:<WebServicePort>/<ServerInstance>/WS/<CompanyName>/Page/<Se
rviceName>
```

The URL for accessing a codeunit published as a web service has the following syntax:

```
http://<Server>:<WebServicePort>/<ServerInstance>/WS/<CompanyName>/Codeunit
/<ServiceName>
```

The company name and service name are all case-sensitive. The following table describes the different URL components:

URL element	Description
`<Server>`	The NAV server name.
`<WebServicePort>`	The TCP port number used to expose a NAV web service (default = 7047). You need to set up a Windows Firewall rule in order to open this post to the clients.
`<ServerInstance>`	The NAV server instance name (defined during installation).
`<CompanyName>`	The NAV name for the company where you want to publish web services. Special characters in the company name must be URL-encoded in order to be properly translated.
`<ServiceName>`	The service name for the exposed page or codeunit. *Please avoid spaces or special characters*.

This is a sample of the available web services (`discovery`) for this server instance via a browser:

In this sample, you can see that there are two codeunits published as web services for this server instance and this company.

If you type the URL for the first web service codeunit, you can see the published functions (methods) defined in the codeunit as a WSDL definition:

If you publish a page as a web service (for example, `Page 21 - Customer Card`), this is the service definition you have by testing on the browser:

For the page, you can also see the native methods exposed to read and update the data:

```
                </xsd:sequence>
              </xsd:complexType>
            </xsd:element>
   -        <xsd:element name="Read_Result">
     -        <xsd:complexType>
       -        <xsd:sequence>
                  <xsd:element name="CustomerCard" type="tns:CustomerCard" maxOccurs="1" minOccurs="0"/>
                </xsd:sequence>
              </xsd:complexType>
            </xsd:element>
   -        <xsd:element name="ReadByRecId">
     -        <xsd:complexType>
       -        <xsd:sequence>
                  <xsd:element name="recId" type="xsd:string" maxOccurs="1" minOccurs="1"/>
                </xsd:sequence>
              </xsd:complexType>
            </xsd:element>
   -        <xsd:element name="ReadByRecId_Result">
     -        <xsd:complexType>
       -        <xsd:sequence>
                  <xsd:element name="CustomerCard" type="tns:CustomerCard" maxOccurs="1" minOccurs="0"/>
                </xsd:sequence>
              </xsd:complexType>
            </xsd:element>
   -        <xsd:element name="ReadMultiple">
     -        <xsd:complexType>
       -        <xsd:sequence>
                  <xsd:element name="filter" type="tns:CustomerCard_Filter" maxOccurs="unbounded" minOccurs="1"/>
                  <xsd:element name="bookmarkKey" type="xsd:string" maxOccurs="1" minOccurs="0"/>
                  <xsd:element name="setSize" type="xsd:int" maxOccurs="1" minOccurs="1"/>
                </xsd:sequence>
              </xsd:complexType>
            </xsd:element>
   -        <xsd:element name="ReadMultiple_Result">
     -        <xsd:complexType>
       -        <xsd:sequence>
                  <xsd:element name="ReadMultiple_Result" type="tns:CustomerCard_List" maxOccurs="1" minOccurs="0"/>
                </xsd:sequence>
              </xsd:complexType>
            </xsd:element>
```

In a Microsoft Dynamics NAV multitenant deployment, since web services are created in the application database, you must create at least one tenant that has write access to the application database. This setting is determined by the *Allow application database writes* parameter when you mount a tenant against a Microsoft Dynamics NAV server instance.

Regarding URLs, in multitenant deployments URLs must specify the tenant that the URL applies to (web services are set up in the application database but you need to consume company-specific and tenant-specific data). The URL can specify the tenant ID or the tenant hostname if you specify hostnames as alternative IDs for tenants. For example, `http://localhost:7048/DynamicsNAV/OData/Company('CRONUS%20International %20Ltd.')/Customer?Tenant=Tenant1` consumes the **Customer** OData web service for a specific tenant.

Summary

In this chapter, we have seen what types of web services you have with Microsoft Dynamics NAV, and what types of protocols they use and we analyzed the differences between them. We have seen how to set up and activate web services in NAV by configuring the service tier and by publishing them from the Windows client, and then how to test whether all is working by using the browser.

After this chapter, you should have a complete knowledge of how to publish NAV business logic to the external applications.

In the next chapter, we'll see how to create an application that will use published NAV web services.

3
Creating an Application Using NAV Web Services

In the previous chapter, we have seen how to configure and publish NAV objects as web services.

In this chapter, we want to create a small application with Visual Studio and C# in order to use a published NAV object as web service. The sample application will be a Windows console application that reads registered sales orders from NAV and permits to create new sales orders from outside the ERP.

In this chapter, you will learn about the following topics:

- Creating a C# console application that consumes NAV web services
- Reading NAV entities via web services
- Creating and modifying NAV entities via web services
- Using NAV OData web services
- Creating a cross-platform application

Creating the NAV web service

The scope of our application is to read NAV sales orders and create new ones by invoking the NAV business logic. In order to do that, we need to publish the NAV **Sales Order** page as web service and use it.

Let's learn how to create a NAV web service by performing the following steps:

1. Open the Microsoft Dynamics NAV RoleTailored Client and go to the **Web Services** page.
2. Create a new record with these parameters:
   - **Object Type**: `Page`
   - **Object ID**: `42` (**Sales Order** page)
   - **Service Name**: `SalesOrder` (a friendly name for our web service)
   - **Published**: `TRUE`

   The results are shown in the following screenshot:

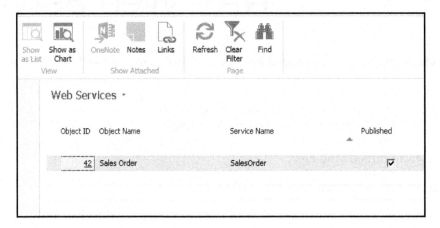

3. When published, NAV immediately gives you the service URL (SOAP and OData). You can test if the web service is correctly working by accessing it directly via the browser (using, for example, the SOAP URL):

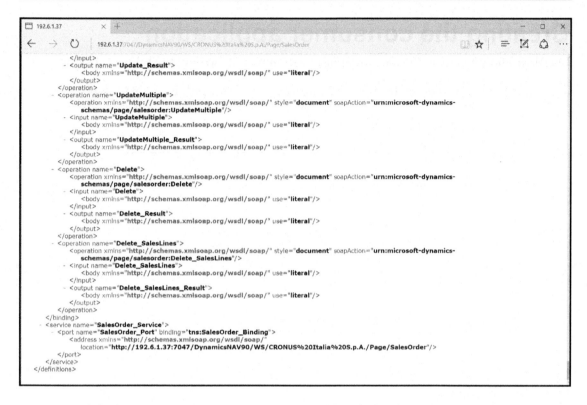

4. If the browser prompts you to insert credentials for the service, access it by using a correctly configured user in NAV.

5. Remember that in order to access the published web services, the service ports (7047 for SOAP web services and 7048 for OData web services if you use the default ones) must be opened to the outside by creating correct rules on the Windows Firewall:

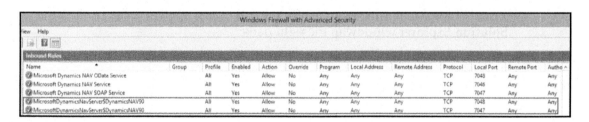

Creating the consumer application

Let's learn how to create the consumer application by performing the following steps:

1. In order to create the application that will use our published NAV web service, open Visual Studio, create a new project, and in the **New Project** window select the **Console Application** project type:

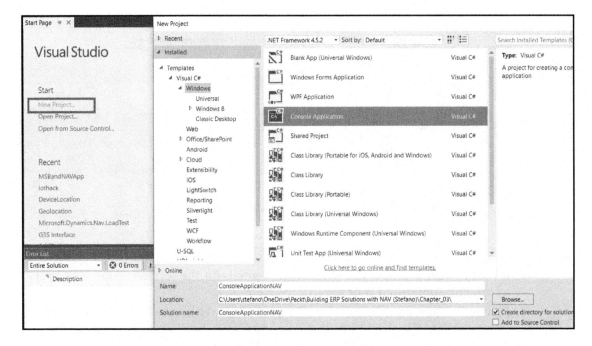

2. Give a desired name to your solution (for example, `ConsoleApplicationNAV`) and click **OK**.
3. Visual Studio creates the template for the solution project. You can see it in the **Solution Explorer** window in the right pane:

4. Here, the `Program.cs` file contains the core of the console application (`Main`) while `App.config` is the application configuration file, an XML file that contains specific settings for the application.

5. Now we have to add a reference to our NAV web service in order to use it. To do this, right-click on your solution file and choose **Add | Service Reference...** as shown in the following screenshot:

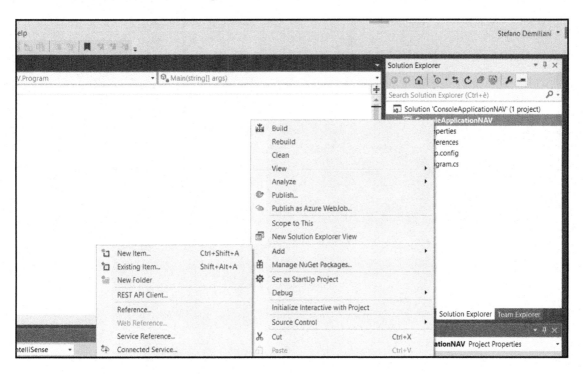

6. Here you can add a reference to one or more **Windows Communication Foundation (WCF)** services in the current solution, locally, on a local area network or on the Internet.

7. For NAV, we don't have a WCF service but instead a SOAP XML web service. For adding a reference to an XML web service, in the **Add Service Reference** window click on **Advanced...**:

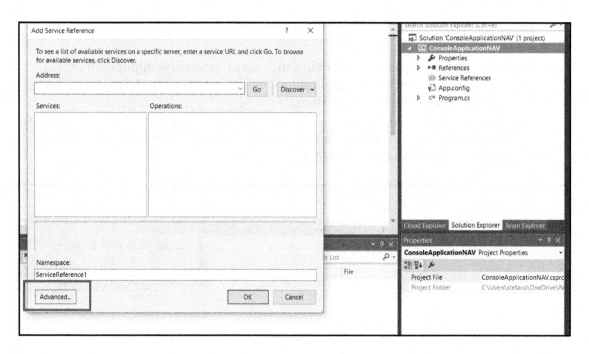

8. And then click on **Add Web Reference…**:

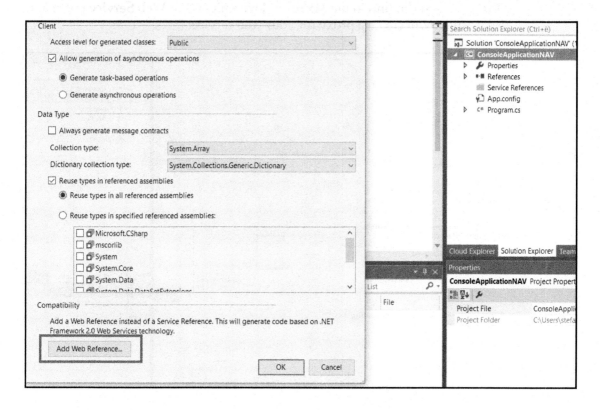

9. In the **Add Web Reference** window, type the URL of your NAV web service (the SOAP URL you can find in the Microsoft Dynamics NAV **Web Service** page) and Visual Studio will create a proxy for your web service:

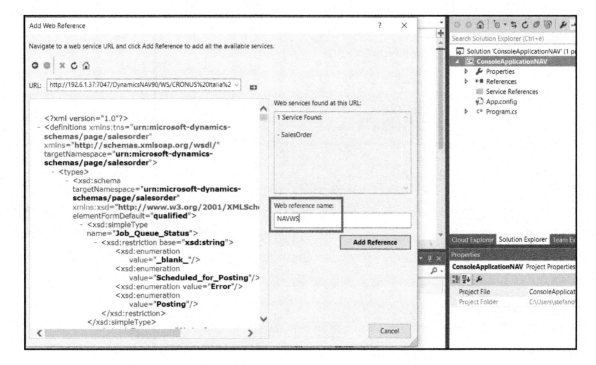

10. To complete the operation, give a desired web reference name (for example, NAVWS) and click **Add Reference**.

Now your solution contains a web reference to your NAV web service:

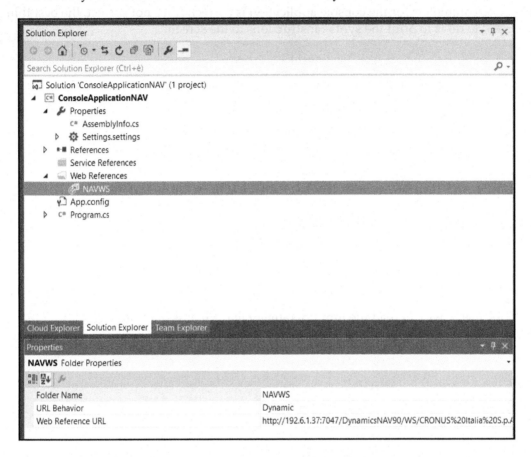

11. We're ready to start writing C# code now. The first thing to do is to write a `using` clause for adding a reference to the `NAVWS` namespace:

```
using ConsoleApplicationNAV.NAVWS;
```

12. Console applications have startup parameters that you can specify as arguments in order to take actions (the `string[] args` parameter in the `Main` function). In this sample application, we want to read sales orders and create new ones, so we want to have a startup parameter, `READ`, to read the NAV registered sales orders and `CREATE` to create a new sales order.

13. In the `Main` function, the first thing to do is to check if the number of startup parameters for the console application is correct. If it's not correct, the best thing to do is to print the syntax instructions to the screen:

```
string OperationType;
//If startup parameters are different from one,
 write the application syntax on screen and exit
if (args.Length != 1)
{
    Console.WriteLine(" Usage:");
    Console.WriteLine(" ConsoleApplicationNAV
    <OperationType>");
    Console.WriteLine(" ------ ");
    Console.WriteLine(" OperationType:");
    Console.WriteLine(" READ: reads NAV Sales
    Orders");
    Console.WriteLine(" CREATE: create a new Sales
    Order on NAV");
    Console.WriteLine(" ------ ");
    return;
}
```

14. Next, we can read the input parameter and process it accordingly:

```
//Reading the Operation Type parameter
OperationType = args[0].ToUpper();

switch(OperationType)
{
    case "READ":
        ReadNAVSalesOrders();
         break;
    case "CREATE":
        CreateNAVSalesOrder();
         break;
    default:
        Console.WriteLine("Wrong parameter!");
         break;
}
```

15. Here, we read the input parameter for our application. If the input parameter is READ, we call the function ReadNAVSalesOrders. If the input parameter is CREATE, we call the function CreateNAVSalesOrder, otherwise an error message is printed:

```
private static void ReadNAVSalesOrders()
    {
        //Here we have to call our NAV web service
        for reading Sales Orders
    }

private static void CreateNAVSalesOrder()
    {
        //Here we have to call our NAV web service for
        creating a Sales Order
    }
```

16. Now we have to write the logic for the preceding two core functions.

Reading NAV sales orders

Let's learn how to read NAV sales orders by performing the following steps:

1. In the ReadNAVSalesOrders function, we have to create an instantiation of the NAV web service and explicitly set the URL for this service:

```
SalesOrder_Service ws = new SalesOrder_Service();
ws.Url = "...";
```

2. I recommend to place the web service URL in the <applicationSettings> section in the app.config file and then to read it from there.
3. To do so, right-click on your project, select **Properties**, and then select **Settings**.
4. Here you can add all the application settings variables you want and these can be loaded at runtime in your application via code.

5. For our example, we can insert a row like the following screenshot:

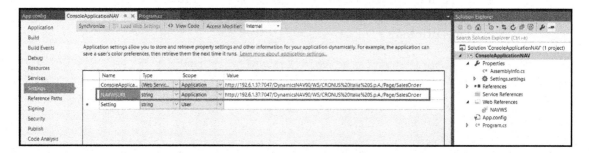

6. Here we have created a setting called NAVWSURL where the type is a string and the value is the URL of our NAV web service.

7. In app.config, Visual Studio creates this entry:

```
<applicationSettings>
    <ConsoleApplicationNAV.Properties.Settings>
        <setting name="NAVWSURL" serializeAs="String">
         <value>
             http://192.6.1.37:7047/DynamicsNAV90/WS/
             CRONUS%20Italia%20S.p.A./Page/SalesOrder
         </value>
        </setting>
    </ConsoleApplicationNAV.Properties.Settings>
 </applicationSettings>
```

8. For dynamically reading this setting, just use this line of code:

```
ws.Url = Properties.Settings.Default.NAVWSURL;
```

9. To access the NAV web service, we also need authentication. We can use explicit credentials (impersonate a particular user) or we can use the default credentials of the user that runs the application. In this case, we want the credentials for the running user, so we use this line:

```
ws.UseDefaultCredentials = true;
```

10. The method for retrieving a set of records from a NAV page web service is called ReadMultiple:

```
Entity [] ReadMultiple(Entity_Filter[] filterArray, string
bookmarkKey, int setSize)
```

11. This method reads a filtered set of records (if filters are applied) and returns an array of entities (objects that represents the page web service). The parameters are as follows:

Parameter	Description
`filterArray`	**Type:** `Entity_Filter[]` An array of record filters.
`bookmarkKey`	**Type:** `String` The last record bookmark of the page that was previously read. To return the first page of results, set `bookmarkKey` to NULL.
`setSize`	**Type:** `Integer` The size of the set to be returned. To return the complete set of results, set `setSize` to zero. To reverse the order of the results, set `setSize` to negative.

12. For our sample application, we want to retrieve all orders for the customer code `10000` (Cannon Group SpA). Accordingly to the `ReadMultiple` method's definition, we have to define an array of filters to apply for the sales order entity (exposed by the web service) and then call the method itself by passing this filter array.

    The piece of code that does the work is this:

    ```
    //Setting filters on the table
    List<SalesOrder_Filter> filterArray = new
    List<SalesOrder_Filter>();
    SalesOrder_Filter filter = new SalesOrder_Filter();
    filter.Field = SalesOrder_Fields.Sell_to_Customer_No;
    filter.Criteria = "10000";
    filterArray.Add(filter);

    //Reading sales orders
    List<SalesOrder> orderList =
    ws.ReadMultiple(filterArray.ToArray(), null, 0).ToList();
    ```

13. We have created a `SalesOrder_Filter` array with a filter on the NAV field, `Sell To Customer No. = 10000`, and then we have called the `ReadMultiple` method of the web service by passing the filter array, NULL as bookmarKey (we want the first page of the recordset) and 0 as `setSize` (we want the complete result set).

14. The `ReadMultiple` method returns a `SalesOrder` array, so here we have used the `.ToList()` extension of `List<T>` in order to directly have a `List` of `SalesOrder` objects and loop through it for printing the details.

The complete function code is as follow:

```
private static void ReadNAVSalesOrders()
{
    //Here we have to call our NAV web service for reading Sales
    Orders

    //Web Service instantiation
    SalesOrder_Service ws = new SalesOrder_Service();
    ws.Url = Properties.Settings.Default.NAVWSURL;
    ws.UseDefaultCredentials = true;

    //Setting filters on the table
    List<SalesOrder_Filter> filterArray = new
    List<SalesOrder_Filter>();
    SalesOrder_Filter filter = new SalesOrder_Filter();
    filter.Field = SalesOrder_Fields.Sell_to_Customer_No;
    filter.Criteria = "10000";
    filterArray.Add(filter);

    //Reading sales orders
    List<SalesOrder> orderList =
    ws.ReadMultiple(filterArray.ToArray(), null, 0).ToList();

    //Printing the results
    if (orderList!=null)
    {
        foreach(SalesOrder order in orderList)
        {
            Console.WriteLine("Order No.: " + order.No);
            Console.WriteLine("Order Date: " +
            order.Order_Date);
            Console.WriteLine("----------------");
        }
        //Waiting user input to terminate
        Console.ReadKey();
    }
}
```

Creating a NAV sales order

In the `CreateNAVSalesOrder` function, we use the NAV page web service for creating a sales order with two lines on NAV. This task requires some steps in order to be completed on NAV:

1. As a first step, we need to instantiate the NAV web service as previously described:

   ```
   SalesOrder_Service ws = new SalesOrder_Service();
   ws.Url = Properties.Settings.Default.NAVWSURL;
   ws.UseDefaultCredentials = true;
   ```

2. Now we have to call the NAV web service in order to create the sales header and having the order header initialized with its order number (here it is exactly like pressing the **NEW** button in the **Sales Order Card** page in NAV):

   ```
   SalesOrder order = new SalesOrder();
   ws.Create(ref order);
   ```

3. For this task, we call the `Create` method by passing a reference to the `SalesOrder` object to initialize:

   ```
   void Create(ref Entity entity)
   ```

4. After this first call, the `SalesOrder` object is created and we have the order number from NAV.

5. Now we can update the sales header with all the details and we can initialize the sales lines:

   ```
   //Update the Sales Header with details
   order.Sell_to_Customer_No = "10000";
   order.Order_Date = DateTime.Now;

   //Create the Sales Lines array and initialize the lines
   order.SalesLines = new Sales_Order_Line[2];
   for (int i=0; i<2; i++)
   {
       order.SalesLines[i] = new Sales_Order_Line();
   }

   ws.Update(ref order);
   ```

6. After that we can create the lines:

```
//First line
Sales_Order_Line line = order.SalesLines[0];
line.Type = NAVWS.Type.Item;
line.No = "1000";
line.Quantity = 5;
//Second line
line = order.SalesLines[1];
line.Type = NAVWS.Type.Item;
line.No = "1001";
line.Quantity = 10;
```

7. At the end we can update the order lines:

```
ws.Update(ref order);
```

8. The complete function code is as follows:

```
private static void CreateNAVSalesOrder()
{
  //Here we have to call our NAV web service for creating a
  Sales Order

  //Web Service instantiation
  SalesOrder_Service ws = new SalesOrder_Service();
  ws.Url = Properties.Settings.Default.NAVWSURL;
  ws.UseDefaultCredentials = true;

  //Create the Sales Header
  SalesOrder order = new SalesOrder();
  ws.Create(ref order);

  //Here the Sales Order is created and we have the order No.


  //Update the Sales Header with details
  order.Sell_to_Customer_No = "10000";
  order.Order_Date = DateTime.Now;

  //Create the Sales Lines array and initialize the lines
  order.SalesLines = new Sales_Order_Line[2];
  for (int i=0; i<2; i++)
    {
      order.SalesLines[i] = new Sales_Order_Line();
    }

  ws.Update(ref order);
```

```
//First line
//Sales_Order_Line line = new Sales_Order_Line();
Sales_Order_Line line = order.SalesLines[0];
line.Type = NAVWS.Type.Item;
line.No = "1000";
line.Quantity = 5;
//Second line
line = order.SalesLines[1];
line.Type = NAVWS.Type.Item;
line.No = "1001";
line.Quantity = 10;
//Update the order lines with all the informations
ws.Update(ref order);

Console.WriteLine("Order {0} created successfully.",
order.No);

}
```

All this code does not contain error handling functions, but you need ALWAYS to enclose every call in a TRY...CATCH block and handling exceptions accordingly.

Testing the application

In order to test the application for the two described scenarios (orders retrieval and order creation), our console application must receive the correct defined parameter (READ, CREATE) at startup.

Let's learn how to test the application by performing the following steps:

1. To do so, right-click on the solution name, click **Properties**, and then choose **Debug**. In the **Debug** window, you can specify the startup parameters:

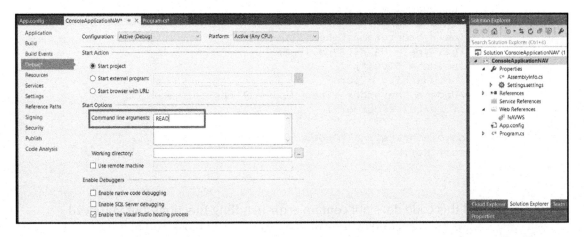

2. Let's test the application by passing the READ parameter as input.
3. The application code has to retrieve all the sales orders for Customer No. = 10000 (Cannon Group SpA) and this is the situation that we have on NAV:

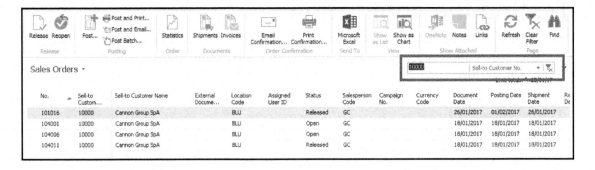

4. If you place a breakpoint (by pressing *F9*) after the lines that calls the NAV web service, you can see the retrieved records in the **Debug** window:

```
ConsoleApplicationNAV*         Program.cs  ⊞ ✕
ApplicationNAV                      ▾  ⚛ ConsoleApplicationNAV.Program                  ▾  ⊕ₐ ReadNAVSalesOrders()
            TILTCIAIIay.Auu(TILTCI);

        //Reading sales orders
        //SalesOrder[] orders = ws.ReadMultiple(filterArray.ToArray(), null, 100);
        List<SalesOrder> orderList = ws.ReadMultiple(filterArray.ToArray(), null, 0).ToList();

        //Printing the results
    if (orderList!=null)
        {       ▷ ● orderList  Count = 4
            foreach(SalesOrder order in orderList)
            {
                Console.WriteLine("Order No.: " + order.No);
                Console.WriteLine("Order Date: " + order.Order_Date);
                Console.WriteLine("----------------");
            }
            //Waiting user input to terminate
            Console.ReadKey();
        }
    }
```

5. The final output on the console shows you the details for all the retrieved sales orders:

```
Starting execution...
Order No.: 101016
Order Date: 26/01/2017 00:00:00
----------------
Order No.: 104001
Order Date: 18/01/2017 00:00:00
----------------
Order No.: 104006
Order Date: 18/01/2017 00:00:00
----------------
Order No.: 104011
Order Date: 18/01/2017 00:00:00
----------------
■
```

6. Now change the application startup parameter and use CREATE in order to call the function for creating a sales order on NAV:

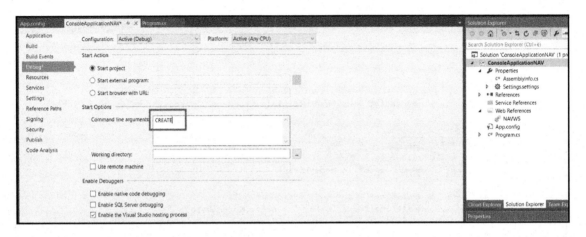

7. We placed a breakpoint after the first NAV web service Create call to check the correct order initialization (NAV must give us the Order No.). While debugging (Visual Studio stops the execution at your breakpoint) select the order object on the code, right-click, and choose **QuickWatch...**.

8. In the **QuickWatch** window in Visual Studio, you can see all the object details and you can check the Order No. returned by NAV:

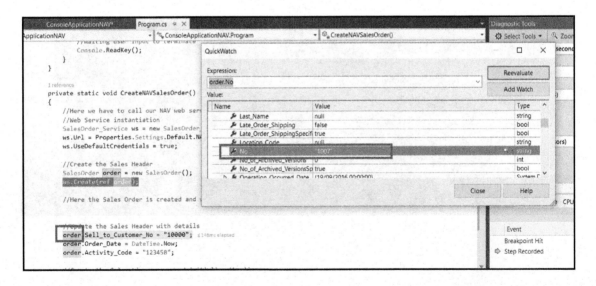

9. This is the final result on NAV:

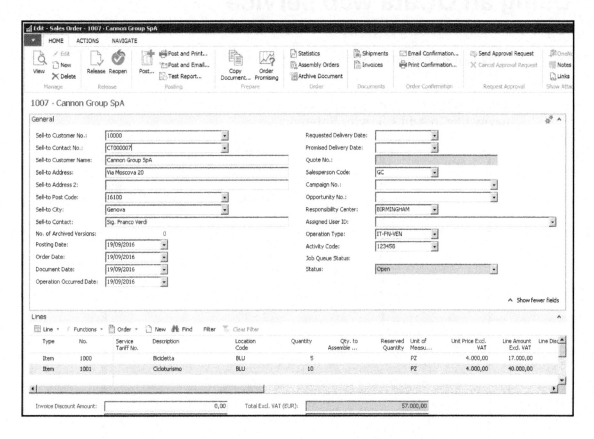

Using an OData web service

As you previously learned, a page web service has also an OData URL.

Let's learn how to use OData web service by performing the following steps:

1. To use an OData web service, we need to reference it in our Visual Studio by going to the project name in **Solution Explorer**, right-clicking on it, and navigating to **Add | Service Reference…**:

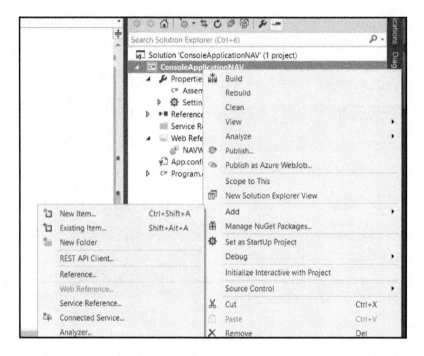

2. In the **Add Service Reference** window, add the OData service URL at `http://servername:port/NAVInstance/OData/`.
3. `servername` is the name (or IP address) of your NAV server, `port` is the OData web service port, and `NAVInstance` is the name of your NAV instance.
4. In this sample, our service URL is `http://VMEID31:7048/DynamicsNAV90/OData/`.
5. Give a friendly namespace for the service (in this sample, we use `NAVODATA`):

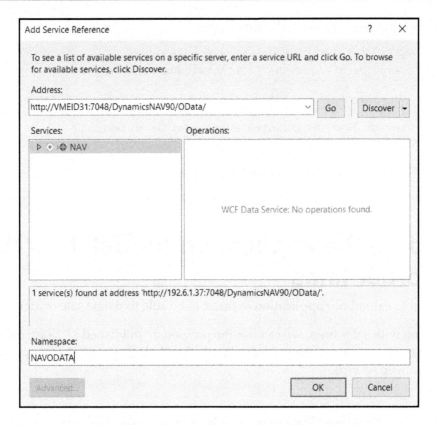

6. Now you can use the ODATA service in your application. First, add a reference to:

```
using System.Data.Services.Client;
```

7. Then set the ODATA service URL by reading it from your `app.config` file:

```
string serviceUri =
ConfigurationManager.AppSettings["NAVODATAUrl"];
```

8. Now you can call the ODATA service:

```
DataServiceContext context = new DataServiceContext(new
Uri(serviceUri));

NAVODATA.NAV Nav = new NAVODATA.NAV(new Uri(serviceUri));
Nav.Credentials = new
System.Net.NetworkCredential("yourusername", "yourpassword",
"yourdomain");
```

9. And then read the orders in this way:

```
DataServiceQuery<NAV_ODATA.SalesOrder> q =
theNav.CreateQuery<NAV_ODATA.SalesOrder>("SalesOrder");

List<NAV_ODATA.SalesOrder> orderList = q.Execute().ToList();

foreach (NAV_ODATA.SalesOrder order in orderList)
 {
    Console.WriteLine(string.Format("Order No: {0} Date: {1}",
    order.No, order.Order_Date));
 }
```

Extending the application for deleting NAV sales order lines

Here we want to extend our application in order to be able to delete sales order lines.

When working with sales lines, we can use the previously published `SalesOrder Page` web service (`Page 42`) or we can publish directly the NAV `Page 46` (`Sales Order Subform`) as a web service.

Using the SalesOrder web service (Page 42)

You can delete a sales order and/or its sales order lines by using the `SalesOrder Page` web service:

```
//Web Service instantiation
SalesOrder_Service ws = new SalesOrder_Service();
ws.Url = Properties.Settings.Default.NAVWSURL;
ws.UseDefaultCredentials = true;
```

To delete a sales order (given the order number to delete) you have first to read the sales order and then delete it via its `Key` field. The steps in the code are these:

```
//Read the Sales Order given its Order Number
SalesOrder so = ws.Read(SalesOrderNo);

//delete the Sales Order
ws.Delete(so.Key);
```

If you want to delete all the sales order lines (but not the header), you have to first read the sales order, and then loop through the lines and delete them using the `Delete_SalesLines` method:

```
//Read the Sales Order
SalesOrder so = ws.Read(SalesOrderNo);

//delete ALL the order lines
foreach (Sales_Order_Line line in so.SalesLines)
    {
        ws.Delete_SalesLines(line.Key);
    }
```

If you want to delete a specific sales line (given the line number), you can do something like this:

```
//Read the Sales Order
SalesOrder so = ws.Read(SalesOrderNo);
//Delete a specific order line
int lineToDelete = 10000;
foreach (Sales_Order_Line line in so.SalesLines)
    {
        if (line.Line_No == lineToDelete)
        {
            ws.Delete_SalesLines(line.Key);
        }
    }
```

Here are the complete functions:

```
//Delete a Sales Order
private static void DeleteSalesOrder(string SalesOrderNo)
{
    //Web Service instantiation
    SalesOrder_Service ws = new SalesOrder_Service();
    ws.Url = Properties.Settings.Default.NAVWSURL;
    ws.UseDefaultCredentials = true;

    //Read the Sales Order
    SalesOrder so = ws.Read(SalesOrderNo);

    //Delete the Sales Order
    ws.Delete(so.Key);
}

//Delete a Sales Order Line
private static void DeleteSalesOrderLine(string SalesOrderNo, int
LineNo)
```

```
    {
        //Web Service instantiation
        SalesOrder_Service ws = new SalesOrder_Service();
        ws.Url = Properties.Settings.Default.NAVWSURL;
        ws.UseDefaultCredentials = true;

        //Read the Sales Order
        SalesOrder so = ws.Read(SalesOrderNo);

        //Delete the specific order line
        foreach (Sales_Order_Line line in so.SalesLines)
        {
            if (line.Line_No == LineNo)
            {
                ws.Delete_SalesLines(line.Key);
            }
        }
    }

}
```

Using the sales order subform web service (Page 46)

Let's learn how to use the sales order subform web service by performing the following steps:

1. If we want to use the sales order subform, we have to publish it as a web service from NAV, so we have to create a new entry in the **Web Services** page:

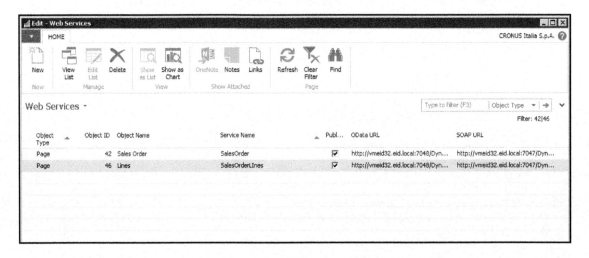

2. After publishing the service (here I've used `SalesOrderLines` as the service name), we have to reference it in our Visual Studio application.

3. Right-click on your project in **Solution Explorer**, choose **Add Service Reference** | **Advanced** | **Add Web Reference**, and in the **Add Web Reference** window copy the SOAP URL of your newly created web service:

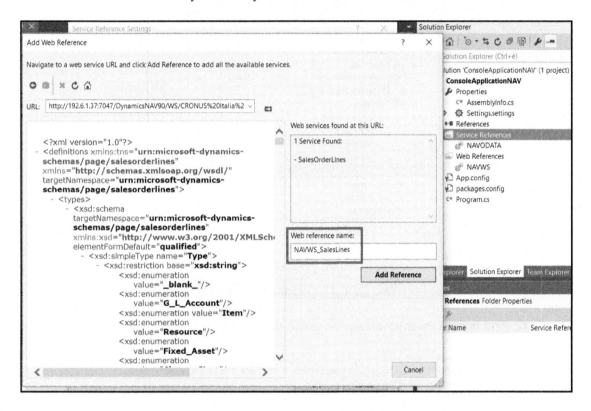

4. Give your service a proper name in Visual Studio (here I've used `NAVWS_SalesLines`) and click **Add Reference**. Visual Studio will create the service reference on your project:

5. And it adds an entry on `app.config` with the service URL:

```
<setting
    name="ConsoleApplicationNAV_NAVWS_SalesLines_
    SalesOrderLInes_Service"
    serializeAs="String">
  <value>
      <YourWSURL>
  </value>
</setting>
```

6. Place a reference of your web service namespace in your code:

```
using ConsoleApplicationNAV.NAVWS_SalesLines;
```

7. We can create a function that receives as input the sales order number and line number to delete and then deletes the line. The signature will be this:

```
DeleteSalesOrderLinePage46(string SalesOrderNo, int LineNo)
```

8. As a first step, we need to create an instance for the `Page 46` web service (`NAVWS_SalesLines` web service in our Visual Studio project):

```
//Web Service instantiation
SalesOrderLines_Service ws = new SalesOrderLines_Service();

ws.Url =
Properties.Settings.Default.
ConsoleApplicationNAV_NAVWS_SalesLines_SalesOrderLines_Service;

ws.UseDefaultCredentials = true;
```

9. Now we have to read the sales line using the input parameters:

```
SalesOrderLInes line = ws.Read(SalesOrderNo, LineNo);
```

10. After that we have a reference to the sales line to delete. We can delete it using the `Delete` method of the NAV web service by passing `line.Key`:

```
ws.Delete(line.Key);
```

11. The complete function code is as follow:

```
private static void DeleteSalesOrderLinePage46(string
SalesOrderNo, int LineNo)
{
    //Web Service instantiation
    SalesOrderLines_Service ws = new SalesOrderLines_Service();

    //Web Service URL settings

    ws.Url = Properties.Settings.Default.
    ConsoleApplicationNAV_NAVWS_
    SalesLines_SalesOrderLines_Service;

    //Authentication as default
    ws.UseDefaultCredentials = true;

    //Reading the Sales Line to delete
    SalesOrderLines line = ws.Read(SalesOrderNo, LineNo);

    //Delete the Sales Line
    if (ws.Delete(line.Key))
    {
        Console.WriteLine("Line deleted.");
    }
}
```

Creating a cross-platform application

We have previously discovered how to use NAV web services from a console application written using C# and the full .NET Framework. This application can run on all the Windows systems.

But how we can interact with NAV web services from other platforms, for example from a Linux or a Mac OS machine? We can use **.NET Core**!

.NET Core is a new open source subset of the .NET Framework. It shares a common baseline with the full .NET stack and it's composed of the following parts:

- A .NET runtime
- A set of base .NET Framework libraries, APIs that are available on all platforms and .NET runtimes
- A set of SDK tools and compilers
- The `dotnet` application host, used to execute .NET Core applications

Let's take a look at the following steps to create a cross-platform application:

1. In the following figure, you can find a schema for the actual .NET development platform:

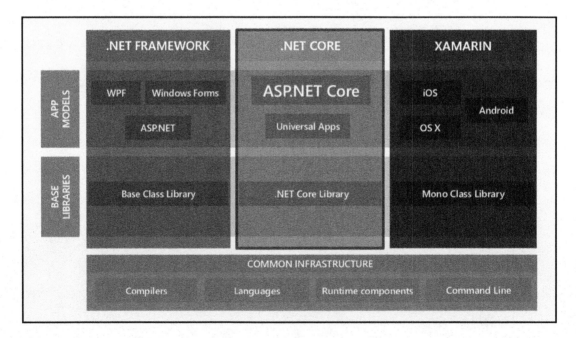

2. You can download and install .NET Core SDK from the following link:
   `https://microsoft.com/net/core`.

3. The best way to work with .NET Core is by using **Visual Studio Code**, a source code editor (open source) developed by Microsoft and available on any platform. You can download Visual Studio Code from the following link:
   `https://code.visualstudio.com`.

4. After downloading and installing .NET Core SDK and Visual Studio Code, I suggest that you launch Visual Studio Code and install the C# extension (it permits you to have C# support with IntelliSense and syntax highlighting). This could be done by clicking the **Extensions** menu and selecting the desired extension from the list of all available extensions.

5. To initiate a new C# project with .NET Core, open Command Prompt (or Terminal if you're on a non-Windows machine), navigate to the folder where you want to create the project, and type the following command:

   ```
   dotnet new
   ```

6. Enter the preceding command in the command prompt as shown in the following screenshot:

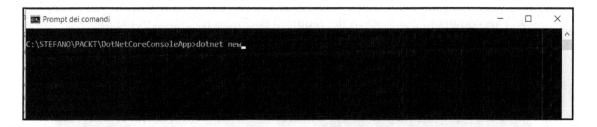

7. This command creates a new C# project with an *Hello World* sample:

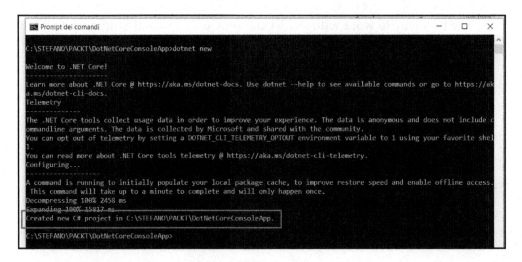

8. Now always from Command Prompt type:

```
dotnet restore
```

9. This command pulls down the required packages (declared in the `project.json` file):

10. You can open Visual Studio Code and after selecting the project folder you can see the files created. The `project.json` file contains all the program requirements and dependencies:

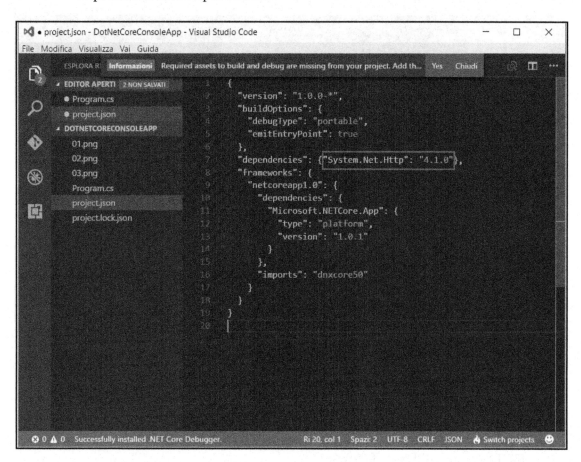

11. You can start writing your application directly in Visual Studio Code. Here, we don't have the complete tools and features that we have in Visual Studio, so we can't directly add a web reference to the NAV web services.

12. To call a NAV web service, we can use the .NET Framework `HttpClient` class:

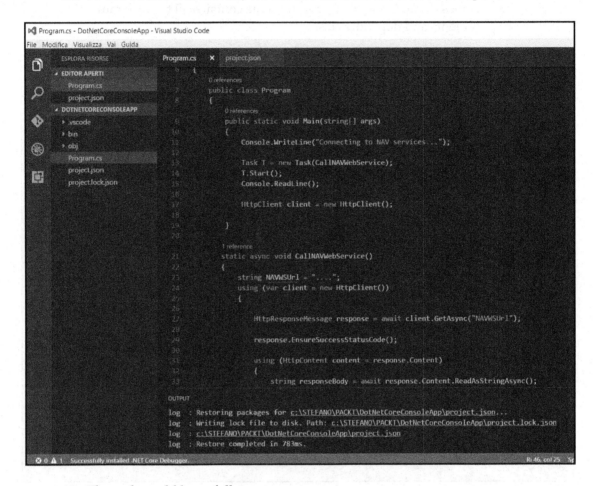

13. The code could be as follows:

```
using System;
using System.Net.Http;
using System.Threading.Tasks;

namespace ConsoleApplication
{
    public class Program
    {
        public static void Main(string[] args)
        {
            Console.WriteLine("Connecting to NAV services...");
```

```
            Task T = new Task(CallNAVWebService);
            T.Start();
            Console.ReadLine();

            HttpClient client = new HttpClient();
        }

    static async void CallNAVWebService()
    {
        string NAVWSUrl = "....";
        using (var client = new HttpClient())
        {
            HttpResponseMessage response = await
            client.GetAsync("NAVWSUrl");
            response.EnsureSuccessStatusCode();
              using (HttpContent content = response.Content)
            {
                string responseBody = await
                response.Content.ReadAsStringAsync();
                  Console.WriteLine("Reading the NAV
                  response");
                //Here you can parse the NAV WS response
            }
        }
    }
}
}
```

14. To launch the application, use the following command from Command Prompt:

    dotnet run

15. The preceding command will compile and run the application. If all is correct, you will see the following result:

16. After successfully testing the application, in order to release it to a production environment, you have to execute the following command:

```
dotnet publish -f netcoreapp1.0 -c release
```

17. You will receive the following output after inserting the preceding command in the command prompt:

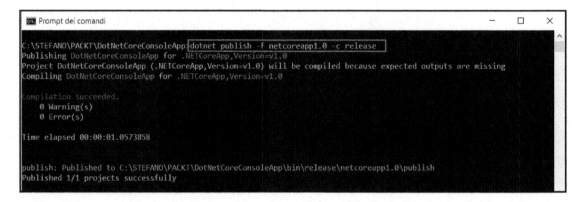

18. After this command, you can find a `publish` subfolder in your project's folder:

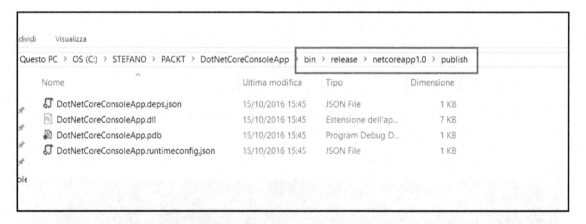

19. This folder contains all the files that can be deployed on the production environment to execute your application (you can just copy them). This application can be executed on every environment where .NET Core is installed (Windows, Linux, and maxOS).

Tips and tricks

When using NAV web services from external applications, I would recommend the following:

- Direct exposure of NAV web services to the external application should be done only if the consumer application is in your local network and if you manage that application
- If you want to expose NAV web services to external applications on the Internet, it's better to write a *proxy application* (middle tier) that permits you to not directly expose NAV to the outside world
- With a *proxy service* (a custom web service between NAV and the client application), you can expose only the desired method with the desired signatures, not the entire NAV entity
- For authentication with NAV web services, I recommend to impersonate a dedicated user with the desired permission
- Place all your settings (web service URLs) in `app.config` or `web.config`

Summary

This chapter shows how to expose a NAV object as a web service (in this case the **Sales Order** page) and how to create an application with Visual Studio and .NET in order to use this published web service.

You learned how to create a console application with Visual Studio, how to reference a published NAV web service in Visual Studio, and then how to use the web service methods and objects to perform operations such as retrieving and deleting data from NAV and creating new records on NAV (sales orders) with indirect calls to all the NAV business logic.

The chapter also shows you how to use an OData web service (endpoint) for reading NAV data and how to create a cross-platform application by using the new .NET core framework.

Now you have all you need to know in order to use NAV web services from custom applications. In the next chapters, we'll see how to use all these concepts in real-world applications.

4
Using NAV Web Services with Microsoft Power BI

In 2009, Microsoft came up with the idea to introduce a self-service business intelligence platform by announcing several BI add-ins for Microsoft Excel, such as **Power Pivot**, **Power Query**, and **Power View**. Following this, the Microsoft BI platform has silently evolved and Microsoft has presented a complete platform called Microsoft Power BI.

Microsoft Power BI is a growing platform for business reporting and data analysis. In this chapter, we want to discover how to use Power BI services to analyze data from Microsoft Dynamics NAV. The data from the NAV ERP will be published as web services to the Power BI platform. Here you will learn about the following topics:

- An overview of Power BI platform
- Publishing Microsoft Dynamics NAV data to Power BI
- Creating rich BI dashboards and reports with Power BI and NAV data
- Embed Power BI reports into a Microsoft Dynamics NAV page

Introducing Microsoft Power BI

Microsoft Power BI is a cloud-based platform that can be used for reporting and data analysis from a wide range of data sources. The platform is made up of several different components (that you can use independently or in a combination):

- **Power Query**: This is a tool for data discovery and transformation, and is able to work with data that comes from different data sources
- **Power Pivot**: This is an in-memory tabular data modeling tool

- **Power View**: This is a data visualization tool
- **Power Map**: This is a 3D geo-spatial data visualization tool
- **Power Q&A**: This is a natural language question and answering engine for Power BI
- **Power BI Desktop**: This is a desktop development tool for Power BI analysis and reporting
- **PowerBI.com website**: This is the **Power BI portal** (cloud service) where you can publish data analysis and reports and share them with your team
- **Power BI Mobile Apps**: These are the mobile applications for Power BI (Android, iOS, and Windows Mobile)

Power BI is currently available as part of the Office 365 Enterprise E5 version but you can start using it with a free plan (with a data capacity of 1 GB/user and other limitations) and upgrade it in the future to a Pro plan for $9.99 per user/per month.

These are the main differences between the Free and Pro versions:

	Free	Pro
Data capacity limit	1 GB/user	10 GB/user
Create, view, and share your personal dashboards and reports with other Power BI users	•	•
Author content with the Power BI Desktop	•	•
Explore data with natural language	•	•
Access your dashboards on mobile devices using native applications for iOS, Windows, and Android	•	•
Consume curated content packs for services such as Dynamics, Salesforce, and Google Analytics	•	•
Import data and reports from Excel, CSV, and Power BI Desktop files	•	•
Publish to the web	•	•

The differences with respect to data refresh are as follows:

Consume content that is scheduled to refresh	Daily	Hourly
Consume streaming data in your dashboards and reports	10 K rows/hour	1 M rows/hour
Consume live data sources with full interactivity		•

Access on-premises data using the Data Connectivity Gateways (Personal and Data Management)		•

For collaboration, the differences between the Free and Pro versions are:

Collaborate with your team using Office 365 groups in Power BI		•
Create, publish, and view organizational content packs		•
Manage access control and sharing through Active Directory groups		•
Shared data queries through the Data Catalog		•
Control data access with row-level security for users and groups		•

When you open the PowerBI.com portal or the **Power BI Desktop application**, you will have a workspace organized in different zones:

The zones highlighted are as follows:

- Navigation bar
- Dashboard with tiles
- Q&A question box
- Help and feedback buttons
- Dashboard title
- Office 365 app launcher
- Power BI home buttons
- Additional dashboard actions

The main parts of Power BI are **Datasets**, **Reports**, and **Dashboards**:

- A dataset is a set of data that you import or connect to from an external system. Each dataset represents a single source of data and you can use it on many different analyses.
- A report is a page of data visualization that comes from a single dataset and it contains charts, graphs, images, tables and so on. A report can be edited (if you have the permission to do so) or just viewed.
- A dashboard is something like a canvas that can display visualizations from many different datasets and many different reports. You can see it as a workspace with all the content for an analysis.

Here we don't want to go in to more detail about Power BI (it's beyond the scope of this book). For more information, you can check `https://powerbi.microsoft.com/en-us/`.

In the next sections, we'll see how to publish data from NAV (by using web services) and how to use them on the Power BI platform. We'll start by using the Power BI Desktop application and finally we'll publish the data on the cloud platform.

Publishing NAV data for Power BI

In order to use NAV data from Power BI, we need to publish it as OData web services (we want to absolutely avoid direct access to SQL Server tables). The best way to work is to use `Query` objects. This permits you to query the NAV database and retrieve fields from a single table or from multiple tables (by using `join` clauses):

1. We can start by using the standard NAV `Query` object with `ID = 102`(Item Sales by Customer):

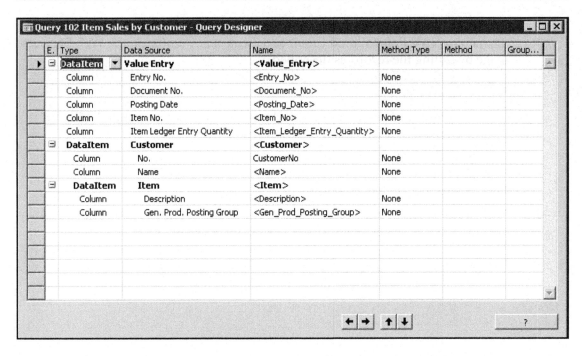

2. You can directly run the `Query` object from the NAV Development Environment and see the following result set:

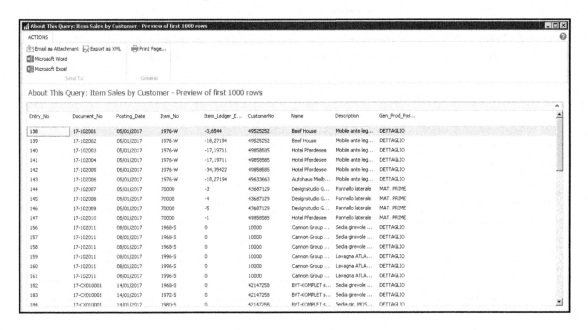

3. When your Query is ready to be published, you've to access the Microsoft Dynamics NAV RoleTailored Client and create a new entry on the **Web Services** page by setting the record as described:

- **Object Type**: Query
- **Object ID**: 102
- **Service Name**: Your desired service name, recommended without using spaces (here it is ItemSalesByCustomer)
- **Published**: TRUE

Your record will appear as follows:

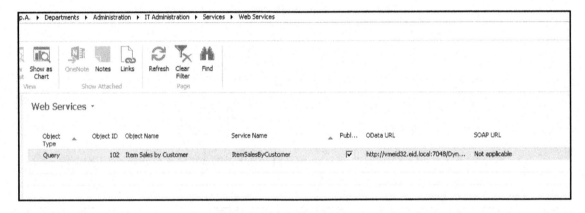

4. When published, NAV gives you the OData URL. You can check the URL on your browser and what you'll obtain is a feed of data in XML format:

```
<?xml version="1.0" encoding="utf-8"?><feed xml:base="http://192.6.1.37:7048/DynamicsNAV90/OData/" xmlns="http://www.w3.org/2005/Atom" xmlns:d="http://schemas.microsoft.com/
xmlns:m="http://schemas.microsoft.com/ado/2007/08/dataservices/metadata"><id>http://192.6.1.37:7048/DynamicsNAV90/OData/Company('CRONUS%20Italia%20S.p.A.')/ItemSalesByCustom
22T15:45:27Z</updated><link rel="self" title="ItemSalesByCustomer" href="ItemSalesByCustomer" /><entry><id>http://192.6.1.37:7048/DynamicsNAV90/OData/Company('CRONUS%20Itali
W',CustomerNo='49525252',Entry_No=138)</id><category term="NAV.ItemSalesByCustomer" scheme="http://schemas.microsoft.com/ado/2007/08/dataservices/scheme" /><link rel="edit"
href="Company('CRONUS%20Italia%20S.p.A.')/ItemSalesByCustomer(AuxiliaryIndex1='1976-W',CustomerNo='49525252',Entry_No=138)" /><title /><updated>2016-09-22T15:45:27Z</updated
<d:Entry_No m:type="Edm.Int32">138</d:Entry_No><d:Document_No>17-102001</d:Document_No><d:Posting_Date m:type="Edm.DateTime">2017-01-05T00:00:00</d:Posting_Date><d:Item_No>1
m:type="Edm.Decimal">-3.6544</d:Item_Ledger_Entry_Quantity><d:CustomerNo>49525252</d:CustomerNo><d:Name>Beef House</d:Name><d:Description>Mobile ante legno INNSBRUCK</d:Desc
<d:AuxiliaryIndex1>1976-W</d:AuxiliaryIndex1></m:properties></content></entry><entry><id>http://192.6.1.37:7048/DynamicsNAV90/OData/Company('CRONUS%20Italia%20S.p.A.')/ItemS
</id><category term="NAV.ItemSalesByCustomer" scheme="http://schemas.microsoft.com/ado/2007/08/dataservices/scheme" /><link rel="edit" title="ItemSalesByCustomer" href="Comp
W',CustomerNo='49525252',Entry_No=139)" /><title /><updated>2016-09-22T15:45:27Z</updated><author><name /></author><content type="application/xml"><m:properties><d:Entry_No
<d:Posting_Date m:type="Edm.DateTime">2017-01-05T00:00:00</d:Posting_Date><d:Item_No>1976-W</d:Item_No><d:Item_Ledger_Entry_Quantity m:type="Edm.Decimal">-18.27194</d:Item_L
House</d:Name><d:Description>Mobile ante legno INNSBRUCK</d:Description><d:Gen_Prod_Posting_Group>DETTAGLIO</d:Gen_Prod_Posting_Group><d:AuxiliaryIndex1>1976-W</d:AuxiliaryI
<id>http://192.6.1.37:7048/DynamicsNAV90/OData/Company('CRONUS%20Italia%20S.p.A.')/ItemSalesByCustomer(AuxiliaryIndex1='1976-W',CustomerNo='49858585',Entry_No=140)</id><cate
scheme="http://schemas.microsoft.com/ado/2007/08/dataservices/scheme" /><link rel="edit" title="ItemSalesByCustomer" href="Company('CRONUS%20Italia%20S.p.A.')/ItemSalesByCus
/><updated>2016-09-22T15:45:27Z</updated><author><name /></author><content type="application/xml"><m:properties><d:Entry_No m:type="Edm.Int32">140</d:Entry_No><d:Document_No
05T00:00:00</d:Posting_Date><d:Item_No>1976-W</d:Item_No><d:Item_Ledger_Entry_Quantity m:type="Edm.Decimal">-17.19711</d:Item_Ledger_Entry_Quantity><d:CustomerNo>49858585</d
INNSBRUCK</d:Description><d:Gen_Prod_Posting_Group>DETTAGLIO</d:Gen_Prod_Posting_Group><d:AuxiliaryIndex1>1976-W</d:AuxiliaryIndex1></m:properties></content></entry><entry>
<id>http://192.6.1.37:7048/DynamicsNAV90/OData/Company('CRONUS%20Italia%20S.p.A.')/ItemSalesByCustomer(AuxiliaryIndex1='1976-W',Company('CRONUS%20Italia%20S.p.A.')/ItemSalesByCus
/><updated>2016-09-22T15:45:27Z</updated><author><name /></author><content type="application/xml"><m:properties><d:Entry_No m:type="Edm.Int32">141</d:Entry_No><d:Document_No
05T00:00:00</d:Posting_Date><d:Item_No>1976-W</d:Item_No><d:Item_Ledger_Entry_Quantity m:type="Edm.Decimal">-17.19711</d:Item_Ledger_Entry_Quantity><d:CustomerNo>49858585</d
INNSBRUCK</d:Description><d:Gen_Prod_Posting_Group>DETTAGLIO</d:Gen_Prod_Posting_Group><d:AuxiliaryIndex1>1976-W</d:AuxiliaryIndex1></m:properties></content></entry><entry>
<id>http://192.6.1.37:7048/DynamicsNAV90/OData/Company('CRONUS%20Italia%20S.p.A.')/ItemSalesByCustomer(AuxiliaryIndex1='1976-W',CustomerNo='49858585',Entry_No=142)</id><cate
scheme="http://schemas.microsoft.com/ado/2007/08/dataservices/scheme" /><link rel="edit" title="ItemSalesByCustomer" href="Company('CRONUS%20Italia%20S.p.A.')/ItemSalesByCus
/><updated>2016-09-22T15:45:27Z</updated><author><name /></author><content type="application/xml"><m:properties><d:Entry_No m:type="Edm.Int32">142</d:Entry_No><d:Document_No
05T00:00:00</d:Posting_Date><d:Item_No>1976-W</d:Item_No><d:Item_Ledger_Entry_Quantity m:type="Edm.Decimal">-34.39422</d:Item_Ledger_Entry_Quantity><d:CustomerNo>49858585</d
INNSBRUCK</d:Description><d:Gen_Prod_Posting_Group>DETTAGLIO</d:Gen_Prod_Posting_Group><d:AuxiliaryIndex1>1976-W</d:AuxiliaryIndex1></m:properties></content></entry><entry>
<id>http://192.6.1.37:7048/DynamicsNAV90/OData/Company('CRONUS%20Italia%20S.p.A.')/ItemSalesByCustomer(AuxiliaryIndex1='1976-W',CustomerNo='49858585',Entry_No=143)</id><cate
scheme="http://schemas.microsoft.com/ado/2007/08/dataservices/scheme" /><link rel="edit" title="ItemSalesByCustomer" href="Company('CRONUS%20Italia%20S.p.A.')/ItemSalesByCus
/><updated>2016-09-22T15:45:27Z</updated><author><name /></author><content type="application/xml"><m:properties><d:Entry_No m:type="Edm.Int32">143</d:Entry_No><d:Document_No
05T00:00:00</d:Posting_Date><d:Item_No>1976-W</d:Item_No><d:Item_Ledger_Entry_Quantity m:type="Edm.Decimal">-18.27194</d:Item_Ledger_Entry_Quantity><d:CustomerNo>49633663</d
legno INNSBRUCK</d:Description><d:Gen_Prod_Posting_Group>DETTAGLIO</d:Gen_Prod_Posting_Group><d:AuxiliaryIndex1>1976-W</d:AuxiliaryIndex1></m:properties></content></entry><entry>
<id>http://192.6.1.37:7048/DynamicsNAV90/OData/Company('CRONUS%20Italia%20S.p.A.')/ItemSalesByCustomer(AuxiliaryIndex1='70000',CustomerNo='43687129',Entry_No=144)</id><categ
scheme="http://schemas.microsoft.com/ado/2007/08/dataservices/scheme" /><link rel="edit" title="ItemSalesByCustomer" href="Company('CRONUS%20Italia%20S.p.A.')/ItemSalesByCus
/><updated>2016-09-22T15:45:27Z</updated><author><name /></author><content type="application/xml"><m:properties><d:Entry_No m:type="Edm.Int32">144</d:Entry_No><d:Document_No
05T00:00:00</d:Posting_Date><d:Item_No>70000</d:Item_No><d:Item_Ledger_Entry_Quantity m:type="Edm.Decimal">-3</d:Item_Ledger_Entry_Quantity><d:CustomerNo>43687129</d:Custome
laterale</d:Description><d:Gen_Prod_Posting_Group>MAT. PRIME</d:Gen_Prod_Posting_Group><d:AuxiliaryIndex1>70000</d:AuxiliaryIndex1></m:properties></content></entry><entry>
<id>http://192.6.1.37:7048/DynamicsNAV90/OData/Company('CRONUS%20Italia%20S.p.A.')/ItemSalesByCustomer(AuxiliaryIndex1='70000',CustomerNo='43687129',Entry_No=145)</id><categ
```

5. Now you're ready to use this OData URL for using your NAV data with the Power BI Desktop.

Loading NAV data on the Power BI desktop

Let's see how the NAV data loads on the Power BI desktop by performing the following steps:

1. The Power BI Desktop can be downloaded for free from the PowerBI.com website at https://powerbi.microsoft.com/en-us/desktop/.

   The download starts automatically for your Windows OS version you have on your machine.

2. After it's installed (it's a simple wizard), launch the Power BI Desktop:

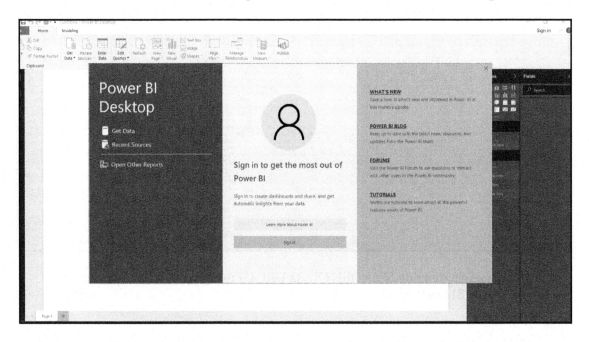

The application starts by presenting a blank desktop. This is the point to start to create an analysis.

3. In the ribbon toolbar, click the **Get Data** button and then select **OData Feed**:

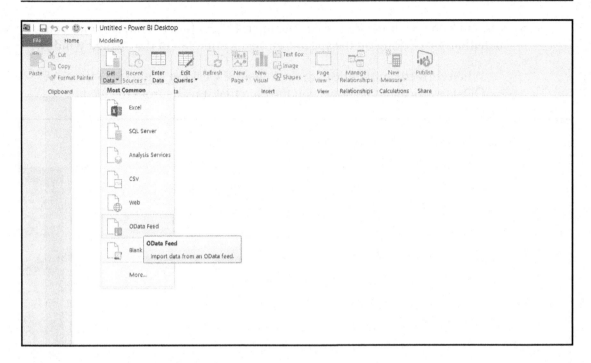

4. In the **OData Feed** window, insert the OData URL that comes from NAV:

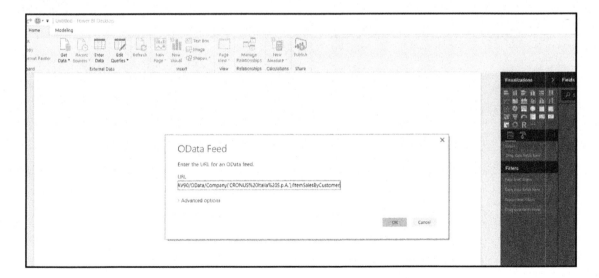

5. Now click on **OK**. If the Power BI Desktop asks you for credentials, enter your credentials by clicking on the specific authentication tab in the opened window.

When correctly authenticated, the Power BI Desktop connects to the NAV OData service and it shows you the data that it reads from the feed:

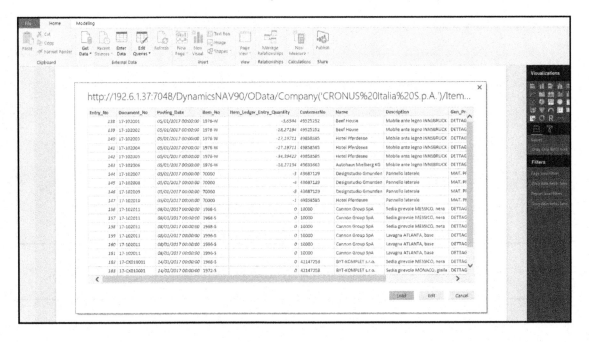

6. Now click on **Load** to load the NAV data. Power BI will create a dataset and you can see all the available data fields in the right panel:

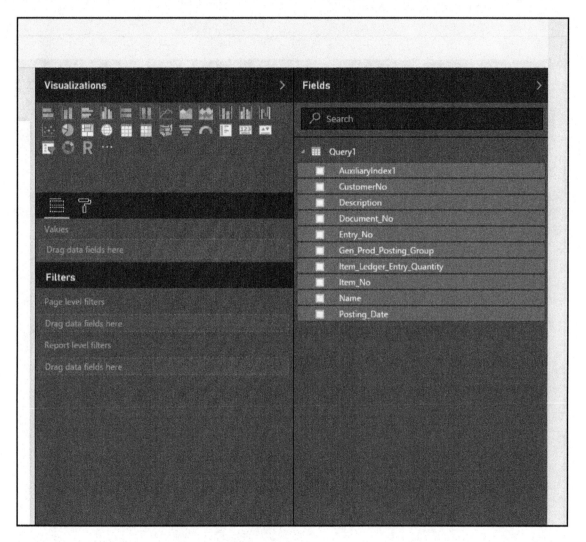

Now we're ready to analyze our NAV data with the Power BI Desktop.

7. Let's try to analyze the number of sales for customer and display them on a pie chart. Click on **Visualizations** to select the type of data visualization you want. Here we select **Pie chart**:

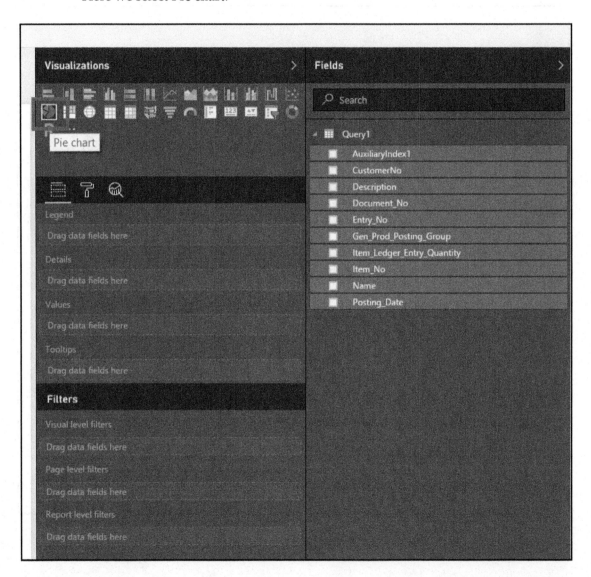

8. Now select the measures. Click on `CustomerNo` (or drag the field to the **Legend** section) and then drag the `Item_Ledger_Entry_Quantity` field on the **Values** section. Then drag the `Name` field on the **Details** section:

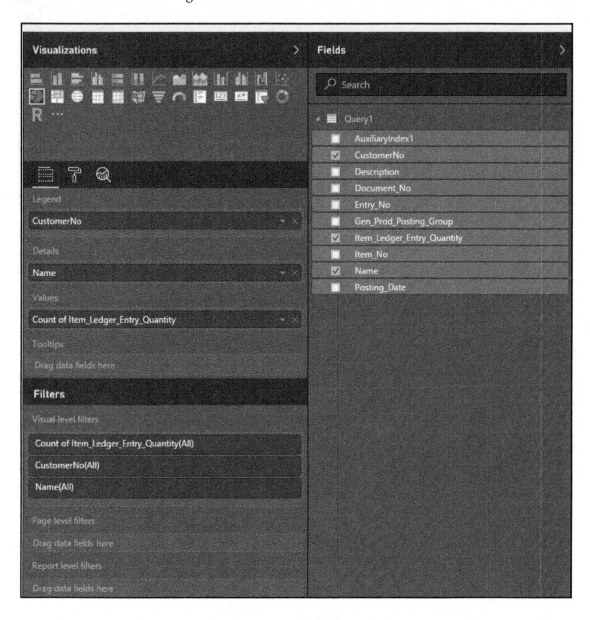

Power BI will display a chart like the following:

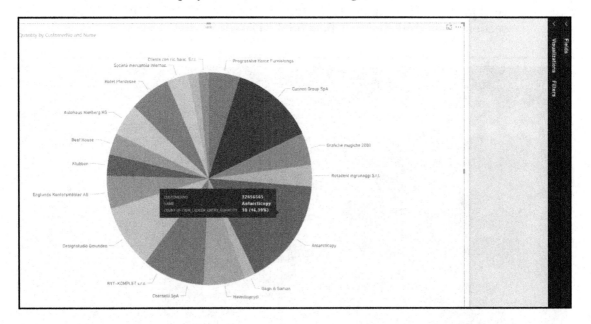

If we want to see the *number of sales per date* in a line chart, refer to the following screenshot:

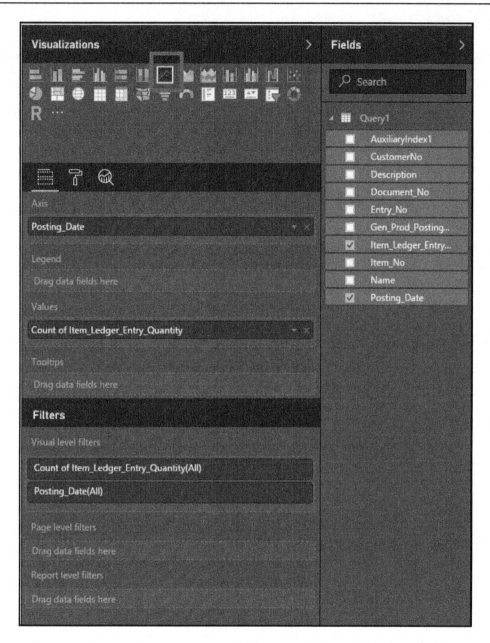

And this is the result:

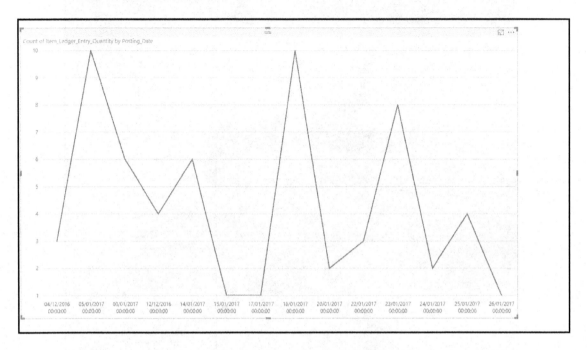

We can now create a dashboard by adding more graphs (**Visuals** in Power BI terms).

9. Click on the**New Visual** button on the ribbon:

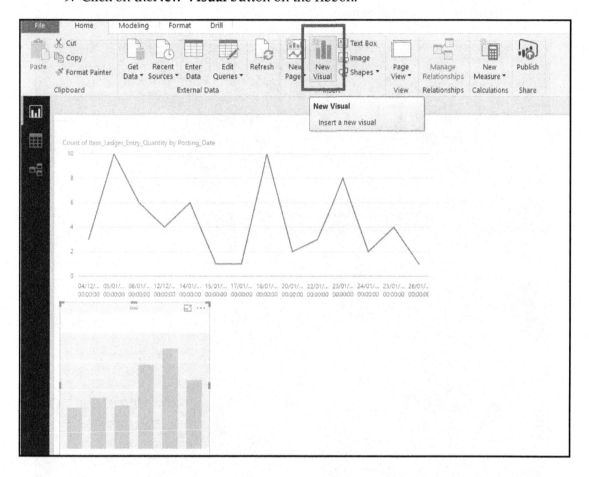

10. Select the newly added Visual object and add, for example, a pie chart with the details of the sales for items:

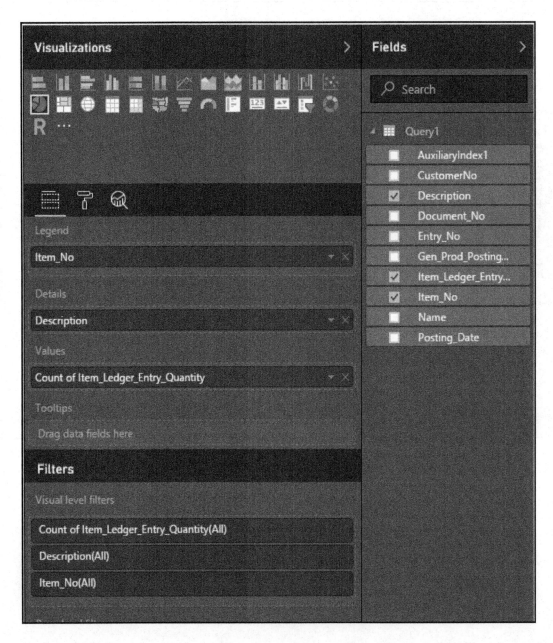

11. You can format the legend for every chart (and other details) by clicking the **Format** button and go to the desired section:

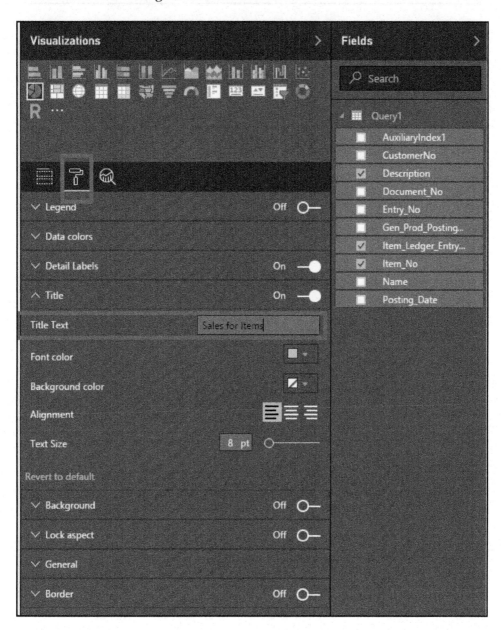

And now your dashboard appears as follow:

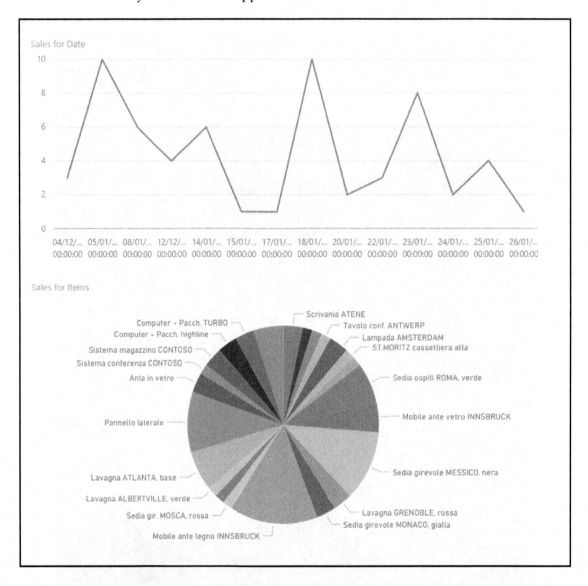

Publishing your NAV dashboard to the Power BI portal

After the creation of a Power BI report with the desktop application, here we want to create a Power BI dashboard and publish it on the PowerBI.com website by performing the following steps:

1. Let's start by opening the Microsoft Dynamics NAV Development Environment and for this sample we'll use the NAV query, Top Customer Overview (object ID = 100):

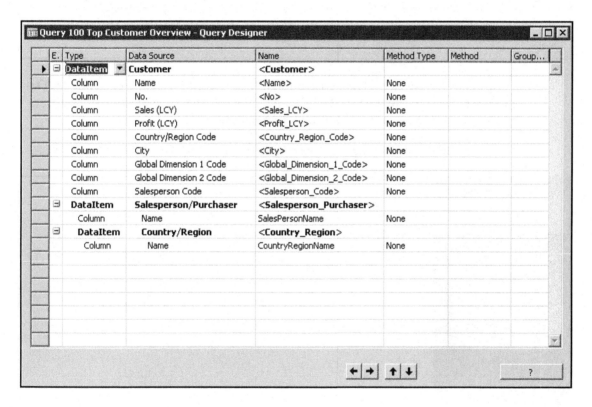

2. From the NAV RoleTailored Client, open the **Web Services** page and publish this `Query` object as a web service:

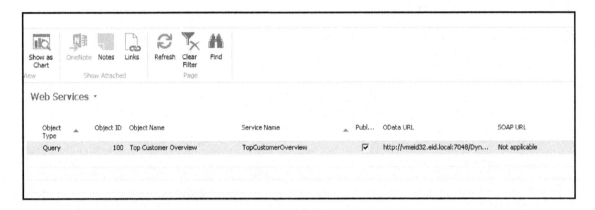

3. Copy the web service OData URL and on the Power BI Desktop click on **Get Data | OData Feed**. Paste the OData URL and click **OK** (here I've used the IP address but it's better to use a fully qualified domain name).

The Power BI Desktop may show you this message:

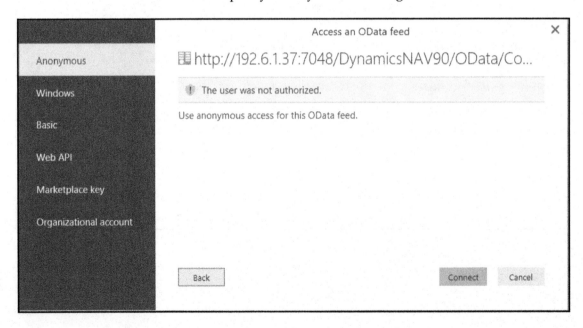

4. If so, click on the desired authentication tab on the left and insert the correct credentials:

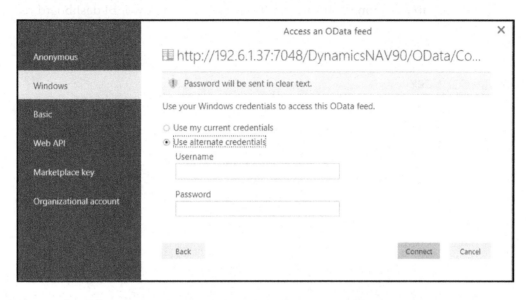

Power BI will load the NAV data via the OData web service and you will see the dataset in the right pane:

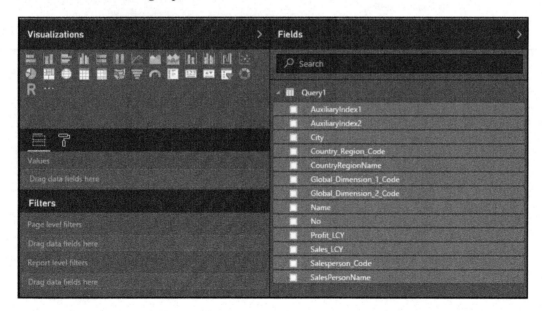

5. We can start adding visuals, for example, **SALES BY COUNTRY** and by **SALES BY SALES PERSON** and a visual map of all sales (because in the dataset we have the **Country Region Code**) and at the end we have a Power BI dashboard ready to use:

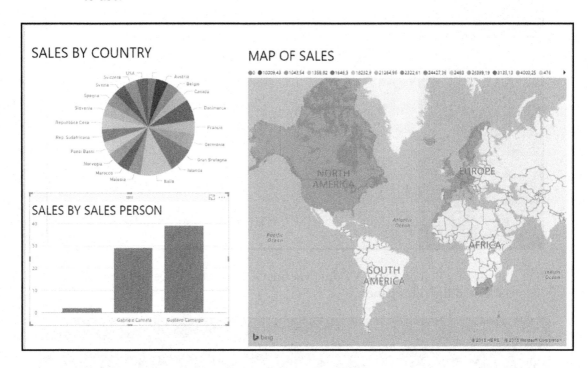

6. The magic of a Power BI dashboard is that everything is filtered by context. If you click, for example, on a sales person's name, all the dashboard will be filtered accordingly:

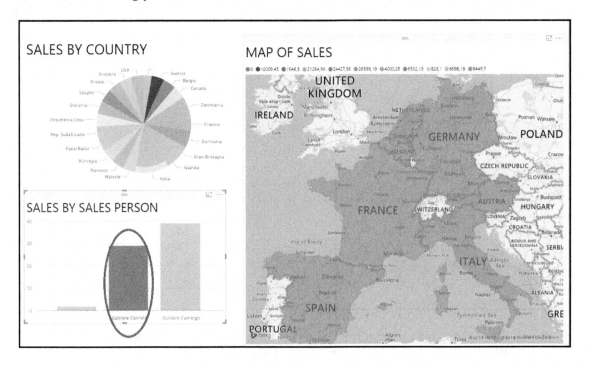

7. Who sells in the USA? Just click on the map:

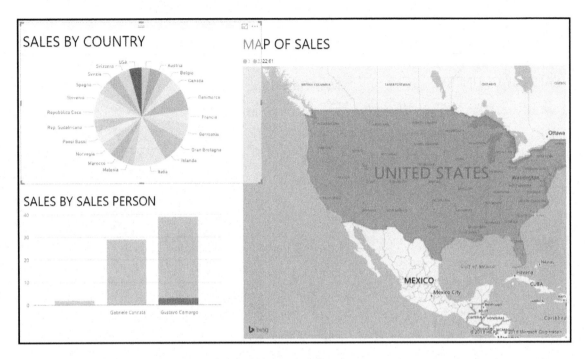

8. The dashboard can be refreshed by clicking the **Refresh** button on the toolbar (Power BI will refresh the data via the OData service):

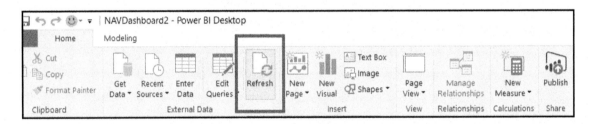

9. Now we want to publish our new dashboard to the PowerBI.com portal for sharing and collaboration with people outside our office or organization. To do this, click on the **Publish** button or the Power BI Desktop ribbon:

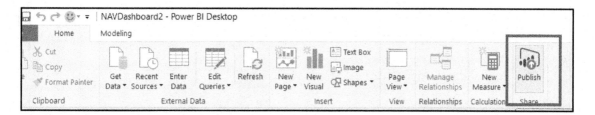

10. If you're not signed on the PowerBI.com portal, you will be required to log in:

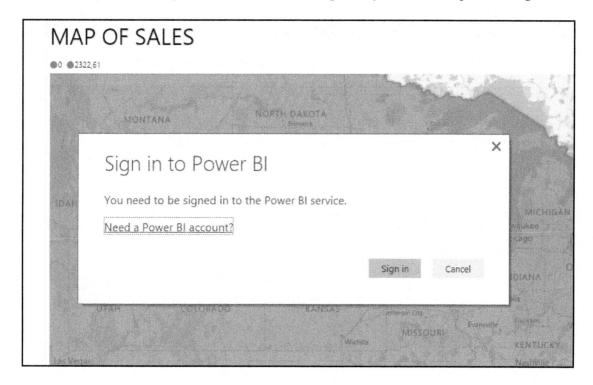

After entering your credentials, the publishing process starts:

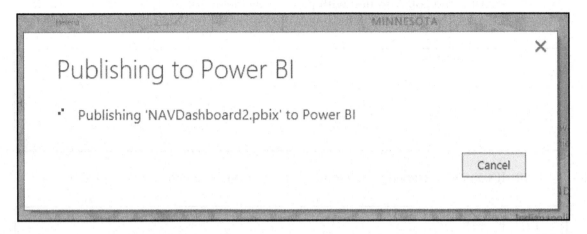

And if all is OK, when your dashboard is published you will receive this message:

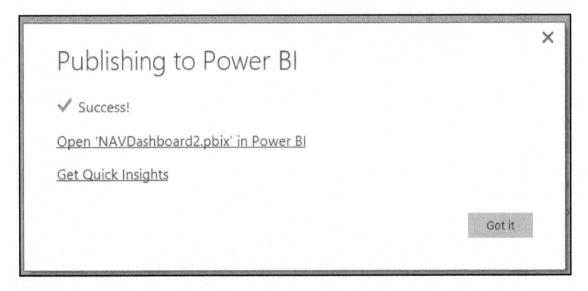

11. Now you can log in to the PowerBI.com portal (or just click the link on the previous message window) and you will see your new dashboard/report and the published NAV dataset (ready for creating new analysis directly from the web portal):

12. On your Power BI.com portal, you have all your loaded datasets and all your saved reports and dashboards (not only the ones you've just published).

Microsoft Dynamics NAV content pack for Power BI

Starting from NAV 2016, Power BI has a special content pack for NAV (freely available) that contains ready-to-go dashboards and reports for NAV financials and sales data. You can find details about the Microsoft Dynamics NAV content pack for Power BI at
https://powerbi.microsoft.com/en-us/integrations/microsoft-dynamics-nav/.

Let's see how we can use Microsoft Dynamics NAV content pack for Power BI by performing the following steps:

1. In order to use this content pack on PowerBI.com, after connecting to the portal you've to click on the **Get Data** button on the left pane:

2. And then in the **Services** box, select the **Get** button:

3. Now select the **Microsoft Dynamics NAV** content pack and click **Get**:

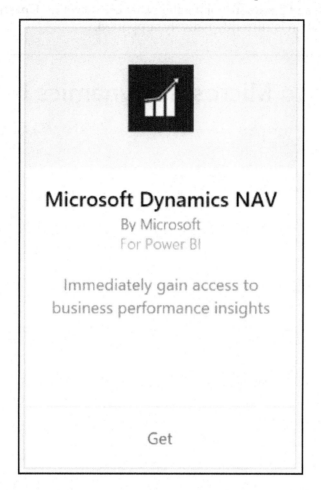

4. After the content pack selection, Power BI prompts you to enter the NAV OData URL. The URL has this schema:

```
https//navservername:port/NAV_Instance/OData/
Company('CRONUS%20International%20Ltd.')
```

Where `navservername` is the NAV server name, `port` is the OData port (`default = 7048`), and `NAV_Instance` is the NAV server instance name.

5. In the **Authentication Method** window, you've to choose **Basic** and insert the username and password for a valid NAV user account. Unfortunately, only basic authentication is currently natively supported:

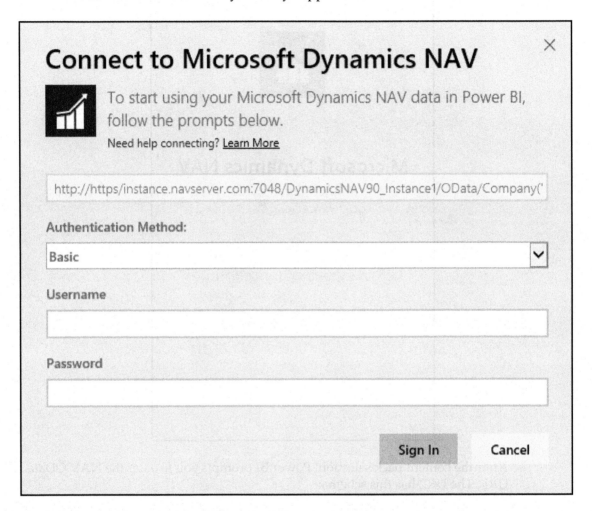

If the connection is OK, Power BI will retrieve the data from your NAV database and it creates a pre-defined dashboard and a set of reports ready to use:

6. As mentioned before, actually the NAV content pack for Power BI *supports only basic authentication* out of the box, so you have to configure a NAV server instance in order to use the **NavUserPassword** authentication.

   The Power BI Desktop will allow you to avoid this, but the NAV content pack is not available for the desktop version (so there are no pre-built dashboards).

7. For enterprise customers who need an efficient way to use the Power BI platform, actually the use of the Power BI Desktop in conjunction with a **Power BI Data Gateway** is the best solution.

8. The data Gateway acts as a bridge, providing quick and secure data transfer between your NAV data and Power BI. You can have one single connection with your NAV OData service and this connection can be shared across all the Power BI objects you create (**Datasets**, **Reports**, and **Dashboards**).

Starting from version 2017, Microsoft Dynamics NAV permits you to embed a Power BI report directly into **Role Center**:

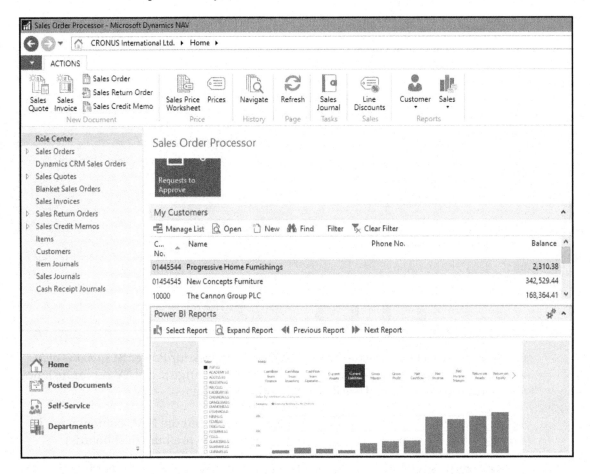

9. In NAV 2017, you have a new **Active Directory Setup Wizard** where you can link an Azure Active Directory account to a NAV account. This setup registers the NAV application on Azure and generates an application ID and key that you will use on the new NAV 2017 Power BI assisted wizard in order to set up the connection with PowerBI.com.

10. To launch this setup from NAV, navigate to **Departments | Administration | Application Setup | General | Assisted Setup** and choose **Set up Azure Active Directory**:

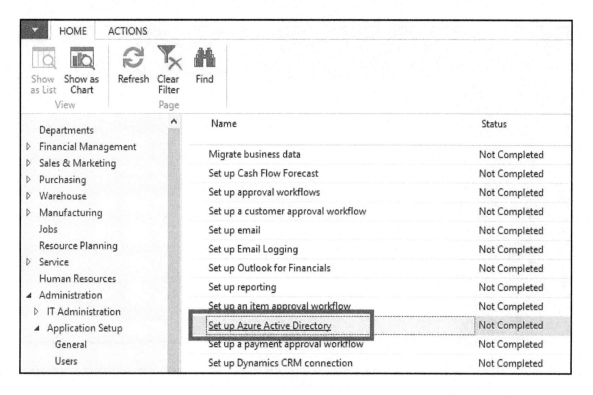

11. In the Azure portal, you've to click on **Azure Active Directory** and create a new application registration. In the **App Registrations** window, copy the **Reply URL** that NAV shows you when you launch the **Active Directory Setup Wizard**:

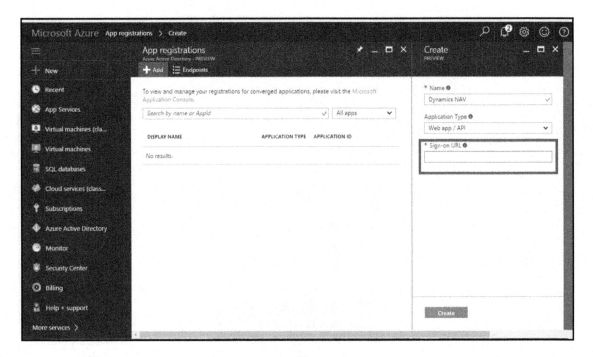

12. Then you have to set the permissions for the Power BI service, so select your app and navigate to **Required Permission** | **Add** | **Select an API** | **Power BI Service (Power BI)**:

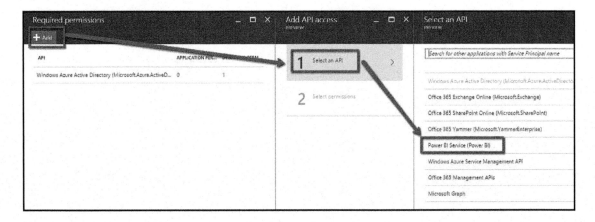

13. Provide the required permissions to the Power BI service and click **Select**:

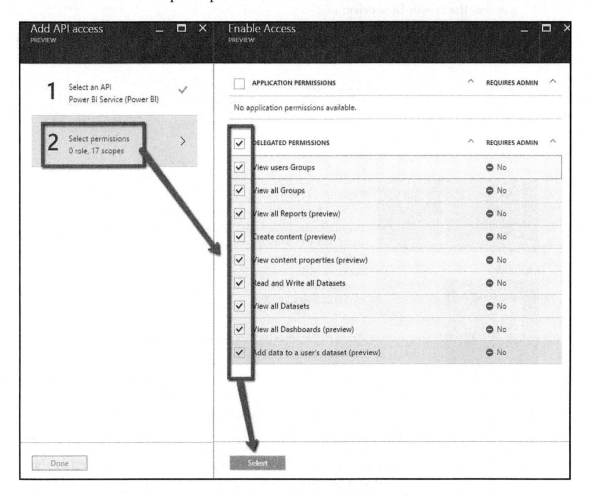

14. When registered, go to **Settings** and select **Keys** to create an application key. Azure gives you the **Application ID** and **Key** that you have to provide on NAV in the **Setup Azure Active Directory Wizard** window.

15. The last step with NAV is to authorize the **Azure Active Directory Service** to access the Power BI service:

16. After this setup, you can select what Power BI report you want to embed in your NAV **Role Center** and you can directly navigate your report from NAV (there is no need to switch the environment).

Summary

In this chapter, we have covered the first real-world usage of NAV web services: publishing your data to the Microsoft cloud business intelligence platform (Power BI).

We have discovered what Power BI is and what you can do with the Microsoft BI service (desktop application and cloud portal).

We have learned how to publish NAV data to the Power BI Desktop application by using NAV OData web services and how to create reports and dashboards from that application. Next, we have learned how to publish a dashboard to the cloud portal of Power BI.

Finally, we discovered the Microsoft Dynamics NAV content pack for Power BI and looked at how to use it and what the actual limits are.

In the next chapter, we'll see a real-world case of integration between NAV and external applications by using web services.

5
Integrating NAV Web Services and External Applications

As described in the previous chapters, an external application can interact with NAV business logic by directly using its published web services. But in the real world, normally you don't want to directly expose a NAV web service to the outside world and your external application could have requirements that NAV web services cannot completely satisfy.

In this chapter, we'll see a real-world integration scenario between NAV and an external application. We'll see how we can decouple NAV web services from external clients and how we can create an integration framework that is client-independent. This chapter covers the following topics:

- Handling integration business logic in NAV and decoupling it from the outside world
- Writing a RESTful WCF service
- A service interacting with NAV by using JSON and XML
- Deploying a real-world integration solution between NAV and a B2B website

An overview of the business scenario

A sales company needs to integrate its core **ERP** (**Microsoft Dynamics NAV**) with an external B2B website in order to have a complete web shop (e-commerce). The business requirements are as follows:

- The items catalog must be read from NAV.
- Every item has a **BRAND** dimension.
- Customers' details and their shipment addresses must be read from NAV.
- Only customers properly enabled on NAV should be exposed to the B2B website.
- Customers in NAV have a dimension called CUSTOMER_TYPE. This dimension value will affect a behavior on the B2B website (they can see a different menu item, only prices, prices + discounts, and so on).
- Items availability must be obtained in real-time from the NAV inventory.
- Items sales prices must be obtained from NAV in real-time according to the ERP sales price logic.
- When a user from the B2B website confirms a sales order, this must be transmitted to NAV for processing.
- The B2B website is located on an external server (no LAN communication).

To satisfy this scenario and in order to create an open interface, our architecture will be implemented with these guidelines:

- NAV business logic and entities will be exposed as web services.
- NAV web services will not be directly exposed to the Internet.
- The B2B website will connect to NAV by using a proxy service (WCF service). This WCF service will expose to the external application (B2B) only the required functions.
- All the service calls must be handled in a secure way (authentication in the SOAP header).
- The messages between NAV and the external application (B2B) will be available as XML and JSON format.

Our software architecture is illustrated in the following diagram:

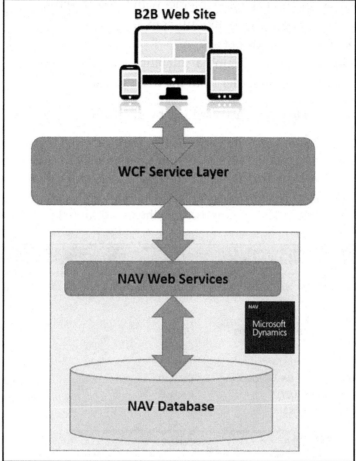

Creating NAV business logic

The first step we have to do to develop our solution is to provide the business logic functionalities in NAV.

Our NAV must provide to the external application (B2B website) the following features:

- A list of customers enabled to interact with the B2B website
- For every customer, a list of its shipment addresses
- A list of items with their details
- A function to retrieve an item's availability and sales prices
- A function to insert an order from the B2B website

Let's see how we can create NAV business logic by performing the following steps:

1. To enable a customer entity to be visible to the external B2B website, we can add a `Boolean` field called `Web Active` on **Customer Card**. All customers with `Web Active` set as `true` will be visible to the external application.

2. Open the Microsoft Dynamics NAV Development Environment, go to the `Customer` table (`ID = 18`), and create the `Boolean` field:

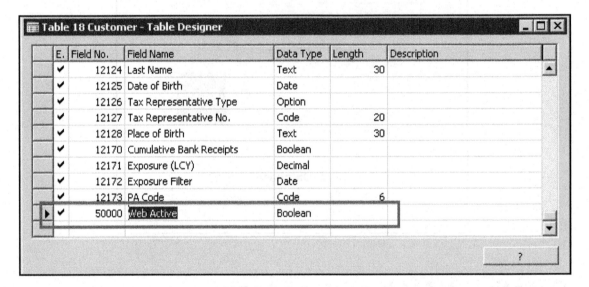

3. After that, open `Page 21 – ` **Customer Card** and add this new field to the user interface.

4. To expose a list of customers to the B2B website, we have to design a `Query` object on NAV. The `Query` object must retrieve all customers where `Web Active = TRUE` and for every customer the corresponding `CUSTOMER_TYPE` dimension value must be returned.

    The `Query` object can be designed as follows:

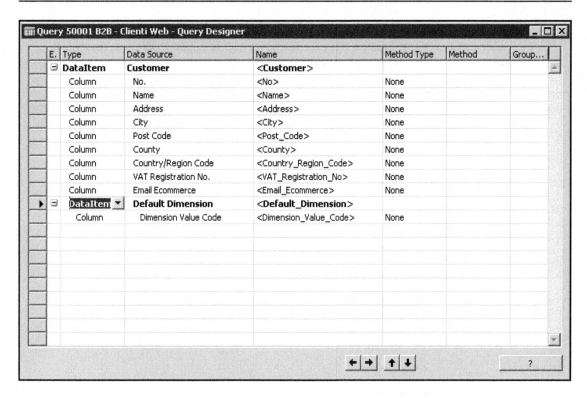

5. For the `Customer DataItem`, we have to apply the appropriate
   `DataItemTableFilter` value:

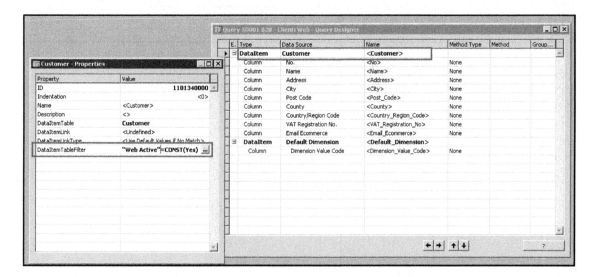

6. For every customer, we have to retrieve the corresponding `Default Dimension` table entry where `Dimension Code` is `CUSTOMER_TYPE`. We can do this as follows:

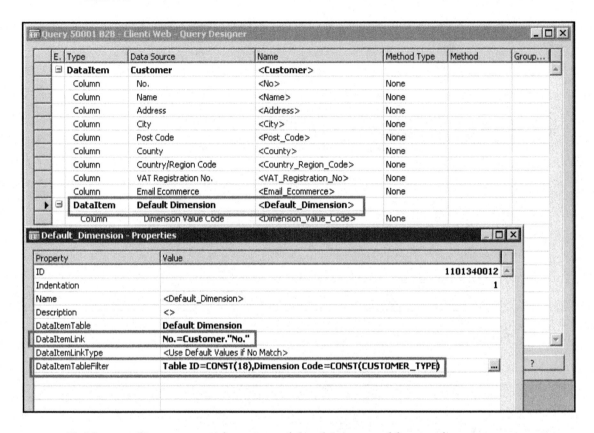

7. Now we have to provide a view of the shipment addresses for every customer. This can be done simply by creating a `Query` object like this:

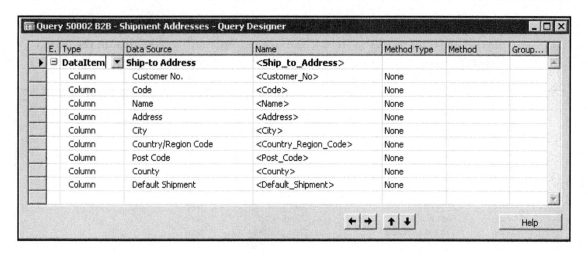

8. For retrieving an item's details, we can write a new `Query` object as shown in the following screenshot:

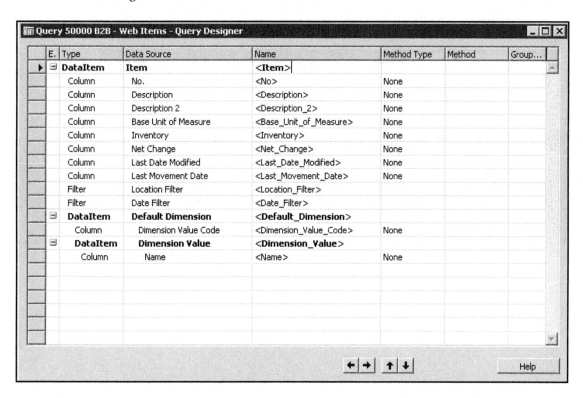

9. We need to also retrieve the **BRAND** dimension associated to the Item record (as the Default Dimension in NAV). We can apply a filter like this on the Query object:

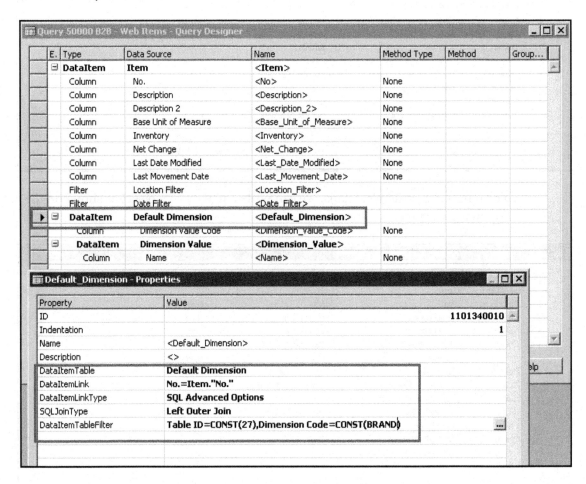

10. With `DataItemLinkType` we set a data item link by creating an SQL `join`. The `SQLJoinType` property is set to `Left Outer Join`. The resulting dataset contains every record from the upper `DataItemTable`, even if a record does not have a matching value in the lower data item for fields that are linked by the `DataItemLink` property. Then from the `Default Dimension` value, we can retrieve the `Dimension Value` (the **BRAND** name) by using the `Dimension Code` with a `DataItemTableLink` property as follows:

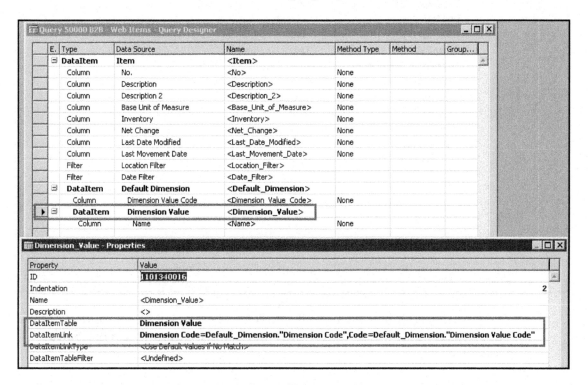

11. Now we have to create a NAV table for storing **Sales Orders** that arrives from the B2B website (you can see them as *drafts* and they must be checked and converted to real **Sales Orders** inside NAV). In NAV, we can create a table like this:

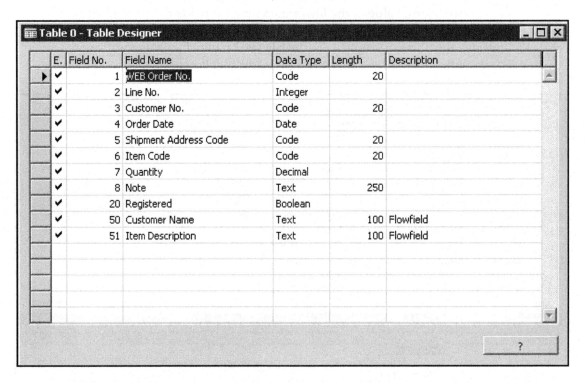

These B2B Sales Orders will be visible to NAV operators in an appropriate NAV Page object and with a proper function they could transform them to a **Sales Order** inside NAV.

12. The last piece of work inside NAV is to build the business logic that we have to expose to the B2B application. As an architectural choice, we decide to write a single codeunit with all the functions that must be available to the external application. This codeunit will be then exposed as a web service in NAV (single service).

13. The functions that we have to implement in the NAV codeunit are as follows:

   - GetSalesPrice: This gets the item sales price for a particular customer in a particular date
   - GetSalesDiscount: This gets the item sales discount for a particular customer at a particular date
   - GetItemInventory: This gets the item inventory at the current date
   - InsertOrderB2B: This permits you to insert a sales order from an external application to NAV

This is the C/AL code for the functions previously described in the GetSalesPrice parameters:

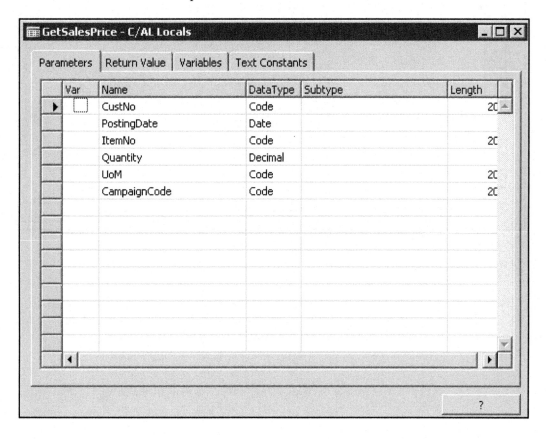

Let's take a look at the GetSalesPrice local variables in the following screenshot:

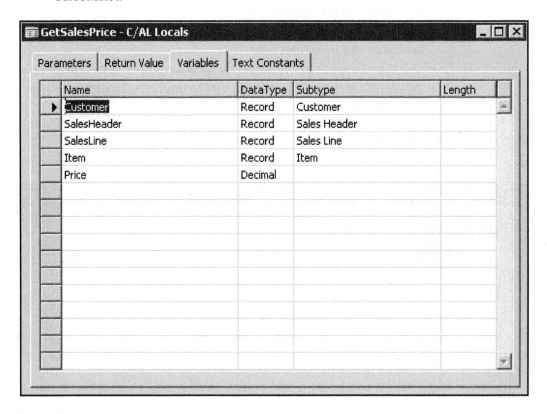

This is the NAV codeunit C/AL code that we expose as a web service:

```
GetSalesPrice(CustNo : Code[20];PostingDate : Date;ItemNo :
Code[20];Quantity : Decimal;UoM : Code[20];CampaignCode :
Code[20]) : Decimal
Price := 0;
IF Customer.GET(CustNo) AND Item.GET(ItemNo) THEN
BEGIN
  //Here we create a Sales Order
  //with a special code that will avoid primary key violation
    and
  //that persists only for the duration of this transaction
  SalesHeader."Document Type" := SalesHeader."Document
  Type"::Order;
  SalesHeader."No.":='B2B';
  SalesHeader.VALIDATE("Sell-to Customer No.",CustNo);
  SalesHeader.VALIDATE("Posting Date",PostingDate);
  SalesHeader.VALIDATE("Document Date", PostingDate);
  SalesHeader.VALIDATE("Shipment Date", PostingDate);
  SalesHeader."Campaign No.":=CampaignCode;
  SalesHeader.INSERT(TRUE);

 //Sales Line creation
  SalesLine."Document Type":=SalesLine."Document Type"::Order;
  SalesLine."Document No.":='B2B';
  SalesLine."Line No.":=10000;
  SalesLine.VALIDATE("Sell-to Customer No.",CustNo);
  SalesLine.Type:=SalesLine.Type::Item;
  SalesLine.VALIDATE("No.",ItemNo);
  SalesLine.VALIDATE("Unit of Measure",UoM);
  SalesLine.VALIDATE("Shipment Date", PostingDate);
  SalesLine.VALIDATE(Quantity,Quantity);
  SalesLine.INSERT(TRUE);

  Price := SalesLine."Unit Price";

 //Delete temporary data
  SalesHeader.GET(SalesHeader."Document Type"::Order,'B2B');
  SalesHeader.DELETE(TRUE);

 END;
 EXIT(Price);
```

Let's take a look at the `GetSalesDiscount` parameters in the following screenshot:

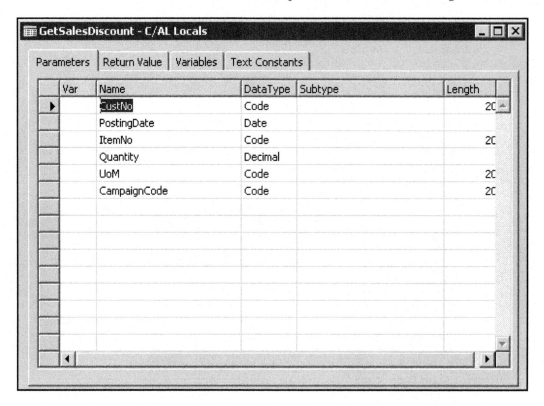

Let's take a look at the `GetSalesDiscount` local variables in the following screenshot:

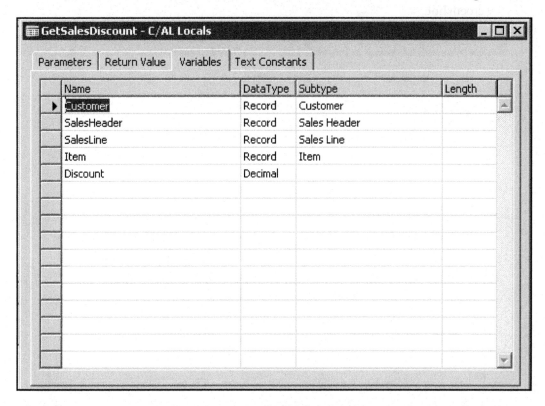

The `GetSalesDiscount` C/AL code is omitted here (it's the same as the previous function except that it returns the `SalesLine Line Discount %` value.

14. In these two functions, we create a temporary **Sales Order** with all the input parameters. Here we don't use a temporary table but we prefer to create a real **Sales Order** with a custom number (used only from a single transaction from the B2B). This *virtual sales order* will be deleted at the end of the transaction. From the virtual `Sales Line` created, we return the `Sales Price` and the `Sales Discount`. This trick permits us to rely on standard NAV logic in order to calculate the desired sales parameters.

Let's take a look at the GetItemInventory parameters in the following screenshot:

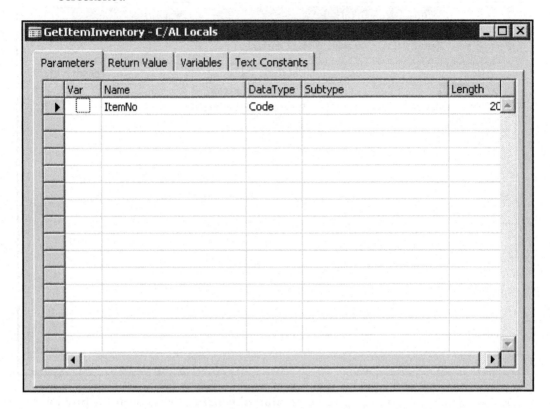

Let's take a look at the `GetItemInventory` local variables in the following screenshot:

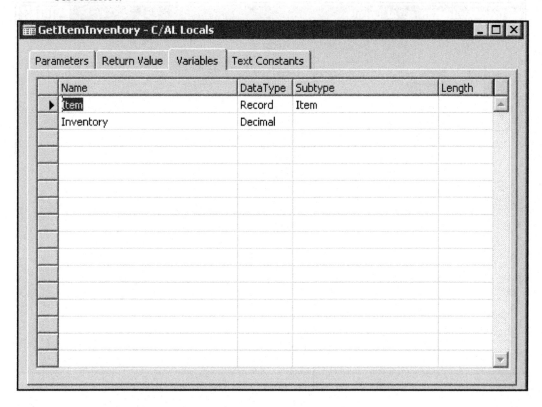

The C/AL code for the function is as follows:

```
GetItemInventory(ItemNo : Code[20]) : Decimal
Inventory:=0;
IF Item.GET(ItemNo) THEN
BEGIN
  //Default location (place it on setup table)
  Item.SETFILTER("Location Filter",'SEDE');
  Item.SETFILTER("Date Filter",'%1',TODAY);
  Item.CALCFIELDS(Inventory);
  Inventory := Item.Inventory;
END;
EXIT(Inventory);
```

Let's take a look at the **InsertOrderB2B** parameters in the following screenshot:

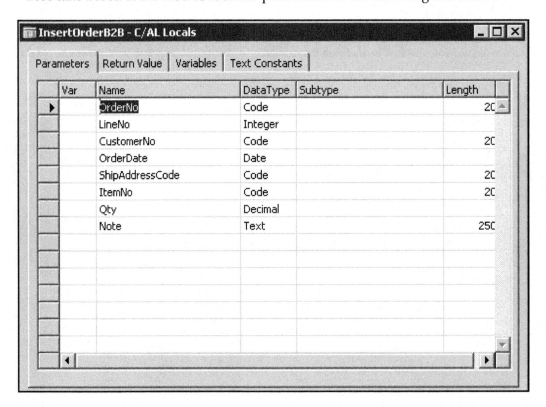

Let's take a look at the `InsertOrderB2B` local variables:

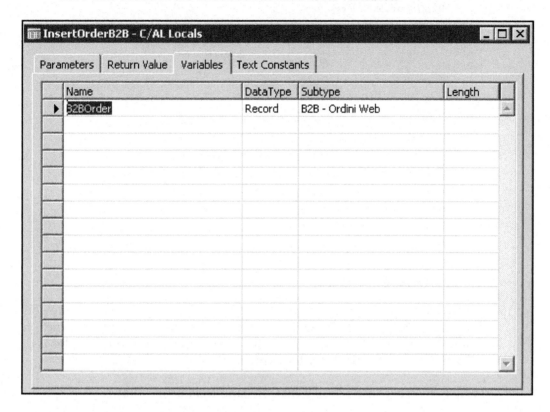

The C/AL code for the function is as follows:

```
InsertOrderB2B(OrderNo : Code[20];LineNo : Integer;CustomerNo :
Code[20];OrderDate : Date;ShipAddressCode : Code[20];ItemNo :
Code[20];Qty : Decimal;Note : Text[250]) : Text[100]
IF B2BOrder.GET(OrderNo,LineNo) THEN
BEGIN
  IF B2BOrder.Registered THEN
    EXIT(txtErrorRegistered)
  ELSE
  BEGIN
    //Row Update
    B2BOrder."Customer No." := CustomerNo;
    B2BOrder."Order Date" := OrderDate;
    B2BOrder."Shipment Address Code" := ShipAddressCode;
    B2BOrder."Item Code" := ItemNo;
    B2BOrder.Quantity := Qty;
    B2BOrder.Note := Note;
```

```
          B2BOrder.Registered:=FALSE;
          B2BOrder.MODIFY;
        END
      END
      ELSE
      BEGIN
        //Insert
        B2BOrder.INIT;
        B2BOrder."WEB Order No." := OrderNo;
        B2BOrder."Line No." := LineNo;
        B2BOrder."Customer No." := CustomerNo;
        B2BOrder."Order Date" := OrderDate;
        B2BOrder."Shipment Address Code" := ShipAddressCode;
        B2BOrder."Item Code" := ItemNo;
        B2BOrder.Quantity := Qty;
        B2BOrder.Note := Note;
        B2BOrder.Registered:=FALSE;
        B2BOrder.INSERT;
      END;

      EXIT('OK');
```

15. This function checks if the B2B sales order line (input parameter) was previously registered in NAV as a **Sales Order**. If the order is not registered, the function permits you to update the row (if it exists) or to create a new one. All this is done by writing in the B2B **Sales Order Table** in NAV.

    The error messages are a local **Text Constant** declared as follows:

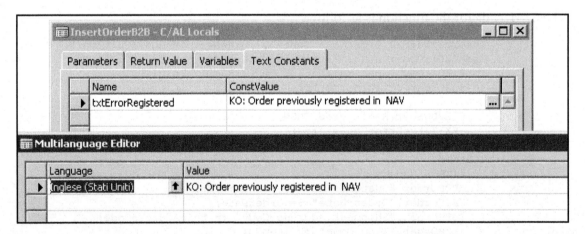

16. Save the `codeunit` object with an object ID where you have permission.

Publishing the NAV objects

To expose the NAV business objects and entities we have previously created to an external world, we need to publish them as a web service:

1. To do so, we can open the **Web Service** page in NAV and create the new entries (with `Published = TRUE`) for the `Codeunit` object:

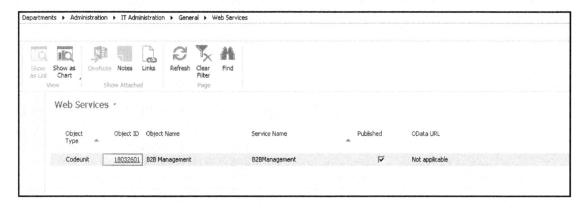

2. Here we need to set the following parameters:
   - **Object Type**: `Codeunit`
   - **Object ID**: ID of our previously created codeunit in NAV (obviously, the object ID can be a standard range or a custom range)
   - **Service Name**: This is the name of our codeunit web service (without spaces!)
   - **Published**: `TRUE`
3. When published, NAV gives the SOAP URL. We can test if all is working by opening a browser and load the returned URL.
4. For every `Query` object to publish, we need to create an entry in the **Web Services** page with:
   - **Object Type**: `Query`
   - **Object ID**: ID of our previously created Query in NAV
   - **Service Name**: This is the name of our `Query` web service (without spaces!)
   - **Published**: `TRUE`

This is the final result:

Object Type		Object ID	Object Name	Service Name		Published
Query	▲	50000	B2B - Articoli Web	B2BArticoliWeb	▲	☑
Query		50001	B2B - Clienti Web	B2BClientiWeb		☑
Query		50002	B2B - Indirizzi Spedizione	B2BShipAddress		☑

Web Services ▾

5. After publishing a `Query` object, NAV gives the ODATA URL. We can test if all is working by copying the ODATA URL, cutting the string after the word `OData/`, opening a web browser, and copying this URL. The URL to test will be in the `http://ServerName:ODataPort/NAVInstance/OData/` format:

Creating the service layer

As described in the architectural diagram of our solution, we don't want to directly expose the NAV web services (business logic) to an external application. We want to create a WCF service that will be something like an integration layer between NAV and the B2B application. This will permit us to have the following things:

- NAV objects (`Query` and `Codeunit`) and their methods not directly published to the B2B website
- Custom authentication from the B2B application to access the business functions
- Custom methods exposed to the B2B application, not directly binded to the NAV entities, with the possibilities to use protocols such as XML or JSON

The information's flow will be as represented in the following diagram:

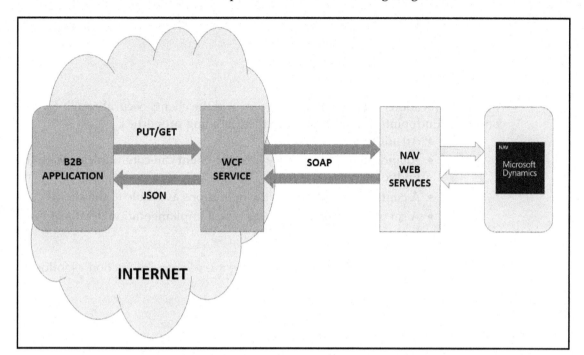

Let's start to write the WCF service now by perfomring the following steps:

1. Open Visual Studio, select the WCF template, and go to **File** | **New** | **Project...** | **WCF Service Application** in order to create the project solution.
2. We want to create a WCF service that is able to use XML and JSON as response protocols and is able to have REST methods.

   A WCF service has a `Service Contract` (interface) that describes to clients what the service does.

Our WCF service has the following interface definition:

```
namespace RestService
{
    [ServiceContract]
    public interface IB2BService
    {
```

- All communications between a WCF service and the clients occur through the concept of Endpoints. An Endpoint has the following properties:
  - An address
  - A binding used to specify how the client can communicate with the Endpoint
  - A contract that identifies the operations available to the client
  - A set of behaviors that specify local implementation details of the Endpoint

We have to modify our `web.config` file in the `ServiceModel` section as follows:

```
<system.serviceModel>
  <services>
    <service behaviorConfiguration="ServiceBehaviour"
     name="RestService.B2BService">
    <endpoint address="" behaviorConfiguration="web"
     binding="webHttpBinding"
    contract="RestService.IB2BService" />
    </service>
  </services>

  <behaviors>
    <serviceBehaviors>
      <behavior name="ServiceBehaviour">
        <!-- To avoid disclosing metadata information, set
         the value below to false and remove the metadata
         endpoint above before deployment -->
        <serviceMetadata httpGetEnabled="true"/>
        <!-- To receive exception details in faults for
         debugging purposes, set the value below to true.
         Set the value above to false before deployment to
         avoid disclosing exception information -->
        <serviceDebug
        includeExceptionDetailInFaults="false"/>
      </behavior>
    </serviceBehaviors>
            <endpointBehaviors>
            <behavior name="web">
```

```
            <webHttp/>
          </behavior>
        </endpointBehaviors>
      </behaviors>
      <serviceHostingEnvironment
        multipleSiteBindingsEnabled="true" />
    </system.serviceModel>
```

The `webHttpBinding` permits you to have a WCF service that responds to HTTP requests instead of SOAP messages (with REST Endpoints). This is used in conjunction with `webHttp` in the behavior configuration as shown previously.

Our Visual Studio solution will be organized as follows:

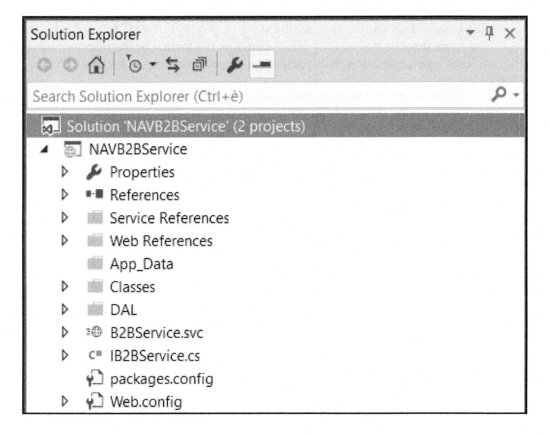

- The contents of this project are as follows:
  - `IB2BService.cs`: This contains the service contract (interface)
  - `B2BService.cs` (the source file under `B2BService.svc`): This contains the method's definition (implementation)
  - `Classes`: This will contain all the object's definitions
  - `DAL`: This will contain the data access layer code (a software layer that will manage all the calls to NAV web services)

3. We have to define our service interface now. In a WCF service, all methods that define operations in a service contract are declared with the `OperationContract` attribute. In order to have our methods able to be invoked by the WCF REST model, we have also to decorate the methods with the `WebInvoke` tag. The `Method` attribute (`GET`, `POST`) is the HTTP method used for the request while `ResponseFormat` contains the format of the response message (it uses an enumeration that specifies the message format as JSON or XML).

The methods that we want to expose in the service contract and their declarations are the following (C# definition):

```
namespace RestService
    {
        [ServiceContract]
        public interface IB2BService
        {
            [OperationContract]
            [WebInvoke(Method = "GET",ResponseFormat =
            WebMessageFormat.Xml,BodyStyle =
            WebMessageBodyStyle.Wrapped,UriTemplate =
            "getItemsXML")]
            List<Item> GetItemsXML();

            [OperationContract]
            [WebInvoke(Method = "GET", ResponseFormat =
            WebMessageFormat.Json, BodyStyle =
            WebMessageBodyStyle.Wrapped, UriTemplate =
            "getItemsJSON")]
            List<Item> GetItemsJSON();

            [OperationContract(Name = "GetItemsXMLbyDate")]
            [WebInvoke(Method = "GET", ResponseFormat =
            WebMessageFormat.Xml, BodyStyle =
            WebMessageBodyStyle.Wrapped, UriTemplate =
            "getItemsXML?date={ModifiedDate}")]
            List<Item> GetItemsXML(string ModifiedDate); //Format
```

```
YYYY-MM-DD

[OperationContract(Name = "GetItemsJSONbyDate")]
[WebInvoke(Method = "GET", ResponseFormat =
WebMessageFormat.Json, BodyStyle =
WebMessageBodyStyle.Wrapped, UriTemplate =
"getItemsJSON?date={ModifiedDate}")]
List<Item> GetItemsJSON(string ModifiedDate);

[OperationContract]
[WebInvoke(Method = "GET", ResponseFormat =
WebMessageFormat.Xml, BodyStyle =
WebMessageBodyStyle.Wrapped, UriTemplate =
"getCustomersXML")]
List<Customer> GetCustomersXML();

[OperationContract]
[WebInvoke(Method = "GET", ResponseFormat =
WebMessageFormat.Json, BodyStyle =
WebMessageBodyStyle.Wrapped, UriTemplate =
"getCustomersJSON")]
List<Customer> GetCustomersJSON();

[OperationContract]
[WebInvoke(Method = "GET", ResponseFormat =
WebMessageFormat.Xml, BodyStyle =
WebMessageBodyStyle.Wrapped, UriTemplate =
"getShipmentAddressesXML")]
List<ShipmentAddress> getShipmentAddressesXML();

[OperationContract]
[WebInvoke(Method = "GET", ResponseFormat =
WebMessageFormat.Json, BodyStyle =
WebMessageBodyStyle.Wrapped, UriTemplate =
"getShipmentAddressesJSON")]
List<ShipmentAddress> getShipmentAddressesJSON();

[OperationContract]
[WebInvoke(Method = "GET", ResponseFormat =
WebMessageFormat.Xml, BodyStyle =
WebMessageBodyStyle.Wrapped, UriTemplate =
"getPriceXML?cust={CustomerNo}&date={OrderDate}&item=
{ItemNo}&qty={Quantity}")]
decimal GetSalesPriceXML(string CustomerNo, string
OrderDate, string ItemNo, decimal Quantity);
//Date Format = GG-MM-AAAA

[OperationContract]
```

```
[WebInvoke(Method = "GET", ResponseFormat =
WebMessageFormat.Json, BodyStyle =
WebMessageBodyStyle.Wrapped, UriTemplate =
"getPriceJSON?cust={CustomerNo}&date={OrderDate}&item=
{ItemNo}&qty={Quantity}")]
decimal GetSalesPriceJSON(string CustomerNo, string
OrderDate, string ItemNo, decimal Quantity);
//Date Format = GG-MM-AAAA

[OperationContract]
[WebInvoke(Method = "GET", ResponseFormat =
WebMessageFormat.Xml, BodyStyle =
WebMessageBodyStyle.Wrapped, UriTemplate =
"getDiscountXML?cust={CustomerNo}&date=
{OrderDate}&item={ItemNo}&qty={Quantity}")]
decimal GetSalesDiscountXML(string CustomerNo, string
OrderDate, string ItemNo, decimal Quantity);
//Date Format = GG-MM-AAAA

[OperationContract]
[WebInvoke(Method = "GET", ResponseFormat =
WebMessageFormat.Json, BodyStyle =
WebMessageBodyStyle.Wrapped, UriTemplate =
"getDiscountJSON?cust={CustomerNo}&date=
{OrderDate}&item={ItemNo}&qty={Quantity}")]
decimal GetSalesDiscountJSON(string CustomerNo, string
OrderDate, string ItemNo, decimal Quantity);
//Date Format = GG-MM-AAAA

[OperationContract]
[WebInvoke(Method = "GET", ResponseFormat =
WebMessageFormat.Xml, BodyStyle =
WebMessageBodyStyle.Wrapped, UriTemplate =
"getItemDetailXML?cust={CustomerNo}&date=
{OrderDate}&item={ItemNo}&qty={Quantity}")]
ItemDetail GetItemDetailXML(string CustomerNo, string
OrderDate, string ItemNo, decimal Quantity);
//Date Format = GG-MM-AAAA

[OperationContract]
[WebInvoke(Method = "GET", ResponseFormat =
WebMessageFormat.Json, BodyStyle =
WebMessageBodyStyle.Wrapped, UriTemplate =
"getItemDetailJSON?cust={CustomerNo}&date=
{OrderDate}&item={ItemNo}&qty={Quantity}")]
ItemDetail GetItemDetailJSON(string CustomerNo, string
OrderDate, string ItemNo, decimal Quantity);
//Date Format = GG-MM-AAAA
```

```
[OperationContract]
[WebInvoke(Method = "POST", RequestFormat =
WebMessageFormat.Xml, ResponseFormat =
WebMessageFormat.Xml, BodyStyle =
WebMessageBodyStyle.Bare, UriTemplate =
"/insertOrderXML")]
string InsertOrderXML(Order order);

[OperationContract]
[WebInvoke(Method = "POST", RequestFormat =
WebMessageFormat.Json, ResponseFormat =
WebMessageFormat.Json, BodyStyle =
WebMessageBodyStyle.Bare, UriTemplate =
"/insertOrderJSON")]
string InsertOrderJSON(Order order);
    }
  }
```

4. For every method defined in the service contract (interface), we need to define its implementation (in the file B2BService.cs). This file contains a class that implements the previously defined IB2BService interface:

```
public class B2BService : IB2BService
```

The methods implementation will be as follow (C# code for only the JSON methods):

```
public class B2BService : IB2BService
  {
      #region ITEMS

  public List<Item> GetItemsJSON()
     {
         if (!CheckBasicAuthentication())
            {
                throw new
                WebFaultException(HttpStatusCode.Unauthorized);
            }

            DALItems DAL = new DALItems();
            return DAL.GetItems("");
     }


  public List<Item> GetItemsJSON(string ModifiedDate)
     {
         if (!CheckBasicAuthentication())
            {
```

```
            throw new
            WebFaultException(HttpStatusCode.Unauthorized);
        }

        DALItems DAL = new DALItems();
        return DAL.GetItems(ModifiedDate);
}

        #endregion

        #region CUSTOMERS


    public List<Customer> GetCustomersJSON()
        {
            if (!CheckBasicAuthentication())
                {
                    throw new
                    WebFaultException
                    (HttpStatusCode.Unauthorized);
                }

                    DALCustomers DAL = new DALCustomers();
                    return DAL.GetCustomers();
            }

            #endregion

            #region SHIPMENT ADDRESSES


    public List<ShipmentAddress> getShipmentAddressesJSON()
        {
            if (!CheckBasicAuthentication())
            {
                throw new
                WebFaultException
                (HttpStatusCode.Unauthorized);
            }

                DALShipmentAddresses DAL = new
                DALShipmentAddresses();
                return DAL.GetShipmentAddresses();
        }

                #endregion

                #region PRICES AND DISCOUNTS
```

```
public decimal GetSalesPriceJSON(string CustomerNo,
string OrderDate, string ItemNo, decimal Quantity)
    {
        if (!CheckBasicAuthentication())
            {
                throw new
                WebFaultException(HttpStatusCode.
                Unauthorized);
            }

                DateTime _dtOrdine =
                Convert.ToDateTime(OrderDate);
                DALPrices DAL = new DALPrices();
                decimal _price = DAL.GetPrice(CustomerNo,
                _dtOrdine, ItemNo, Quantity, "PZ", "");
                return _price;
        }

public decimal GetSalesDiscountJSON(string CustomerNo,
string OrderDate, string ItemNo, decimal Quantity)
    {
        if (!CheckBasicAuthentication())
          {
            throw new
            WebFaultException(HttpStatusCode.
            Unauthorized);
          }

            DateTime _dtOrdine =
            Convert.ToDateTime(OrderDate);
            DALPrices DAL = new DALPrices();
            decimal _discount = DAL.GetDiscount(CustomerNo,
            _dtOrdine, ItemNo, Quantity, "PZ", "");
            return _discount;
    }


public ItemDetail GetItemDetailJSON(string CustomerNo,
string OrderDate, string ItemNo, decimal Quantity)
    {
        if (!CheckBasicAuthentication())
            {
                throw new
                WebFaultException(HttpStatusCode.
                Unauthorized);
            }

                ItemDetail DET = new ItemDetail();
```

```
                        DALPrices DAL = new DALPrices();
                        DateTime _dtOrdine =
                        Convert.ToDateTime(OrderDate);
                        DET.ItemNo = ItemNo;
                        DET.Price = DAL.GetPrice(CustomerNo,
                        _dtOrdine, ItemNo, Quantity, "PZ", "");
                        DET.Discount = DAL.GetDiscount(CustomerNo,
                        _dtOrdine, ItemNo, Quantity, "PZ", "");
                        return DET;
                }


                #endregion

                #region SALES ORDERS


        public string InsertOrderJSON(Order order)
            {
                if (!CheckBasicAuthentication())
                    {
                        throw new
                        WebFaultException(HttpStatusCode.
                        Unauthorized);
                    }

                try
                 {
                        DALOrders DAL = new DALOrders();
                        string result = DAL.InsertOrder(order);

                        return result;
                 }
                catch (Exception ex)
                 {
                        throw ex;
                 }
            }

                #endregion
        }
```

5. As a requirement, to call our WCF service, a client must create a message with proper credentials passed in the HTTP request header (username and password with basic authentication).

- Every method defined in the WCF service as a first step calls the `CheckBasicAuthentication` function that performs these actions:
  - Reads the credentials (app key to access our WCF service) from the `web.config` file (they could be encrypted if required).
  - Checks the authorization header from the incoming HTTP request.
  - Extracts the client credentials from the authorization header (our security key that the client application must know in order to access our service).
  - If the client credentials match, the client is authorized to access the service (return TRUE).
  - If the client credentials don't match, the client is not authorized and an exception with HTTP Status Code = 401 (unauthorized) is triggered.

The code for this function is as follows:

```
//Check WS Authentication in HTTP Request Header
private Boolean CheckBasicAuthentication()
{
    try
    {
        string userKEY =
        ConfigurationManager.AppSettings["WS_User"];
        string pwdKEY =
        ConfigurationManager.AppSettings["WS_Pwd"];
        string auth =
        WebOperationContext.Current.IncomingRequest.
        Headers[HttpRequestHeader.Authorization];
        if (auth != null)
        {
            if (auth.StartsWith("Basic "))
            {
                string cred =
                Encoding.UTF8.GetString(Convert.
                FromBase64String(auth.Substring("Basic
                ".Length)));
                string[] parts = cred.Split(':');
                string userName = parts[0];
                string password = parts[1];
                if ((userName == userKEY) && (password ==
                    pwdKEY))
                {
                    return true;
                }
                //return string.Format("User: {0}, password:
```

```
                    {1}", userName, password);
            }
        }

        return false;
    }
        catch (Exception)
        {
            return false;
        }
    }
```

As you can see, after checking the client credentials, every method calls a proper **Data Access Layer** (**DAL**) function to perform the desired action on NAV. There's no direct NAV web service access on the service code.

The following schema represents the data flow of the solution:

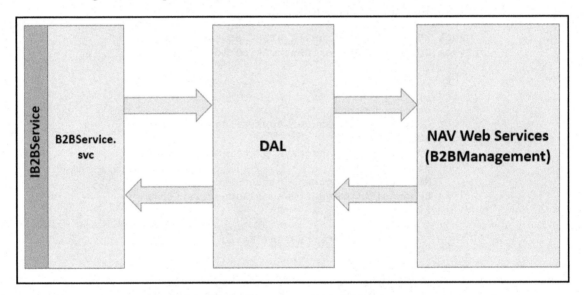

6. To interact with the published NAV web service (our NAV `codeunit`), we need to add a web service reference on the Visual Studio solution. In our project, we have two types of NAV web service to reference:
   - SOAP web service for the NAV `Codeunit` objects
   - ODATA web service for the NAV `Query` objects

7. To add a reference to the NAV SOAP web service, in Solution Explorer, right-click on the project name and select **Add | Service Reference...**. In the **Add Service Reference** window, click **Advanced** and then **Add Web Reference**.

8. Now, in the **Add Web Reference** window, copy the NAV web service SOAP URL and Visual Studio will load the NAV web service WSDL:

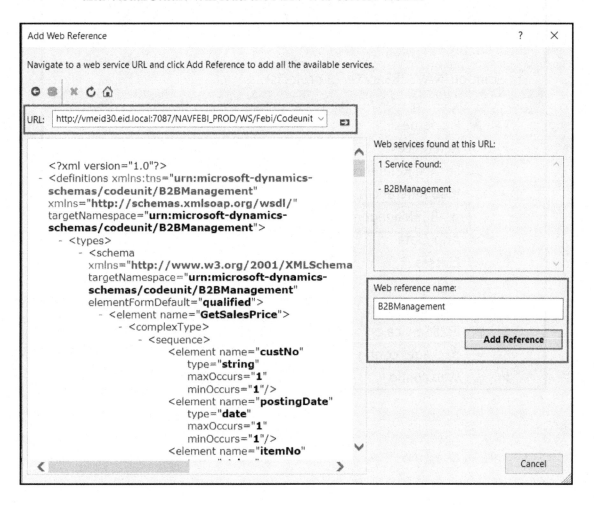

9. Give a proper web reference name (we have used the name B2BManagement) and click **Add Reference**.

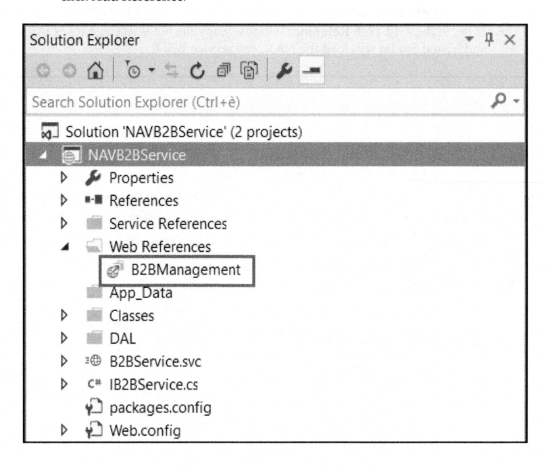

10. To add a reference to the NAV ODATA web service, in **Solution Explorer**, right-click on the project name and select **Add | Service Reference…**. In the **Add Service Reference** window, type the ODATA URL and give the proper service name, then click on **OK**:

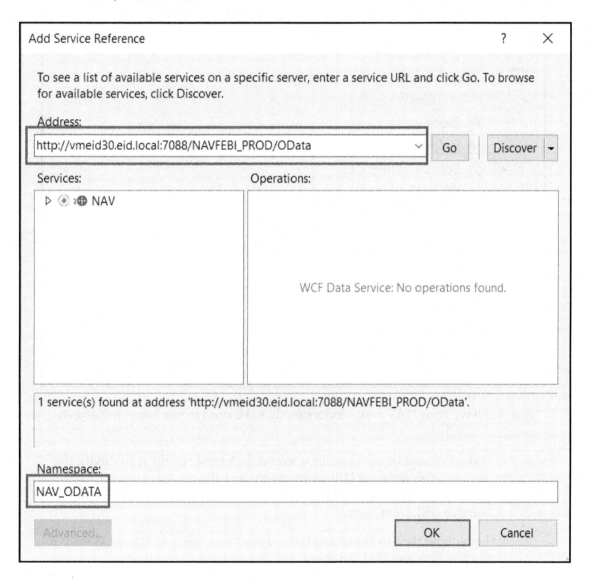

Visual Studio creates a reference to our NAV_ODATA web service:

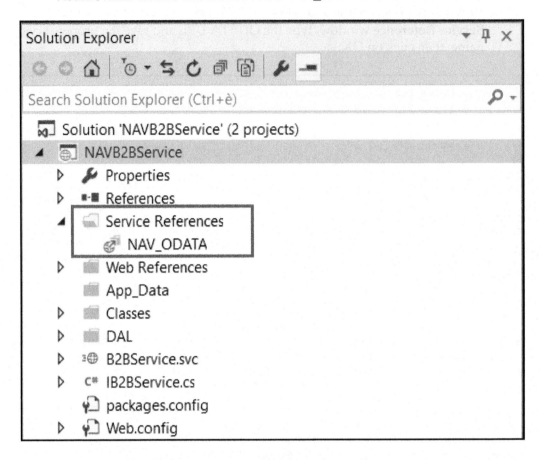

Now you have your NAV web services ready to be used in our Data Access Layer class.

 When you add a web service reference in Visual Studio, it automatically sets the *Web Reference URL* property to the URL you have used. I recommend adding a setting on web.config and always read the web service URL from there.

11. To better split the functional modules of our Data Access Layer class, we create five different DAL classes:
   - DALCustomers.cs: This file contains the logic to retrieve customer details from NAV

- `DALShipmentAddresses.cs`: This file contains the logic to retrieve customer's shipment address details from NAV
- `DALItems.cs`: This file contains the logic to retrieve item details from NAV
- `DALPrices.cs`: This file contains the logic to retrieve item prices, discounts, and inventories from NAV
- `DALOrders.cs`: This file contains the logic to insert a sales order in NAV

The `DAL` folder inside our solution appears as follows:

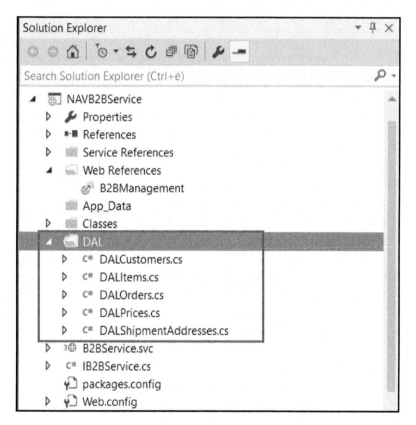

The following sections describe the implementation details for every method/class.

DALCustomers

This implements a `GetCustomers` method. It reads the `web.config` file for retrieving the NAV web service URL and all the NAV parameters for authentication (user's impersonation). Then it creates an instance of the NAV ODATA web service (`Query` object), passes credentials to the instance, executes the NAV `Query` object (Query ID `50001`), and reads the results.

Here is the C# code:

```csharp
public List<Customer> GetCustomers()
{
    string serviceODataURL =
    ConfigurationManager.AppSettings["NAVODATAUrl"];
    string WS_User =
    ConfigurationManager.AppSettings["NAV_User"];
    string WS_Pwd =
    ConfigurationManager.AppSettings["NAV_Pwd"];
    string WS_Domain =
    ConfigurationManager.AppSettings["NAV_Domain"];
    string Company =
    ConfigurationManager.AppSettings["Company"];
    //OData URI creation
    string serviceUri = string.Format(serviceODataURL +
    "/Company('{0}')", Company);

    List<Customer> custListB2B = new List<Customer>();

    try
    {
        DataServiceContext context = new
        DataServiceContext(new Uri(serviceUri));
        //Web service initialization
        NAV_ODATA.NAV theNav = new NAV_ODATA.NAV(new
        Uri(serviceUri));
        //User impersonation
        theNav.Credentials = new
        System.Net.NetworkCredential(WS_User, WS_Pwd,
        WS_Domain);
        //Calls the OData WS (NAV Query)
        DataServiceQuery<NAV_ODATA.B2BClientiWeb> q =
        theNav.CreateQuery<NAV_ODATA.B2BClientiWeb>
        ("B2BClientiWeb");

        List<NAV_ODATA.B2BClientiWeb> custList =
        q.Execute().ToList();
```

```
foreach (NAV_ODATA.B2BClientiWeb cust in custList)
 {
    Customer c = new Customer();
    c.No = cust.No;
    c.Name = cust.Name;
    c.Address = cust.Address;
    c.City = cust.City;
    c.CAP = cust.Post_Code;
    c.Country = cust.Country_Region_Code;
    c.County = cust.County;
    c.FiscalCode = cust.Fiscal_Code;
    c.VATNo = cust.VAT_Registration_No;
    c.EmailEcommerce = cust.Email_Ecommerce;
    c.Active = cust.ActivadoWeb;
    custListB2B.Add(c);
 }
}
catch (Exception)
 {
 }

return custListB2B;
}
```

DALShipmentAddresses

This implements a GetShipmentAddresses method. It reads the web.config file for
retrieving the NAV web service URL and all the NAV parameters for authentication (user's
impersonation). Then it creates an instance of the NAV ODATA web service (Query object),
passes credentials to the instance, executes the NAV Query object (Query ID 50002), and
reads the results.

Here is the C# code:

```
public List<ShipmentAddress> GetShipmentAddresses()
    {
        string serviceODataURL =
        ConfigurationManager.AppSettings["NAVODATAUrl"];
        string WS_User =
        ConfigurationManager.AppSettings["NAV_User"];
        string WS_Pwd =
        ConfigurationManager.AppSettings["NAV_Pwd"];
        string WS_Domain =
        ConfigurationManager.AppSettings["NAV_Domain"];
        string Company =
        ConfigurationManager.AppSettings["Company"];
```

```
string serviceUri = string.Format(serviceODataURL +
"/Company('{0}')", Company);

List<ShipmentAddress> indListB2B = new
List<ShipmentAddress>();

try
{
   DataServiceContext context = new DataServiceContext(new
   Uri(serviceUri));

   NAV_ODATA.NAV theNav = new NAV_ODATA.NAV(new
   Uri(serviceUri));
   theNav.Credentials = new
   System.Net.NetworkCredential
   (WS_User, WS_Pwd, WS_Domain);

   DataServiceQuery<NAV_ODATA.B2BShipAddress> q =
   theNav.CreateQuery<NAV_ODATA.B2BShipAddress>
   ("B2BShipAddress");

   List<NAV_ODATA.B2BShipAddress> addrList =
   q.Execute().ToList();

    foreach (NAV_ODATA.B2BShipAddress addr in addrList)
    {
        ShipmentAddress ind = new ShipmentAddress();
        ind.CustomerNo = addr.Customer_No;
        ind.Code = addr.Code;
        ind.Name = addr.Name;
        ind.Address = addr.Address;
        ind.City = addr.City;
        ind.County = addr.County;
        ind.Country = addr.Country_Region_Code;
        ind.Default = addr.Default_Shipment;

        indListB2B.Add(ind);
    }
}
catch (Exception)
{
}

return indListB2B;
}
```

DALItems

This implements a `GetItems` method. It reads the `web.config` file for retrieving the NAV web service URL and all the NAV parameters for authentication (user's impersonation). Then, it creates an instance of the NAV ODATA web service (`Query` object), passes credentials to the instance, executes the NAV `Query` object (Query ID `50000`), and reads the results.

Here is the C# code:

```csharp
public List<Item> GetItems(string ModifiedDate)
    {
        string serviceODataURL =
        ConfigurationManager.AppSettings["NAVODATAUrl"];
        string WS_User =
        ConfigurationManager.AppSettings["NAV_User"];
        string WS_Pwd =
        ConfigurationManager.AppSettings["NAV_Pwd"];
        string WS_Domain =
        ConfigurationManager.AppSettings["NAV_Domain"];
        string Company =
        ConfigurationManager.AppSettings["Company"];

        string serviceUri = string.Format(serviceODataURL +
        "/Company('{0}')", Company);

        List<Item> itemListB2B = new List<Item>();

        try
            {
            DataServiceContext context = new DataServiceContext(new
            Uri(serviceUri));

            NAV_ODATA.NAV theNav = new NAV_ODATA.NAV(new
            Uri(serviceUri));
            theNav.Credentials = new
            System.Net.NetworkCredential(WS_User, WS_Pwd,
            WS_Domain);

            DataServiceQuery<NAV_ODATA.B2BArticoliWeb> q =
            theNav.CreateQuery<NAV_ODATA.B2BArticoliWeb>
            ("B2BArticoliWeb");

            if (ModifiedDate.Length > 0)
            {
                //OData Filter Expression ge = greater than or
                  equal to
```

```
                              string FilterValue =
                              string.Format("Last_Date_Modified ge
                              datetime'{0}'
                              or Last_Movement_Date ge datetime'{0}'",
                              ModifiedDate);
                              q = q.AddQueryOption("$filter", FilterValue);
                  }

                              List<NAV_ODATA.B2BArticoliWeb> itemList =
                              q.Execute().ToList();

                  foreach (NAV_ODATA.B2BArticoliWeb item in itemList)
                  {
                      Item a = new Item();
                      a.No = item.No;
                      a.Description1 = item.Description;
                      a.Description2 = item.Description_2;
                      a.Inventory = item.Inventory;
                      a.Lot = item.Quantità_Lotto;
                      a.UnitOfMeasure = item.Base_Unit_of_Measure;
                      a.ItemType = item.Linea;
                      a.ItemBrand= item.Dimension_Value_Code;
                      a.BrandDescription = item.Name;
                      itemListB2B.Add(a);
                  }
          }
          catch (Exception ex)
          {
              string exmsg = ex.Message;
          }

          return itemListB2B;
      }
```

DALPrices

This contains the following three methods:

- GetPrice
- GetDiscount
- GetInventory

Every method reads the `web.config` file for retrieving the NAV web service URL and all the NAV parameters for authentication (user's impersonation). Then it creates an instance of the NAV SOAP web service (the published codeunit), passes credentials to the instance, calls the appropriate codeunit's function, and returns the result.

This is the C# code for every method:

```csharp
public decimal GetPrice(string CustomerNo, DateTime PostingDate,
string ItemNo, decimal Quantity, string UoM, string CampaignCode)
    {
        string serviceSOAPURL =
        ConfigurationManager.AppSettings["NAVSOAPUrl"];
        string WS_User =
        ConfigurationManager.AppSettings["NAV_User"];
        string WS_Pwd = ConfigurationManager.AppSettings["NAV_Pwd"];
        string WS_Domain =
        ConfigurationManager.AppSettings["NAV_Domain"];
        string Company =
        ConfigurationManager.AppSettings["Company"];

        string serviceUri = string.Format(serviceSOAPURL, Company);
         try
           {
              B2BManagement.B2BManagement ws = new
              B2BManagement.B2BManagement();
              ws.Url = serviceUri;
              ws.Credentials = new
              System.Net.NetworkCredential(WS_User, WS_Pwd,
              WS_Domain);

              decimal price = ws.GetSalesPrice(CustomerNo,
              PostingDate, ItemNo, Quantity, UoM, CampaignCode);

              return price;
           }
         catch (Exception)
            {
              return 0;
            }

    }


public decimal GetDiscount(string CustomerNo, DateTime PostingDate,
string ItemNo, decimal Quantity, string UoM, string CampaignCode)
    {
        string serviceSOAPURL =
```

```
        ConfigurationManager.AppSettings["NAVSOAPUrl"];
        string WS_User =
        ConfigurationManager.AppSettings["NAV_User"];
        string WS_Pwd = ConfigurationManager.AppSettings["NAV_Pwd"];
        string WS_Domain =
        ConfigurationManager.AppSettings["NAV_Domain"];
        string Company =
        ConfigurationManager.AppSettings["Company"];

        string serviceUri = string.Format(serviceSOAPURL, Company);
         try
          {
            B2BManagement.B2BManagement ws = new
            B2BManagement.B2BManagement();
            ws.Url = serviceUri;
            ws.Credentials = new
            System.Net.NetworkCredential(WS_User, WS_Pwd,
            WS_Domain);

            decimal discount = ws.GetSalesDiscount(CustomerNo,
            PostingDate, ItemNo, Quantity, UoM, CampaignCode);

             return discount;
          }
         catch (Exception)
          {
             return 0;
          }

        }

    public decimal GetInventory(string ItemNo)
        {
        string serviceSOAPURL =
        ConfigurationManager.AppSettings["NAVSOAPUrl"];
        string WS_User =
        ConfigurationManager.AppSettings["NAV_User"];
        string WS_Pwd = ConfigurationManager.AppSettings["NAV_Pwd"];
        string WS_Domain =
        ConfigurationManager.AppSettings["NAV_Domain"];
        string Company =
        ConfigurationManager.AppSettings["Company"];

        string serviceUri = string.Format(serviceSOAPURL, Company);
         try
          {
            B2BManagement.B2BManagement ws = new
            B2BManagement.B2BManagement();
```

```
        ws.Url = serviceUri;
        ws.Credentials = new
        System.Net.NetworkCredential(WS_User, WS_Pwd,
        WS_Domain);

        decimal inventory = ws.GetItemInventory(ItemNo);

        return inventory;
    }
    catch (Exception)
      {
          return 0;
      }


    }
```

DALOrders

This implements an `InsertOrder` method. It reads the `web.config` file for retrieving the NAV web service URL and all the NAV parameters for authentication (user's impersonation). Then it creates an instance of the NAV SOAP web service (the published codeunit), passes credentials to the instance, calls the appropriate codeunit's function, and return the result.

This is the C# code:

```
public string InsertOrder(Order order)
    {
        string serviceSOAPURL =
        ConfigurationManager.AppSettings["NAVSOAPUrl"];
        string WS_User =
        ConfigurationManager.AppSettings["NAV_User"];
        string WS_Pwd = ConfigurationManager.AppSettings["NAV_Pwd"];
        string WS_Domain =
        ConfigurationManager.AppSettings["NAV_Domain"];
        string Company =
        ConfigurationManager.AppSettings["Company"];

        string serviceUri = string.Format(serviceSOAPURL, Company);
         try
          {
            B2BManagement.B2BManagement ws = new
            B2BManagement.B2BManagement();
            ws.Url = serviceUri;
            ws.Credentials = new
            System.Net.NetworkCredential(WS_User, WS_Pwd,
```

```
            WS_Domain);

            string result = ws.InsertOrderB2B(order.OrderNo,
            order.LineNo, order.CustomerNo, order.OrderDate,
    order.ShipmentAddressCode, order.ItemNo, order.Quantity, order.Note);

            return result;
        }
        catch (Exception ex)
        {
            return "KO: " + ex.Message;
        }

    }
```

Testing the solution

Now our interface is complete and we are ready to test it.

The interesting thing about our solution is that it is REST compliant, so we can directly test a method by using a browser, typing the correct URL (according to what is specified in the service contract), and passing the desired parameters.

For example, to test the item's price retrieval with a JSON response, we can use the `http://localhost:35798/B2BService.svc/getPriceJSON?cust=05001041&date=2 016-05-30&item=01001&qty=1` URL (the port number here is the debug port that Visual Studio assigns to the local web server, in bold are the parameters):

The result is this:

To retrieve the items list (modified from a particular date, for example `01/01/2015`) you can type
`http://localhost:35798/B2BService.svc/getItemsJSON?date=2015-01-01` in your browser.

This is the returned JSON response:

If we want to test our methods via code (for example from a C# application), we can create a `HTTP Request` method to our WCF service using the appropriate parameters, content type, and `HTTP Method`.

For example, to test the `GetPrice` method from a C# application take a look at the following code:

```
try
{
    string uri =
    "http://localhost:35798/B2BService.svc/getPriceJSON?
    cliente=05001041&data=2016-05-30&art=01001&qty=1";

    var httpWebRequest = (HttpWebRequest)WebRequest.Create(uri);
    httpWebRequest.ContentType = "application/json";
    httpWebRequest.Method = "GET";
```

```
//Basic Authentication settings (user:password)
string svcCredentials =
Convert.ToBase64String(ASCIIEncoding.ASCII.GetBytes
("xxx" + ":" + "xxx"));
httpWebRequest.Headers.Add("Authorization", "Basic "
+ svcCredentials);
var httpResponse =
(HttpWebResponse)httpWebRequest.GetResponse();
using (var streamReader = new
StreamReader(httpResponse.GetResponseStream()))
    {
        var response = streamReader.ReadToEnd();
        MessageBox.Show("Response: " + response);
    }
}
catch (Exception ex)
    {
        MessageBox.Show("Error: " + ex.Message + " - Details: " +
        ex.InnerException);
    }
```

To test the `InsertOrder` method, we need to make an `HTTP POST Request` to the WCF service and pass an `Order` object. This is the test code:

```
//Create the Order object to insert
B2B.Order order = new B2B.Order();
//Initialize here all the order object fields
try
 {
    string uri = "http://localhost:35798/B2BService.
    svc/insertOrderJSON";
    var httpWebRequest = (HttpWebRequest)WebRequest.Create(uri);
    httpWebRequest.ContentType = "application/json";
    httpWebRequest.Method = "POST";

    //Basic Authentication settings (username:password)
    string svcCredentials =
    Convert.ToBase64String(ASCIIEncoding.ASCII.GetBytes
    ("xxx" + ":" + "xxx"));
    httpWebRequest.Headers.Add("Authorization", "Basic "
    + svcCredentials);
    using (var streamWriter = new
    StreamWriter(httpWebRequest.GetRequestStream()))
        {
            string json = new
            JavaScriptSerializer().Serialize(order);
            streamWriter.Write(json);
            streamWriter.Flush();
```

```
            streamWriter.Close();
        }
            var httpResponse =
            (HttpWebResponse)httpWebRequest.GetResponse();
    using (var streamReader = new
    StreamReader(httpResponse.GetResponseStream()))
        {
            var response = streamReader.ReadToEnd();
        }
    }
catch (Exception ex)
    {
        MessageBox.Show("Error: " + ex.Message + " - Details: " +
        ex.InnerException);
    }
```

Solution deployment

After completing the testing phase, our solution must be deployed on a production Internet information server and published on the Internet. Remember that we don't need to publish on the Internet the NAV web services but only the WCF service (this is one of the interesting feature of the solution).

Let's take a look at the following steps in order to deploy our solution:

1. The first step is to copy all the solution's files (.svc files, web.config and the BIN folder) in a folder on the server's filesystem (for example, C:NAVINTERFACEB2BB2BService):

2. To deploy our WCF service on IIS, open the **Internet Information Services (IIS)** Manager. On your server tree, under the **Sites** folder, you can create a new site or a new application under a previously created site.

3. Here we want to create a new application under the **Default Web Site**, so right-click on **Default Web Site** and choose **Add Application**. In the **Add Application** window, set the parameters as shown in the following screenshot:

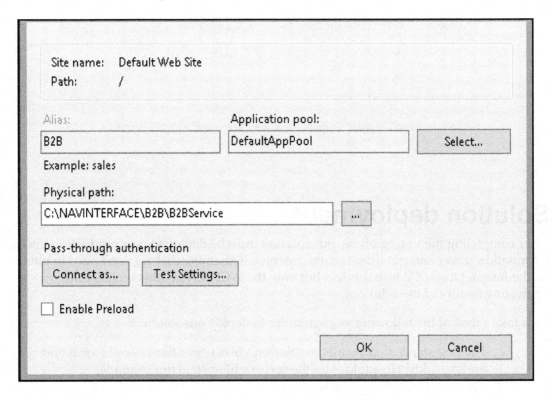

4. The **Application Pool** is extremely important. **Application Pools** on IIS are worker processes used to isolate our web applications from others. Here we are using the IIS default application pool (**DefaultAppPool**) but it's recommended to create a dedicated application pool if you have more than one web application running on this server.

5. Application pools are listed under the **Application Pools** node on IIS. In order to have our application working, we need to set the .NET CLR version of our pool to .NET 4.0 (because we're using WCF and .NET 4.X):

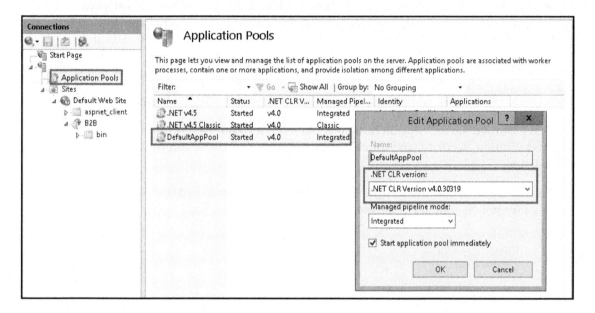

Here are some troubleshooting tips to remember during deployment:

- The IIS Worker Process account (IIS_IUSRS) must have read/write access to the folder where you have deployed the physical files for the solution.
- As described in `Chapter 2`, *Configuring NAV Web Services*, you have to go to the NAV service tier and check the `MaxPageSize` value in the **OData** configuration settings. As default, it is set to `1000` but this could be incorrect for your solution (you don't have the entire result set returned).

Summary

In this chapter, we have seen how to create a real-world interface between Microsoft Dynamics NAV and an external application. As learned in the chapter, it's always recommended not to directly publish NAV web services to an external application but instead use a *middle tier* that wraps the calls and permits flexibility and scalability.

In this chapter, we have covered all the aspects of the interface creation, such as business logic management in NAV, development of a RESTful WCF service that acts as *middle tier* between NAV and the external clients, application testing, and deployment.

We have learned several tips on how to write a modern interface (different responses, layered solution, security, and much more) and now we have a solution ready for production.

The next chapter will show us how to use **Control Add-ins** in order to use the external services from a custom user interface on NAV.

6
Extending NAV Pages with Control Add-ins

During the implementation of a Microsoft Dynamics NAV-based solution, often there are requirements to *extend* the user interface by adding graphical controls that are not natively built-in on the platform.

Microsoft Dynamics NAV offers the ability to create client control add-ins that permit you to add custom functionalities to a NAV page.

In this chapter, we'll see how to solve the requirements of a real-world scenario by using control add-ins. Here you will learn about the following topics:

- Creating a NAV control add-in with Visual Studio
- Publishing a control add-in on NAV

A business case

A manufacturing company is required to interact with a production machine in order to retrieve details for production orders in progress. This data must be displayed on a dedicated NAV page in a graphical way and the final output must be displayed on a big touch screen monitor in the production department.

The technical requirements are as follows:

- Data about production orders must be retrieved from an external production machine
- The production machine returns all the production orders that are in progress and their status (completed or not)
- NAV must receive this data and display the production orders status in a graphical way
- The NAV page must be touch-friendly and must be displayed on a big touch screen
- The operators must have a very simple user interface that permits them to do the following things:
    - Refresh the data (reload it from the external machine)
    - Click on a production order box to see its details

During the analysis, the production staff expressed the desire to have a monitor able to display an interface similar to the this concept:

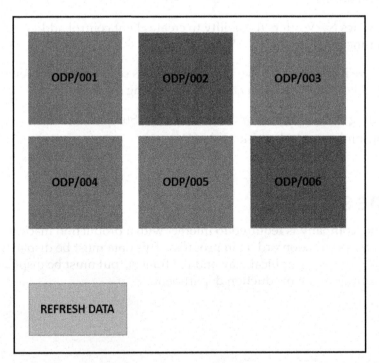

Here we have a box for every production order (with its NAV number). Every box is green in color if the corresponding production order is completed, and red if it's not completed.

On the bottom line of the monitor, there's a big button that permits you to refresh data from an external machine.

Every production order box can be clickable for retrieving its details.

How can we satisfy these requirements?

Microsoft Dynamics NAV offers an **Extensibility Framework** that permits you to extend NAV Role Centers and Pages by adding custom visuals and functionalities that you can't provide with the built-in NAV Development Environment features. These functionalities will be deployed as client control add-ins (.NET Framework assemblies). Starting from NAV 2013R2, the new Extensibility Framework also permits you to use the created add-ins on all the display targets and not only on the Windows client.

NAV control add-ins can be written by using .NET or JavaScript. Control add-ins written in .NET can target the NAV Windows client, while control add-ins written using JavaScript can target any Dynamics NAV client, including the web client and the mobile clients (Universal App).

Remember that JavaScript-based client add-ins in repeater controls (lists, listparts, list subpages, and worksheets) are not supported on any of the Microsoft Dynamics NAV clients.

Control add-ins can be easily deployed and they permit us to satisfy the requirements.

Control add-in implementation

Let's create a control add-in by performing the following steps:

1. To create a Windows client NAV control add-in, open Visual Studio and navigate to **New** | **Project…**.

2. On the **New Project** window, under **Installed** navigate to **Visual C#** | **Class Library**:

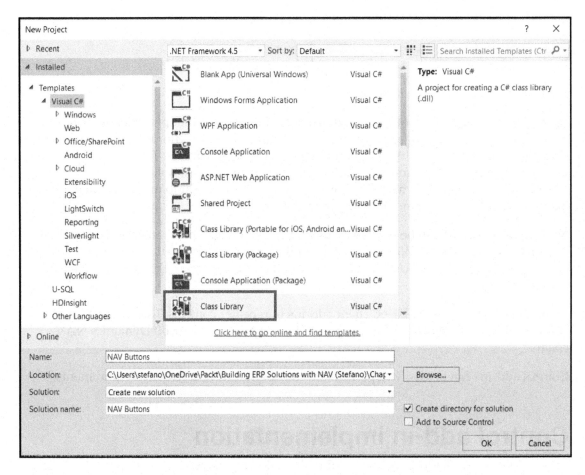

3. Give an appropriate name to your solution and click **OK**. Visual Studio creates an empty class project.

4. To start the add-in creation, we have to add reference to some .NET assemblies. In the **Solution Explorer** pane, right-click on **References** and select **Add Reference…**. In the **Reference Manager** window, navigate to **Assemblies | Framework** and select the following assemblies:

- `System.Drawing`: This is used to draw on our UI
- `System.Windows.Forms`: This is used for creating a UI on Windows devices:

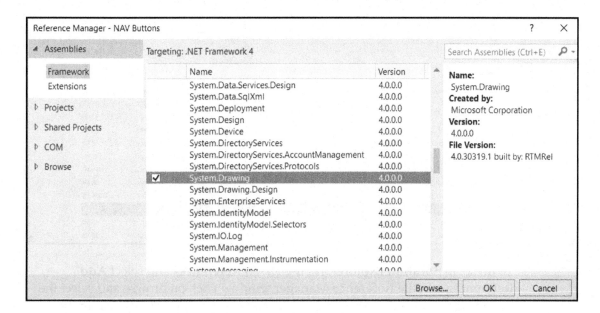

5. We also need to add a reference to the Microsoft Dynamics NAV Extensibility Framework DLL, which is located in the `C:\Program Files (x86)\Microsoft Dynamics NAV\<NAVVersionNumber>\RoleTailored Client` folder, where `<NAVVersionNumber>` is the number of your NAV version (for example, 90 for NAV 2016, 100 for NAV 2017, and so on):

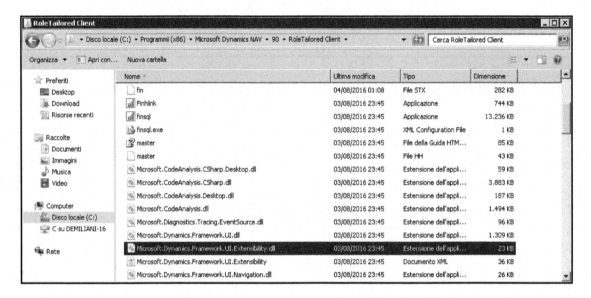

6. To do so, in **Solution Explorer**, right-click on **References** and select **Add Reference...**. In the **Reference Manager** window click on browse and select the `Microsoft.Dynamics.Framework.UI.Extensibility.dll` file from the previously described folder.

7. Now we can create a class for our add-in that inherits from the `StringControlAddinBase` class (the base class for a Windows control add-in that binds a `String` data type and uses events to call the `OnControlAddin` trigger) and implements the `IStringControlAddinDefinition` interface (the base interface for add-ins with a string value type that has a `ControlAddinEventHandler` event). Our add-in will have the following signature:

```
[ControlAddInExport("EID.NAVButtonAddin")] [Description("NAV
Button Controls Add-In")]
public class ContextBindingAddIn : StringControlAddInBase,
IStringControlAddInDefinition
```

8. Microsoft suggests using the following naming convention, `MyCompany.MyProduct.AddInName`, but obviously this is not a requirement. Our class is decorated with two more attributes:
   - `ControlAddInExport`: This defines the add-in name to use in NAV (you need this name in the `AddIn` table in NAV)
   - `Description`: This defines the description for the add-in

9. Now we can start implementing the add-in code. In our project, we override the Windows form `CreateControl` event (this creates the native Windows form control). This method is called when the add-in is displayed on the NAV page.

   Here, we perform the following activities:

10. We call a function to retrieve data from the external production's system. This will be done by calling a method in a proper `Data Access Layer` class (this could be also developed as a new DLL to better decouple the solution).We design the main panel (the content of our UI controls).
11. We design the refresh button (static).
12. For every data retrieved from the external system, we design a button with custom text and event handler.
13. When the control is ready, we trigger an event.

14. So, as the first step, we can implement the `Data Access Layer` class (responsible for retrieving data from an external system). Right-click on the solution and navigate to **Add Reference...**. The newly added class will be called `DAL`:

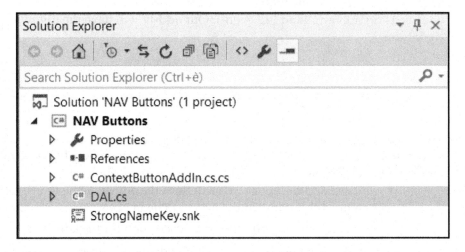

15. In the `DAL` class (defined as `public`), we implement a method that retrieves a list of `Key-value` objects (`string` and `Boolean` dictionary) that represents Production Order Number and its status. Our `DAL` class implements a method such as the following:

```
public Dictionary<string,Boolean> GetItems()
```

This method returns a .NET `Dictionary` object (a tuple with key and value) where the key is `Production Order No.` and the value is a `Boolean` field with these criteria:

- `True`: if the production order is complete
- `False`: if the production order is not complete

The implementation of this method is beyond the scope of this book, but remember that with an *external* class like this we can demand the `Data Access Layer` class implementation to a dedicated staff (other developers) and in Visual Studio we can reference this `DAL` class. In this way, we can retrieve data from an external system in different ways without impacting the development of the add-in itself (we can call a `DLL` file, we can call a web service, and so on.).

16. Our DAL class will be as follows. Remember that the `LoadProductionOrders` method here returns hardcoded values (these are the values that come from an external system):

```
public Dictionary<string,Boolean> GetItems()
    {
        Dictionary<string, Boolean> dict = new Dictionary<string,
        Boolean>();
        LoadProductionOrders(ref dict);
        return dict;
    }

private void LoadProductionOrders(ref Dictionary<string,
Boolean> dict)
    {
        //Fake method to retrive orders list from the external
        machine
        //In real world, here we have to read data from the
        external machine (out of scope)
        dict.Add("ODP16/001", true);
        dict.Add("ODP16/002", true);
        dict.Add("ODP16/003", false);
        dict.Add("ODP16/004", true);
        dict.Add("ODP16/005", false);
        dict.Add("ODP16/006", true);
        dict.Add("ODP16/008", false);
        dict.Add("ODP16/011", false);
        dict.Add("ODP16/023", true);
    }

public ODP GetODPDetails(string ProdOrderNo)
    {
        //Fake method to retrive order's details from the
        external machine
        //In real world, here we have to read data from the
        external machine (out of scope)
        ODP odp = new ODP();
        odp.Code = ProdOrderNo;
        odp.Machine1 = 10;
        odp.Machine2 = 48;
        odp.Machine3 = 32;
        return odp;
    }
```

GetODPDetails retrieves production details for Production Order No. and it returns an ODP object defined in a class as follows:

```
[Serializable]
public class ODP
    {
        public string Code { get; set; }
        public decimal Machine1 { get; set; }
        public decimal Machine2 { get; set; }
        public decimal Machine3 { get; set; }
    }
```

17. Now we can implement the control add-in core.

Our control add-in must implement the CreateControl method to dynamically instantiate the user interface controls.

18. To add an event that will be represented by a new trigger in the C/AL code of a Dynamics NAV Page object, we use the managed attribute, ApplicationVisibleAttribute.

This is the method implementation:

```
//Add-In name for NAV
[ControlAddInExport("EID.NAVButtonAddin")][Description("NAV
Button Controls Add-In")]
public class ContextBindingAddIn : StringControlAddInBase,
IStringControlAddInDefinition
    {
        [ApplicationVisible]
        [field: NonSerialized]
      public event MethodInvoker AddInReady = delegate { };

        [ApplicationVisible]
        [field:NonSerialized]
        public event EventHandler<ODPEventArgs> LoadODP =
        delegate { };
        //Creates the native WinForms control
protected override Control CreateControl()
      {
        DynamicsNAVButtonPanel.DAL DAL = new
        DynamicsNAVButtonPanel.DAL();
        Dictionary<string, Boolean> dict = DAL.GetItems();

        Button buttonRefresh = new Button();
        buttonRefresh.Location = new System.Drawing.Point(0,
        300);
```

```
buttonRefresh.Name = "btnRefresh";
buttonRefresh.Size = new System.Drawing.Size(175, 100);
buttonRefresh.TabIndex = 0;
buttonRefresh.Text = "GET DATA";
buttonRefresh.BackColor =
System.Drawing.Color.OrangeRed;
buttonRefresh.UseVisualStyleBackColor = true;
buttonRefresh.Click += new
System.EventHandler(buttonRefresh_Click);

Panel buttonpanel = new Panel();
buttonpanel.Controls.Add(buttonRefresh);
buttonpanel.Location = new System.Drawing.Point(12, 12);
buttonpanel.Name = "ButtonPanel";
buttonpanel.Padding = new
System.Windows.Forms.Padding(4, 20, 4, 4);
buttonpanel.Size = new System.Drawing.Size(600, 400);
buttonpanel.TabIndex = 0;
buttonpanel.Text = "Global Monitor";

int x = 0, y = 0;
int rowcount = 0, i = 0;
foreach (KeyValuePair<string, bool> kvp in dict)
  {
    i++;
    rowcount++;
    if (rowcount > 3)
        {
            //We want max. 3 rectangles on every lines
            x = 0;
            y += 70;
            rowcount = 1;
        }
    Button button = new Button();
    button.Location = new System.Drawing.Point(x, y);
    button.Name = "btnODP" + i.ToString();
    button.Size = new System.Drawing.Size(50, 50);
    button.Text = kvp.Key;
      if (kvp.Value == true)
        {
            button.BackColor = System.Drawing.Color.Green;
        }
    else
        {
            button.BackColor = System.Drawing.Color.Red;
        }

    x += 70;
```

```
                    button.UseVisualStyleBackColor = true;
                    button.Click += new
                    System.EventHandler(button_Click);

                buttonpanel.Controls.Add(button);

            }

    //The AddInReady event is fired when the control is created
    buttonpanel.HandleCreated += (s, e) => AddInReady();

    return buttonpanel;
        }

    void buttonRefresh_Click(object sender, System.EventArgs e)
        {
            //Here we can call a method to refresh data
            this.RaiseControlAddInEvent(1, "Data refreshed");
        }

    void button_Click(object sender, System.EventArgs e)
        {
            Button button = sender as Button;
            string _ProdOrderNo = button.Text;

            //Launch the event
            DynamicsNAVButtonPanel.DAL DAL = new
            DynamicsNAVButtonPanel.DAL();
            ODP odp = DAL.GetODPDetails(_ProdOrderNo);
            LoadODP(this, new ODPEventArgs(odp));
            //Here we can call a method to refresh data
            this.RaiseControlAddInEvent(2, _ProdOrderNo);
        }

    }
```

This code creates two events (`AddInReady` and `LoadODP`) with the `[ApplicationVisible]` attribute (so NAV can see them):

```
[ApplicationVisible]
[field: NonSerialized]
public event MethodInvoker AddInReady = delegate { };

[ApplicationVisible]
[field:NonSerialized]
public event EventHandler<ODPEventArgs> LoadODP = delegate { };
```

19. After these declarations, inside the override of the `CreateControl` method, we load the production order data by calling the data access layer function. Here a `Dictionary<string, Boolean>` collection is filled.

20. Then, we create a **Refresh** button (`buttonRefresh`) and we attach a `Click` event handler to it:

```
buttonRefresh.Click += new
System.EventHandler(buttonRefresh_Click);
```

21. Next we create a panel (`buttonpanel`) and to this panel we attach the **Refresh** button:

```
Panel buttonpanel = new Panel();
buttonpanel.Controls.Add(buttonRefresh);
```

22. For each production order detail retrieved from the data access layer function, we dynamically create a button with the appropriate color (red or green). Every button created has text appropriate to the corresponding `Production Order No.` and to every button we attach a click event handler (`button_click`). At the end, the created button is added to the panel.

23. When the panel is ready, we trigger the `AddInReady` event:

```
buttonpanel.HandleCreated += (s, e) => AddInReady();
```

24. In the `button_click` event, we retrieve the button that was clicked and do the following things:
    - We read the text of the button (`Production Order No.`)
    - We load the order's details by calling the `Data Access Layer` class (DAL) previously defined
    - We trigger the `LoadODP` event

Let's look at the button_Click event now:

```
void button_Click(object sender, System.EventArgs e)
    {
        Button button = sender as Button;
        string _ProdOrderNo = button.Text;

        //Launch the event
        DynamicsNAVButtonPanel.DAL DAL = new
        DynamicsNAVButtonPanel.DAL();
        ODP odp = DAL.GetODPDetails(_ProdOrderNo);
        LoadODP(this, new ODPEventArgs(odp));
        //Here we can call a method to refresh data
        this.RaiseControlAddInEvent(2, _ProdOrderNo);
    }
```

The LoadODP event has an EventArgs parameter defined as follows:

```
[Serializable]
public class ODPEventArgs: EventArgs
    {
        private readonly ODP _ODP;
        public ODPEventArgs(ODP odp)
            {
                _ODP = odp;
            }

        public ODP ODP
            {
                get { return _ODP;  }
            }
    }
```

Our add-in is now ready to be deployed.

WinForms control add-in

Before deploying the previously created add-in, remember that you can also create a control add-in by creating a class that overrides WinFormsControlAddInBase and then directly design the user interface on Visual Studio by adding a user control to the project.

As a quick example, we can create the following class by performing the following steps:

```
[ControlAddInExport("EID.NAVWinformAddin")][Description("NAV
Button Controls Add-In")]
public class NAVWinformAddin : WinFormsControlAddInBase
```

1. Right-click on the class project in Visual Studio, navigate to **Add** | **Add Reference...**, and then under **Windows Forms** select **User Control**:

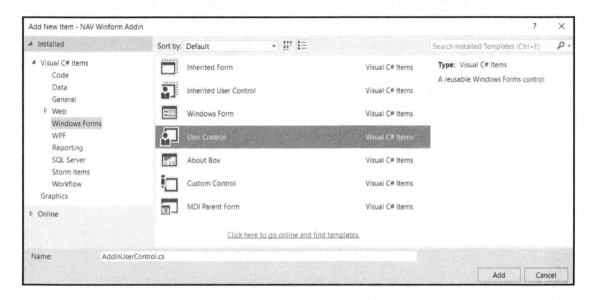

Visual Studio creates an empty **User Control** on your solution with the name you have set:

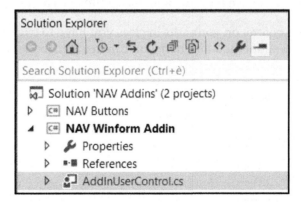

2. If you right-click the user control and select **View Designer**, you can design the UI:

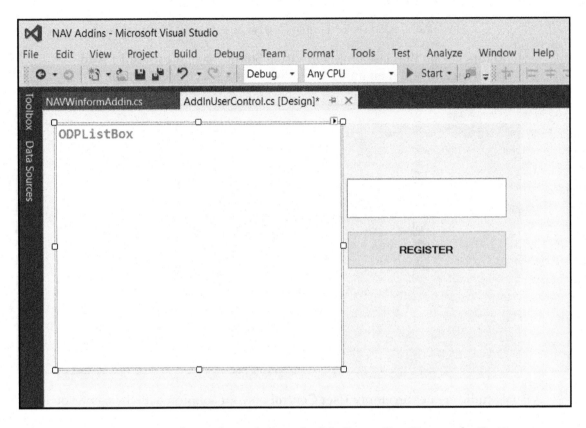

In the preceding sample, we have designed a **ListBox**, a **TextBox**, and a **Button**.

3. As described before, on your add-in class you have to override the `CreateControl` method and here you can instantiate the user control and load the data:

```
public class NAVWinformAddin : WinFormsControlAddInBase
    {
        private Panel _panel;
        private AddInUserControl uc;

        [ApplicationVisible]
        [field: NonSerialized]
    public event MethodInvoker AddInReady = delegate { };
```

```
protected override Control CreateControl()
    {
        uc = new AddInUserControl { Dock = DockStyle.Fill };

        _panel = new Panel
          {
            Dock = DockStyle.Fill,
            Size = new Size(500, 300)
          };

        _panel.Controls.Add(uc);

        //Load the Data from the Data Access Layer class
        DAL _dal = new DAL();
        List<string> ODPlist = _dal.LoadODPData();
        //We call a method defined in the User Control class that
        bind the list to the ListBox control
        uc.LoadData(ODPlist);

        _panel.HandleCreated += (s, e) => AddInReady();

        return _panel;
    }
}
```

Universal control add-in

As previously described, you can also write a NAV client control add-in that targets Windows and a web client.

To do this, you need to perform the following steps:

1. Create the control add-in with Visual Studio as previously described.
2. Sign the add-in assembly.
3. Create a manifest file for the add-in. The manifest file is an XML file that contains add-in information such as resource files, references to JavaScript files, the size of the add-in, and so on. The name of this file must be `Manifest.xml`.
4. Create a JavaScript file for the add-in code.

5. Create one single file containing the manifest and any resource files. This single file is a `.zip` file and it will be registered in the **Client Add-in** page. The `.zip` file must contain a certain structure for it to be recognized by the **Client Add-in** page.

6. Create a `.zip` file containing the manifest and resource files and register this file with the control add-in in Microsoft Dynamics NAV.

 You can find all the references for these tasks on the MSDN site at `https://msdn.microsoft.com/en-us/library/dn182544(v=nav.90).aspx`.

Control add-in deployment

To use a control add-in on NAV, we need to perform the following steps:

1. You first to need to sign the control add-in assembly. Open the Visual Studio Command Prompt and go to the directory where you have the compiled control add-in DLL (usually it's in the `BIN` directory on your project's folder).

   Here you have to launch this command:

   SN.exe -T <NameOfYourDLLAddinFile>

   <NameOfYourDLLAddinFile> is the control add-in DLL file.

   Visual Studio signs the assembly and returns a public key token (a 16-character key):

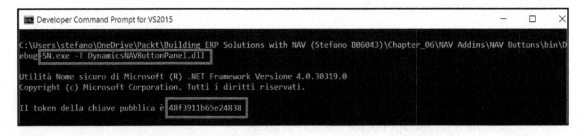

2. Now we have to copy the control add-in files (DLLs) in the Microsoft Dynamics NAV Windows client add-ins folder, which is usually located here:

```
C:\Program Files (x86)\Microsoft Dynamics NAV\
<NAVVersionNumber>\RoleTailored Client\Add-ins
```

`<NAVVersionNumber>` is the number corresponding to the NAV Version (*90 = NAV 2016* and so on).

3. In our solution, we have created a subfolder called `Buttons` on our `Add-ins` folder:

4. After deployment, we have to register the control add-in on NAV. Open the Microsoft Dynamics NAV Development Environment and run the `Add-in` table (`ID = 2000000069`):

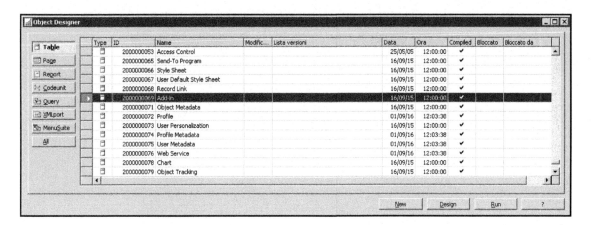

5. On this table, we have to create the following new entries:

- **Add-in Name**: This is the name of your add-in and is similar to the one you have set in Visual Studio in the `ControlAddInExport` attribute
- **Public Key Token**: This is the key returned when signing the assembly
- **Category**: This is `DotNet Control Add-in`
- **Description**: This is the description of your add-in

Take a look at the following screenshot which depicts the preceding mentioned entries:

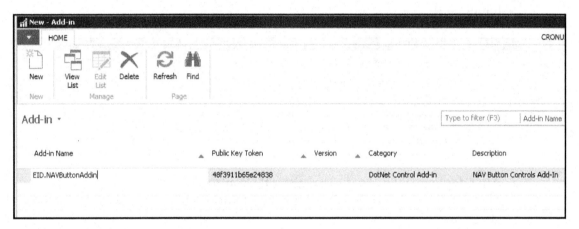

Now the add-in is registered on NAV and we can use it on a NAV page.

6. Let's create a new blank page and here we add a `Field` with an appropriate name (in our example we have used the name `Monitor`). On this field, go to **Property** and on the `ControlAddIn` property select the previously created add-in (by clicking on the `Lookup` field):

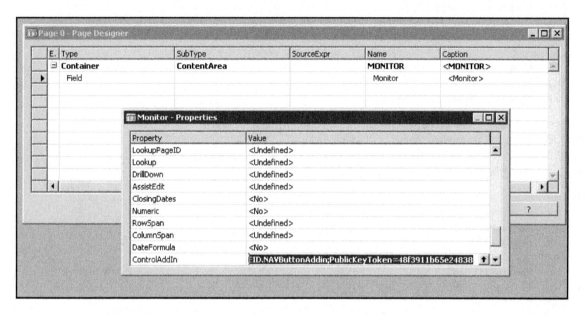

7. If you go on the code view for the page (press *F9* on the previously added field), you can see the add-in triggers.

In the `OnControlAddin` trigger, you can read the data returned by every button pressed on the add-in UI. You can see also the events triggered by our add-in, declared as `ApplicationVisible`:

```
27  ⊟Monitor - OnValidate()
28   ⌊
29  ⊟Monitor - OnLookup(VAR Text : Text) : Boolean
30   ⌊
31  ⊟Monitor - OnDrillDown()
32   ⌊
33  ⊟Monitor - OnAssistEdit()
34   ⌊
35  ⊟Monitor - OnControlAddIn(Index : Integer;Data : Text)
36   MESSAGE('Returned data: ' + Data);
37   ⌊
38  ⊟OnLoadODP(sender : Variant;e : DotNet "NAVButtonAddin.ODPEventArgs")
39   
40   
41   ⌊
42  ⊟Monitor::AddInReady()
43   ready:=TRUE;
44   ⌊
45  ⊟Monitor::LoadODP(sender : Variant;e : DotNet "NAVButtonAddin.ODPEventArgs")
46   IF ready THEN
47   BEGIN
48   
49     OnLoadODP(sender,e);
50   END;
51   ⌊
```

8. If we compile and run the page, the following will be the result:

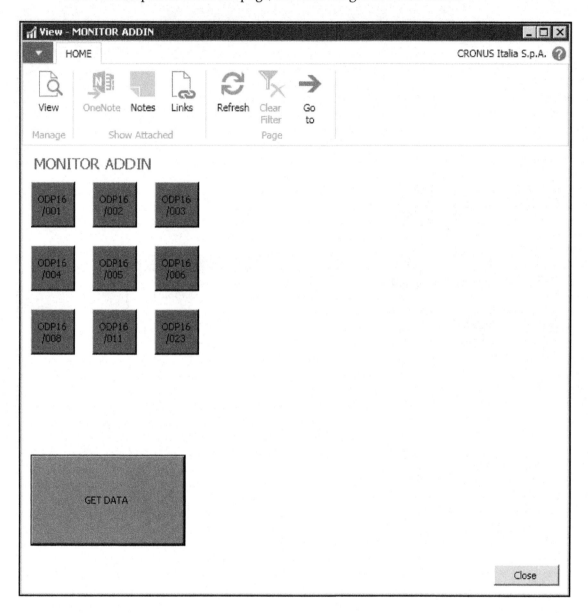

9. If you click on a button, the context is retrieved:

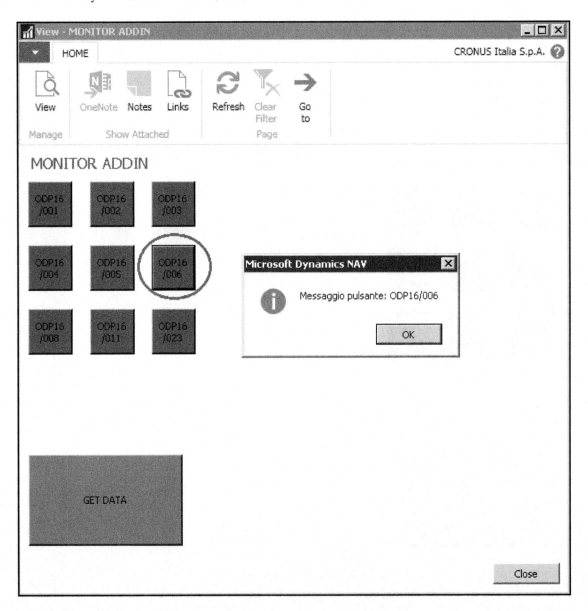

10. From here you can do what you want with your data.

You can deploy a control add-in also by using dedicated PowerShell cmdlets:

- `New-NAVAddin`: This registers a control add-in in the NAV `Add-in` table
- `Get-NAVAddin`: This returns all the information about add-ins registered in NAV
- `Set-NAVAddin`: This permits you to set the resources (DLL files or ZIP) and descriptions associated to an add-in registered in `NAVRemove`
- `NAVAddin`: This removes a previously registered add-in from the NAV `Add-in` table

If a control add-in has the same name as the assembly, you can have an automatic deployment of the add-in and any associated files. As explained on the MSDN site, there are two ways that you set up the automatic deployment of a control add-in:

- You can install the control add-in assembly directly on computers running the Microsoft Dynamics NAV server
- You can import the control add-in assembly into the NAV database

When an operation from the Microsoft Dynamics NAV Windows client requires a control add-in, the control add-in is deployed as follows:

- The client looks for the control add-in assembly in the local `Add-ins` folder (by default in Microsoft Dynamics NAV 2017 the folder is `C:\Program Files (x86)\Microsoft Dynamics NAV\100\RoleTailored Client\Add-ins`) and then:
  - If the assembly is available, it is used
  - If the assembly is not available, the client requests the assembly from the Microsoft Dynamics NAV server

The Microsoft Dynamics NAV server looks for the control add-in assembly in the local `Add-ins` folder (by default in Microsoft Dynamics NAV 2017 the folder is `C:\Program Files\Microsoft Dynamics NAV\100\Service\Add-ins`) and then:

- If the assembly is available, it is deployed to the Microsoft Dynamics NAV Windows client computer. The control add-in is installed in the `%TEMP%\Microsoft Dynamics NAV\Add-Ins` folder of the user who is running the client.
- If the control add-in assembly is not there, the add-in is deployed from the database to the Microsoft Dynamics NAV Windows client.

- The control add-in assembly is streamed from the database to the Microsoft Dynamics NAV server instance and eventually the Microsoft Dynamics NAV Windows client computer.
- On the Microsoft Dynamics NAV Windows client computer, the control add-in is installed in the %TEMP%\Microsoft Dynamics NAV\Add-Ins folder of the user who is running the client.
- The deployed assembly will be then be used whenever the page is run until the control add-in has been updated with a version change.

- If the control add-in assembly is updated and its version number changes, the Microsoft Dynamics NAV server will deploy the updated assembly to the client computer the next time that the client requests the assembly. The updated assembly is put in a subfolder of the %TEMP%\Microsoft Dynamics NAV\Add-Ins folder, where the subfolder has the assembly's version number as its name.

Summary

In this chapter, you have seen how you can use the NAV Extensibility Framework in order to enhance a user interface by developing a control add-in with Visual Studio. You've learned also how to sign, deploy, and activate the add-in.

In the next chapter, we'll see how we can integrate NAV with applications developed for Windows 10 and the Universal Windows Platform.

7
Programming Universal Windows Apps with NAV and Devices

We live in a world where mobility is an emerging requirement for every type of business. In recent years, Microsoft has been continuously investing in creating a unified experience between devices. The goal is to have a platform which allows you to develop an application and run it on every device you have (PC, tablet, smartphone, and so on) by using the different devices's capabilities. Microsoft has reached this goal with Windows 10 and the Unified Windows Platform.

In this chapter, we'll see how we can use the Universal Windows Platform to satisfy real-world business cases where NAV must be integrated with different Windows-based mobile devices. Here you will learn about the following topics:

- An overview of Universal Windows Platform
- Implementing a RESTful interface layer between NAV and a UWP application
- Creating a UWP application for transmitting device locations to NAV
- An interaction with devices from a UWP application

Business case 1 – handling mobile informations with NAV

With an introduction of devices such as Surface, Microsoft has gained ground in its pursuit of enterprise mobility: having a full desktop experience (you can use every desktop application you have on your office machine) on a mobile device (that you can use with a keyboard, with a pen, or simply with a touch of your fingers):

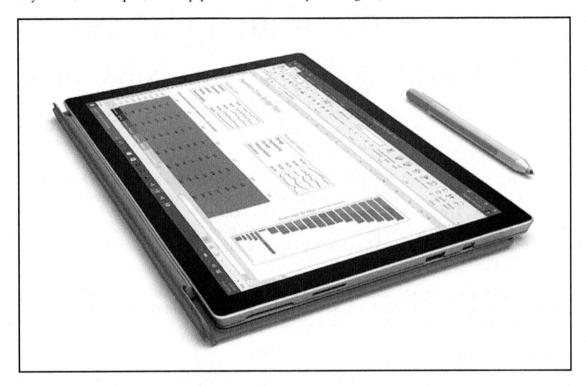

In the transport (logistics) industry, devices such as Microsoft Surface or Windows Mobile tablets are often used by couriers to manage shipments and for a real-time connection with the headquarters' NAV ERP. In the services field, there are more and more companies that use Surface devices in mobility to handle their services to the final customer.

In this business case, a transport company has all its business running on the Microsoft technology stack. In particular, the company utilizes Microsoft Dynamics NAV as the headquarters' ERP. The company has lots of couriers that dispatch goods every day and they need to track in real time the start and the end of a mission for every courier (with their exact location at a given moment).

Every courier has a Windows-based mobile device (many of them have a Surface device, others have a Windows Mobile device) and the company wants to have a simple application that permits the couriers to register the start of a mission (when they collect the goods) and the end of a mission (when they dispatch the goods at the final destination). The application must be easy to use (couriers often are not so able with devices and they're not ERP-addicted). They don't want to expose NAV to the couriers (so no Mobile NAV client or NAV Web client).

Every mission's data is registered in NAV and it is subsequently used for invoicing and for statistics.

The requirements that we have are as follows:

- They need an application to register in real time the start and the end of a delivery, by transmitting the exact location of the courier
- Transmitted data must be stored in the central NAV
- The application must run on the mobile device (Surface or Windows Phone)
- The company doesn't want to give direct access to NAV to the couriers and they don't want to directly expose NAV to the outside world
- The application must be simple to use

How can we satisfy these requirements?

As described in the previous chapters of this book, the architectural idea for the solution is essentially made up with three main pieces:

- Microsoft Dynamics NAV as the company's ERP where we have the business logic and the data repository
- An integration layer (exposed to the Internet) that acts as a *middle tier* between NAV and the client application
- The client application, based on the UWP application)

This is the final schema for the solution:

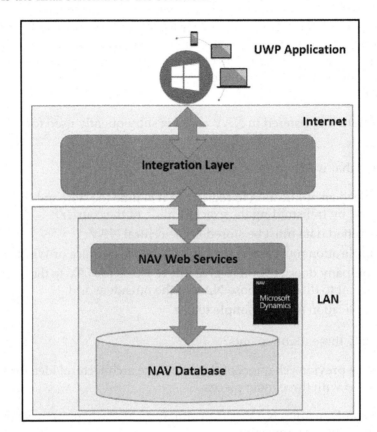

An overview of Universal Windows Platform

The **Universal Windows Platform (UWP)** was first introduced with Windows 8 and its **Windows Runtime (WinRT)**. With Windows 8.1, Microsoft has aligned the WinRT between Windows Phone and Windows by creating a *shared code base* between platforms, and with Windows 10 the UWP was launched.

The UWP provides a common application platform for every device that runs Windows 10.

The idea behind it is that users want to have a consistent experience across devices, despite the type of device they are using (tablet, smartphone, wearable, and so on): you can use the best device for the task you're performing, with its specific features, but an application is *written once and runs everywhere* despite the screen sizes or the interaction models:

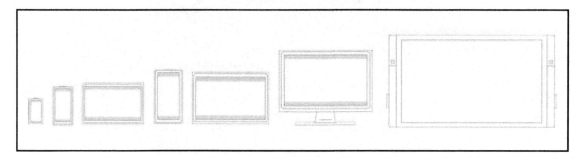

The UWP has the following main characteristics:

- The target is a device family, not the OS
- There's a common API across devices and it's the same for all the Windows family (UWP applications use the native WinRT)
- The UI is adaptive (the UWP has addictive controls and input that uses effective pixels, so every control can adapt itself based on the screen resolution where it runs)
- The application is packaged and distributed using a packaging format (.AppX) that ensures security and is easy to deploy
- You can share your application via the official Windows Store (one store for all devices)
- UWP applications can be developed using different programming languages (such as C# and XAML, JavaScript and HTML, and C++ and DirectX)

The UWP is illustrated in the following schema:

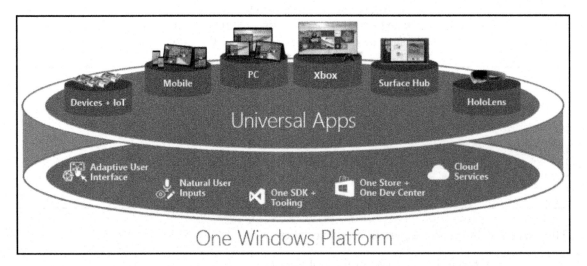

Applications developed for the UWP can use WinRT APIs (common to all devices) and also Win32 and .NET APIs that are specific for the device family where the application is running on.

The Universal Windows Platform has introduced the concept of **device family**: you no longer target a specific operating system but now you target a family of devices.

A device family is a set of APIs that are applicable to a particular device. The UWP starts from the **Universal device family** (a set of APIs present on every OS and on every Windows device) and every new device family adds its own APIs to the **Universal device family** (from which it inherits).

This is a schema of the UWP device families:

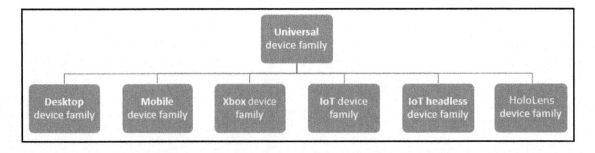

The solution – implementing the NAV business logic

We use NAV to store all the data about the courier's missions and in NAV will reside all the business logic.

For handling our solution we need to do the followings things:

- We need to define the table to handle all the data that comes from devices (upgrade of mission's status)
- We need to define a codeunit with the business logic to register a mission from the external device to NAV
- We need to expose our business logic as a web service

We suppose here that in our NAV database we have a table called `Mission` that contains the details for every mission and the assigned courier, as shown in the following screenshot:

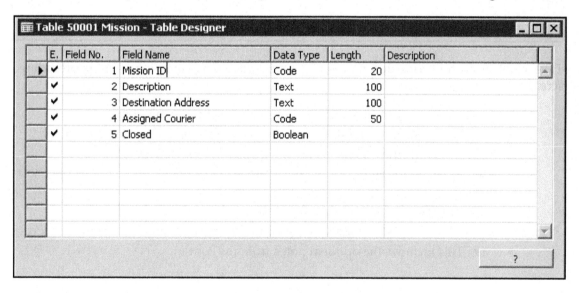

We can open the Microsoft Dynamics NAV Development Environment and here we can design a table called `Mission Tracking`, as shown in the following screenshot:

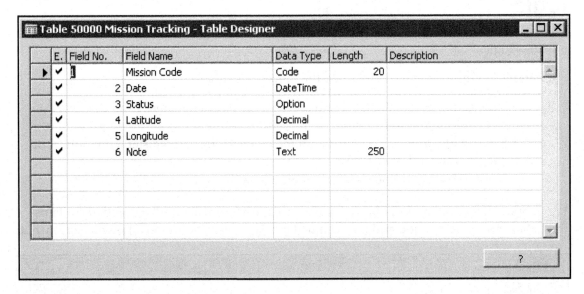

Take a look at the following description of the respective fields mentioned in the preceding screenshot:

- `Mission Code`: This is the unique internal code for the mission.
- `Date`: This is the date and time of the registered status for the mission. Every mission's status update transmitted to NAV will be called a ticket.
- `Status`: This is the status for the mission's ticket (the `OptionString` property is set as `Started`, `In Progress`, or `Delivered`).
- `Latitude`: This is the latitude value of the actual courier's position.
- `Longitude`: This is the longitude value of the actual courier's position.
- `Note`: This includes the optional notes from the courier.

This table has the following composite key:

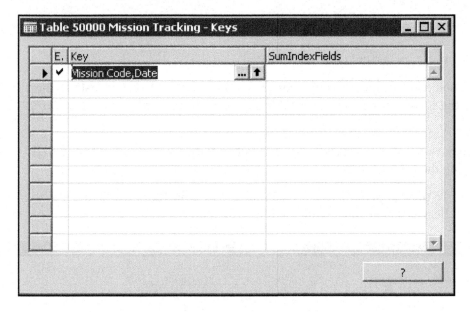

Now we can create a codeunit that has a public function called `RegisterMissionTicket`. This function receives values from an external application and saves the mission to NAV.

This function will be defined as follows (obviously, you can write more complex C/AL code here and you can use text ML constants for error messages):

```
RegisterMissionTicket(MissionCode : Code[20];Date :
DateTime;Status
: Code[20];Latitude : Decimal;Longitude : Decimal;Note :
Text[250])
IF MissionCode='' THEN
  ERROR('No Mission selected!');

  MissionTracking.INIT;
  MissionTracking."Mission Code" := MissionCode;
  MissionTracking.Date := Date;
    CASE Status OF
      'STARTED':
        MissionTracking.Status :=
        MissionTracking.Status::Started;
      'IN PROGRESS':
        MissionTracking.Status := MissionTracking.Status::"In
        Progress";
      'DELIVERED':
        MissionTracking.Status :=
```

```
              MissionTracking.Status::Delivered;
        END;
        MissionTracking.Latitude := Latitude;
        MissionTracking.Longitude := Longitude;
        MissionTracking.Note := Note;
        MissionTracking.INSERT;
```

The function receives the mission record from the service layer. It translates the `Status` value to the correct option string in NAV and saves the record to the `Mission Ticket` table.

Now we have to expose our codeunit as a web service. Let us see how we will do that by performing the following steps:

1. To do so, open Microsoft Dynamics NAV RoleTailored client, go to the **Web Services** page and create the following entry:

2. The `Codeunit` object is here published with `RegisterMissionTicket` in **Service Name**. When published, we have the SOAP URL that we'll use later to add a reference in our service layer implementation.
3. If we want to also expose the missions assigned to a courier, we need also to design a `Query` object and publish it as an OData web service (as explained in `Chapter 5`, *Integrating NAV Web Services and External Applications*).

4. The `Query` object that returns all the active missions is shown in the following screenshot:

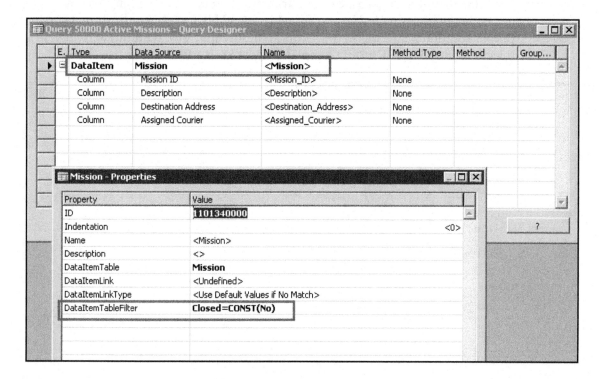

The solution – implementing the integration layer

A key point of our solution architecture is the integration layer that permits the communication between an external application (in this scenario the UWP application) and Microsoft Dynamics NAV. Only this integration layer will be exposed to the outside world (the Internet) and we want to have a RESTful HTTP service.

In `Chapter 5`, *Integrating NAV Web Services and External Applications*, we have seen how to develop a RESTful service tier by using a WCF service. Here we want to use a more **modern** approach for building REST services and we'll use the ASP.NET Web API framework.

The ASP.NET Web API is a framework used to make HTTP REST services that can reach a wide range of clients. It's light weight and easy to configure and it's based on ASP.NET MVC logic.

Take a look at the following steps for implementing the integration layer:

1. Let's start with the development of our integration layer by opening Visual Studio and navigating to **New** | **Project...** | **ASP.NET Web Application**. Give a proper solution name and in the second window that Visual Studio will open (for selecting the ASP.NET project template) select **Web API**:

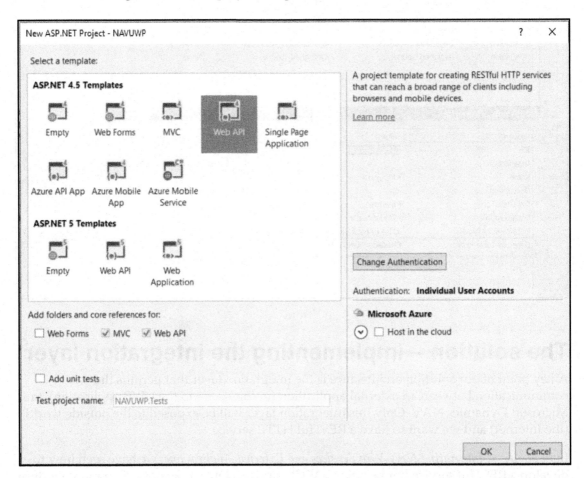

Visual Studio created the following solution:

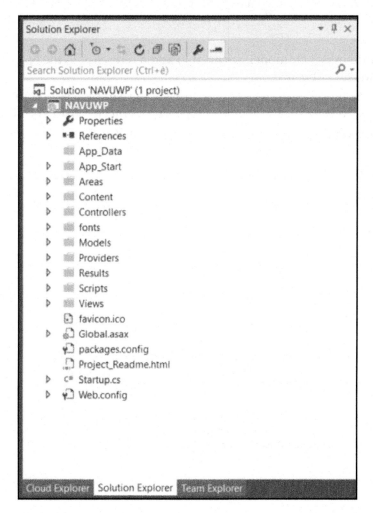

2. As the first step, we have to define our model (the `Mission` entity that represents the data that the service will have to handle and transmit to NAV).

3. Right-click on the `Models` folder in **Solution Explorer** and navigate to **Add** | **Class** to add a class called `Mission`, defined as follows:

```
public class Mission
{
    public string Code { get; set; }
    public DateTime Date { get; set; }
    public string Status { get; set; }
```

```
public Decimal Latitude { get; set; }
public Decimal Longitude { get; set; }
public string Note { get; set; }
}
```

4. After defining our model, we need to add a reference to the NAV web service previously published.

5. In the **Solution Explorer** pane, right-click the **References** node and select **Add Service Reference**, and then navigate to **Advanced** | **Add Web Reference....**.

6. In the **Add Web Reference** window, pass the SOAP URL that comes from NAV (the published codeunit):

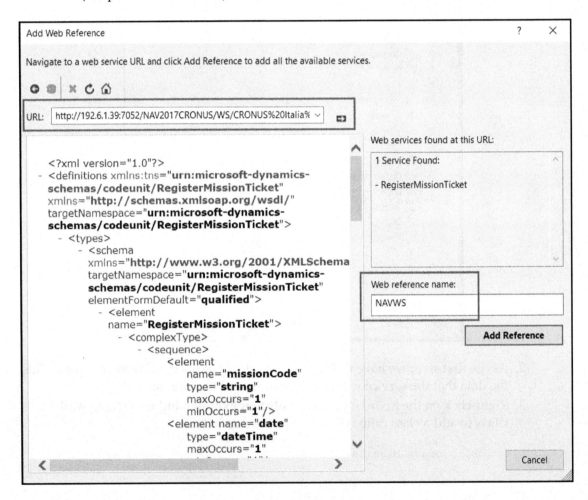

7. When Visual Studio discovers the service, give it a proper name and click on the **Add Reference** button.

8. Now right-click the `Controller` folder and navigate to **Add | Controller** and then select the **Web API 2 Controller – Empty** template:

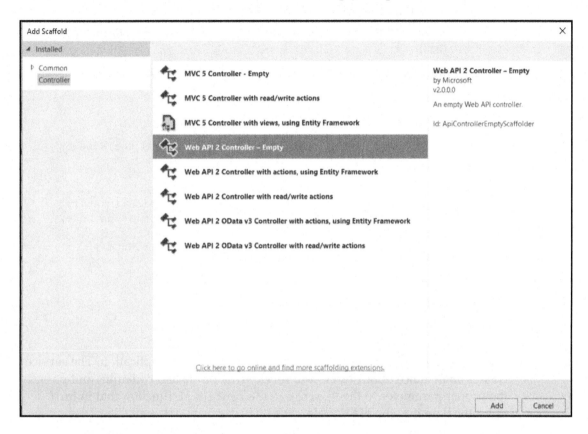

9. Give a name for your controller class (`MissionsController` in our project) and Visual Studio will create the controller class that inherits from `ApiController` (a class from the ASP.NET Web API framework):

```
public class MissionsController : ApiController
    {
        ...
    }
```

10. In the `MissionsController` class, we'll have to implement the logic for the service tier. Here we could handle every CRUD method for our `Mission` entity, but for our solution we will need only the following methods:

    - A method to transmit the mission data to NAV (`HTTP POST`)
    - A method to retrieve all missions (`HTTP GET`)
    - A method to retrieve all missions assigned to a particular user (`HTTP GET`)

11. To post a mission data to NAV, we have to define the following method:

```
[HttpPost]
public void AddMission(Mission mission)
{
   //Here we have to call NAV Web Service and pass the Mission
     data
  try
  {
     RegisterMissionTicket WS = new RegisterMissionTicket();
     WS.CallRegisterMissionTicket(mission.Code, mission.Date,
     mission.Status,
     mission.Latitude, mission.Longitude, mission.Note);
  }
   catch(Exception)
   {
      //Handle exception here
   }
}
```

12. In this code, we receive a `Mission` object from the client application. The service creates an instance of our NAV web service (the published codeunit) and passes the proper parameter to the `RegisterMissionTicket` function that in turn saves the data into the NAV table.

13. Now, if you compile and run the solution on Visual Studio, you will see an ASP.NET MVC page on the screen. To call our Web API, we need to make a `POST` HTTP request to the `http://localhost:54691/api/Missions/AddMission` URL by posting a `Mission` object (the first part of the URL depends of your local environment). This will be done from our UWP application.

14. For retrieving all the missions from NAV, we define the following method:

```
[HttpGet]
public List<Mission> GetMissions()
{
  //Here we have to call the NAV Query Web Service
}
```

15. For retrieving the missions assigned to a particular user ID, we define a method like this:

```
[HttpGet]
[ActionName("GetMissionsForUserID")]
public List<Mission> GetMissions(string UserID)
  {
     //Here we have to call the NAV Query Web Service
  }
```

16. As you can see, these are two instances of the same method but with different parameters (overloading). The second instance has the user ID parameter and it's decorated with an `ActionName` attribute.

17. When an HTTP request is issued, the Web API uses a routing table to determine which action it has to invoke (actions are public methods of `ApiController`).

18. The Web API framework first selects a controller by the `IHttpControllerSelector.SelectController` method and then selects an action method by `IHttpActionSelector.SelectAction`, depending on the matching value in the request URI and configured route table.

19. A routing table can be configured by opening the `App_Start` folder in **Solution Explorer** and editing the `Register` method in the `WebApiConfig.cs` file:

```
public static void Register(HttpConfiguration config)
        {
                // Web API configuration and services
                // Configure Web API to use only bearer token
                   authentication.
                config.SuppressDefaultHostAuthentication();
                config.Filters.Add(new
                HostAuthenticationFilter(OAuthDefaults
                .AuthenticationType));

                // Web API routes
                config.MapHttpAttributeRoutes();

                config.Routes.MapHttpRoute(
                name: "WithActionApi",
```

```
routeTemplate:
"api/{controller}/{action}/{userID}"
                                    );

config.Routes.MapHttpRoute(
name: "DefaultApi",
routeTemplate: "api/{controller}/{id}",
defaults: new { id = RouteParameter.Optional }
                                    );
}
```

20. The `DefaultApi` route is the default one placed by Visual Studio, the other is our custom route for the new action with the parameter.
21. To retrieve all missions, you can make an `HTTP GET` call to `http://localhost:54691/api/Missions/GetMissions`.
22. To retrieve all missions for a given user ID, you can make an `HTTP GET` call to `http://localhost:54691/api/Missions/GetMissionsForUserID/stefano`.
23. The methods themselves in turn make a call to the published `Query` object in NAV and by passing the appropriate filter (the `ODATA` filter) they can read the data from NAV.

The solution – implementing the UWP application

A UWP application is developed by using C# and **Extensible Application Markup Language (XAML)**. By using XAML, you can define a complex user interface for your Windows application, but obviously this is out of the scope of our book.

In our solution, our UWP application will run on every Windows 10 based device and it will have a simple UI. We will have the following things:

- A combo box where you can choose the mission to handle from a list of assigned missions
- A combo box to set the status of this mission
- A textbox for writing notes about the mission
- A button to send the location

Let's learn how to implement the UWP application by performing the following steps :

1. To create a UWP application, open Visual Studio and start a new project by choosing **New** | **Project...** | **Windows** | **Blank App (Universal Windows)** as shown in the following screenshot:

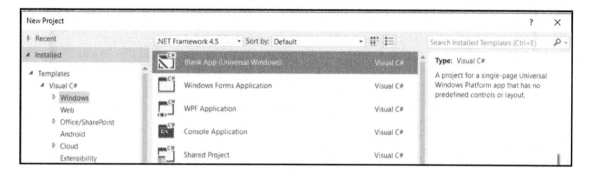

2. Visual Studio prompts you to select the OS target version and the minimum version you will support (some features such as Cortana APIs, Windows Ink, and Windows Hello are available only from the **Build 14393**, for example):

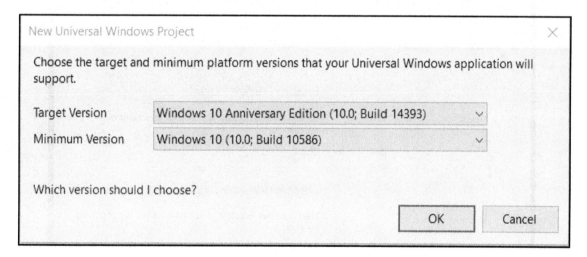

3. Now you have to enable the **Developer mode** option on Windows 10 in order to be able to compile and test the application. You can do this on Windows **Settings**:

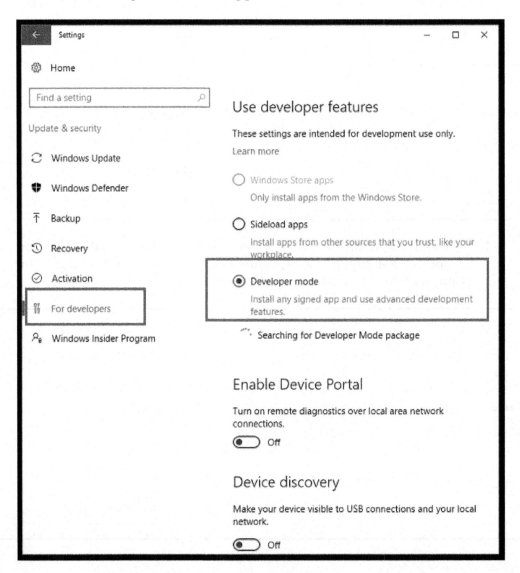

Our Visual Studio project will be created as follows:

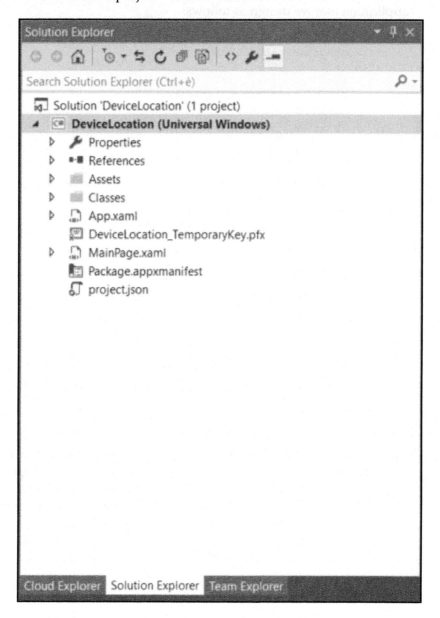

Here, `MainPage.xaml` contains the XAML definition for the UI of our application that we design as follows:

```xaml
<Grid Background="{ThemeResource
ApplicationPageBackgroundThemeBrush}">
<StackPanel>
<ComboBox Name="cmbMissions"
          HorizontalAlignment="Left"
          Margin="10,10,0,0"
          VerticalAlignment="Top"
          Width="300"
          Loaded="ComboBox_Loaded"
          SelectionChanged="ComboBox_SelectionChanged"
          DisplayMemberPath="Code"/>
<TextBox AcceptsReturn="True"
         TextWrapping="Wrap" HorizontalAlignment="Left"
         VerticalAlignment="Top" Margin="10,10,0,0" Width="300"
         Name="txtNote" />
<ComboBox Name="cmbStatus"
          HorizontalAlignment="Left"
          Margin="10,10,0,0"
          VerticalAlignment="Top"
          Width="300"
          Loaded="cmbStatus_Loaded"
          SelectionChanged="cmbStatus_SelectionChanged"/>
<Button Name="btnTransmitLocation" Content="Transmit Location"
        HorizontalAlignment="Left" VerticalAlignment="Top"
        Margin="10,10,0,0" Click="btnTransmitLocation_Click">
</Button>
</StackPanel>
</Grid>
```

Talking in depth about XAML is out of scope of this book, but as you can see, if you know XML, our UI is composed starting from a `Grid` property inside a page. Under the `Grid` property, we have a `StackPanel` (a container that allows you to stack items after items in the specified direction) and then in the `StackPanel` we have a `ComboBox` property for the mission code, a `TextBox` property for the notes, a `ComboBox` property for the mission's status, and a button to transmit the device location to NAV.

4. In the XAML for the first combo box (the one where we load the mission assigned to the user from NAV), the following attribute specifies that in the ComboBox property we want to display an attribute called `Code` for the object that we'll bind to the `ComboBox` in the code-behind (alias the `Code` attribute of our `Mission` object:

```
DisplayMemberPath="Code"
```

This is the UI designer preview in Visual Studio (you can preview it for different devices and form factors):

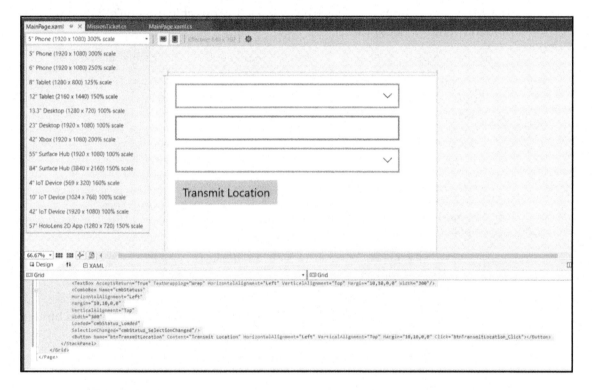

5. After designing the UI, we have to create our data model. We can right-click our project and navigate to **Add** | **Class** and define a class called `MissionTicket` as follows:

```
public class MissionTicket
{
    public string MissionCode { get; set; }
    public DateTime Date { get; set; }
    public string Status { get; set; }
```

```
    public string Note { get; set; }
    public double Latitude { get; set; }
    public double Longitude  { get; set; }
}
```

Now, as you can see in the XAML definition, we have some events bind to the controls (combo box and button) and we need to define the code-behind for these events. In WPF there are different ways to handle control events in an elegant way (such as **Commands** or **EventTriggers**) but here for simplicity we define the logic directly on the event definition.

The `cmbStatus` combo box has fixed values (the possible mission's status) so the binded event is as follows:

```
private void cmbStatus_Loaded(object sender, RoutedEventArgs e)
{
  //Fixed values
  List<string> data = new List<string>();
  data.Add("Started");
  data.Add("In Progress");
  data.Add("Delivered");

  //Get the ComboBox reference.
  var comboBox = sender as ComboBox;

  //Assign the ItemsSource to the List.
  comboBox.ItemsSource = data;

  //Make the first item selected as default.
  comboBox.SelectedIndex = 0;
}
```

The mission's `ComboBox` instead must have values returned from NAV. Its binded event is defined as follows:

```
private async void ComboBox_Loaded(object sender,
RoutedEventArgs e)
  {
    //These data will come by calling the REST service
      var uri = new
      Uri("http://localhost:54691/api/Missions
      /GetMissionsForUserID/stefano");
      var httpClient = new HttpClient();

    // Always catch network exceptions for async methods
      string result=String.Empty;
      List<MissionTicket> model = null;
```

```
        try
          {
             result = await httpClient.GetStringAsync(uri);
           //Here we have to serialize the JSON object to a list
             of Mission objects
             model =
             JsonConvert.DeserializeObject<List<MissionTicket>>
             (result);
          }
        catch(Exception ex)
          {
             //Handle the exception here...
               string dett = ex.Message;
          }
           // Once your app is done using the HttpClient object
             call dispose to
          // free up system resources (the underlying socket and
            memory used for the object)
            httpClient.Dispose();

        //Get the ComboBox reference.
          var comboBox = sender as ComboBox;

       //Assign the ItemsSource to the List.
         comboBox.ItemsSource = model;

      //Make the first item selected as default.
        comboBox.SelectedIndex = 0;
      }
```

This method is called **asynchronously (async-away pattern)** for not blocking the UI on loading data from NAV. The method uses the HTTPClient class to make an HTTP GET request to our previously developed Web API service layer (by calling the relative REST URL and passing the username parameter).

The Web API service returns a JSON response with all the missions assigned to the user (in the following screenshot you can see the debug of the `result` variable):

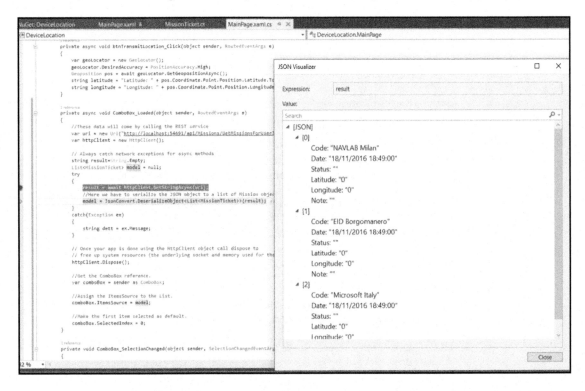

6. Next, we have to serialize the JSON object to a list of the `MissionTicket` objects (our application data model) and to do so we use the **Newtonsoft JSONConvert** package.

7. To reference this package on our Visual Studio project, navigate to **Tools** | **NuGet Package Manager** | **Manage NuGet Packages for Solution...** and search for the `Newtonsoft.Json` package:

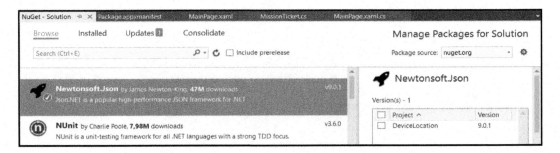

8. Then, we bind the `List<MissionTicket>` object to the `ComboBox` property (and the `Code` field is displayed in the UI).

What about the button for transmitting the device location?

Location access is disabled by default on a UWP application, so we need to activate this feature.Let us see how we can activate the location access in order to enable transmission of device to the desired location by performing the following steps:

1. To do so, right-click the `Package.appxmanifest` file in **Solution Explorer** and click on **View Designer**. Here you can specify all your application settings (the name of the app, device type, supported orientations, icons, and so on) but the most important setting for now is the **Capabilities** tab. Here we have to enable the **Location** feature:

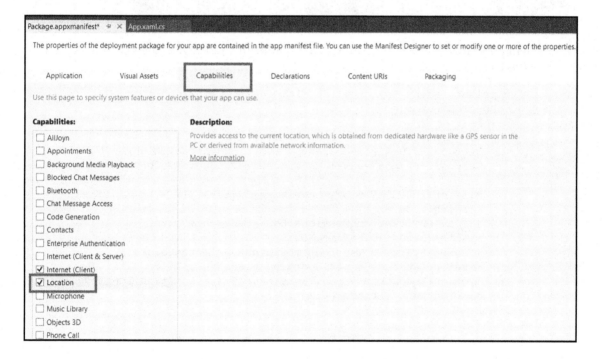

Now when you run the application for the first time, the OS will ask you if you want to enable access to your device location (the message is shown in your OS language):

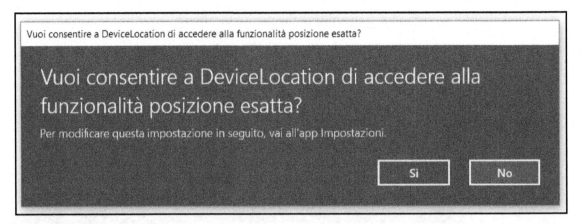

The method to retrieve the device location and transmit the mission's data to NAV is defined as follows:

```
private async void btnTransmitLocation_Click(object sender,
RoutedEventArgs e)
{
  var geoLocator = new Geolocator();
  geoLocator.DesiredAccuracy = PositionAccuracy.High;
  Geoposition pos = await geoLocator.GetGeopositionAsync();

  MissionTicket mission = new MissionTicket();
  mission.Code =
  ((MissionTicket)cmbMissions.SelectedValue).Code;
  mission.Date = DateTime.Now;
  mission.Status = (string)cmbStatuss.SelectedValue;
  mission.Latitude = pos.Coordinate.Point.Position.Latitude;
  mission.Longitude = pos.Coordinate.Point.Position.Longitude;
  mission.Note = txtNote.Text;
  try
    {
      //Makes an HTTP POST to the WEB API service
        var httpClient = new HttpClient();
        var uri = new
        Uri("http://localhost:54691/api/Missions/AddMission");
        var json = JsonConvert.SerializeObject(mission);
        var response = await httpClient.PostAsync(uri, new
        StringContent(json, Encoding.UTF8,
        "application/json"));
```

```
                    response.EnsureSuccessStatusCode();
        }
    catch(Exception ex)
        {
            //Handle exception here...
        }
    }
```

2. Here, we create an instance of the `Geolocator` class (a class on the WinRT APIs that provides access to the current geographic location of the device) and then we retrieve the device location asynchronously.

> The device location is retrieved from the GPS (if you have a GPS-enabled device) or via a Wi-Fi network. Accuracy can be very unreliable if the device does not have a GPS.

3. Then, we create a `MissionTicket` object with the appropriate values. The value for the mission code is read from the `cmbMissions` combo box. If you remember, this combo box was binded to a `List<MissionTicket>` object, so to retrieve the value we need to first cast the `SelectedValue` property to `MissionTicket` and then read the `Code` field.

4. After having created our object to transmit to NAV, we create an instance of the `HTTPClient` class and we make a `POST` request to our REST Web API URL, previously defined. The input to this request is a `JSON` object.

5. Remember that it is extremely important to pass the media type as an argument (here it is `application/json`) or you could receive an error in response:

```
var response = await httpClient.PostAsync(uri, new
StringContent(json, Encoding.UTF8, "application/json"));
```

This is the JSON object passed to the Web API POST request:

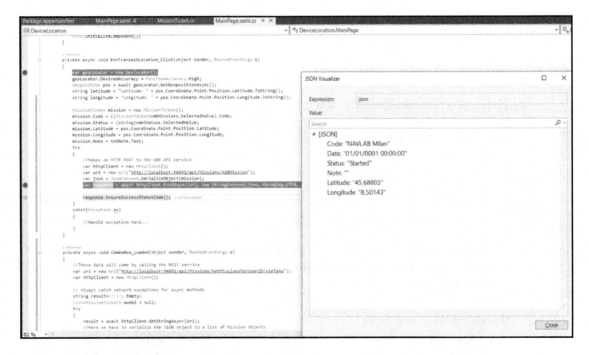

Now our mission data is transferred to NAV and correctly stored on the NAV Mission Tracking table. The courier can now register every step of a mission and from the headquarters with NAV the direction can track every mission and check their status.

6. What would be interesting to do now is to load the Mission Tracking NAV table (via OData) to Power BI (as we learned in Chapter 4, *Using NAV Web Services with Power BI*) and prepare a dashboard with map visualization and a slicer (to filter missions):

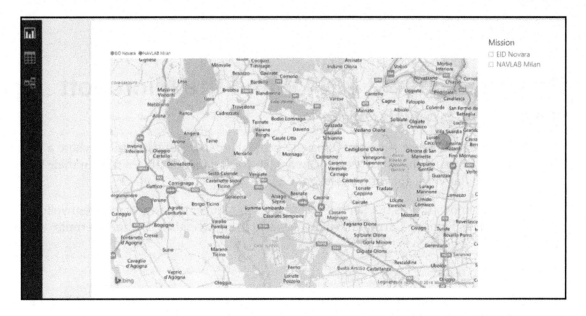

Here you can have the real-time situation and location of all your missions (red balloons indicate where a courier is), you can filter to check for a specific courier, and you can zoom on the map to see the exact detailed location:

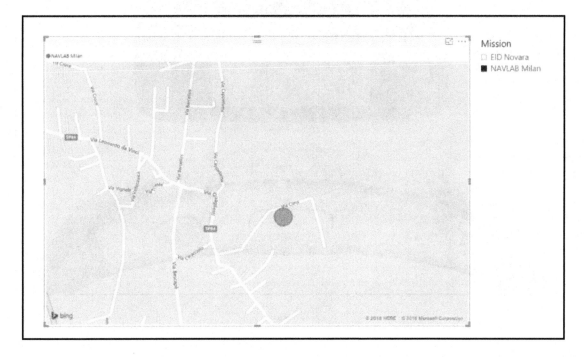

Very interesting isn't it?

Business case 2 – NAV and the Microsoft Band for healthcare

In this second business case, we want to briefly present a particular case study where a fitness-related company (healthcare sector) wants to track patient's fitness data in their ERP system (a particular verticalization based on NAV).

As you already know, fitness tracker are one of the top requested gadgets in recent years. Producers such as Fitbit or Garmin have devices and they have also SDK that permits interacting with a device via the REST API.

What about Microsoft?

Microsoft actually has one of the best fitness trackers on the market: the **Microsoft Band 2**. This is the device form factor:

Source: Microsoft

Unfortunately, Microsoft has recently announced that for the moment they will not release a Band 3 but they will continue to support the actual version. However, they will continue to invest on wearables so be prepared to see something more in the near future.

In this business case, we have a company that uses Microsoft's fitness tracker to collect workout data of their patients (heart rate). Every patient has a Band 2 device connected to a telemetry machine with a custom application that permits transmitting all the data to NAV. Here, the data is collected and analyzed (with Power BI and machine learning tools).

How can we handle an implementation like this? The architecture for the NAV solution will be developed exactly like the previous case as follows:

- In NAV we'll have the tables where we store the data and the business logic to handle them (codeunits)
- The NAV business logic will be exposed as web services
- We'll have a RESTful service layer between NAV and the client application
- The client application will be a UWP app that interacts with the Microsoft Band 2 wearable

We will not repeat here the NAV and the service layer implementation (the logic and the code will be quite the same as the previous ones) but we'll analyze how we can develop the client application.

Business case 2 – developing the Band 2 application

Let's see how to develop the Band 2 application by performing the following steps:

1. To develop a UWP application that interacts with the Microsoft Band 2 fitness tracker, we have to open Visual Studio and create an application by navigating to **New | Project... | Windows | Blank App (Universal Windows)**.

2. Now we need to download from **NuGet Package Manager** (in Visual Studio, navigate to **Tools | NuGet Package Manager**) the Microsoft Band SDK:

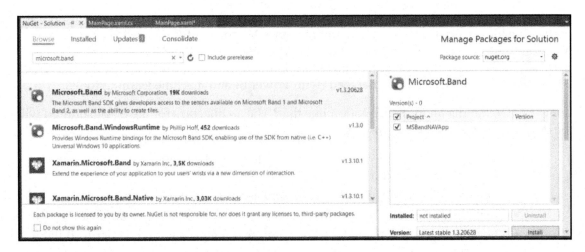

Now our solution appears as follows:

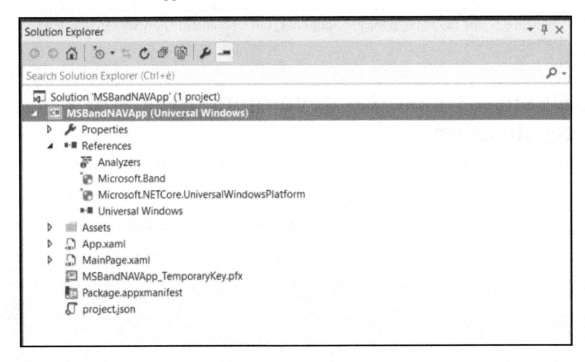

In the `MainPage.xaml` file, we have the UI definition (as previously described):

```xml
<Grid Background="{ThemeResource
ApplicationPageBackgroundThemeBrush}">
  <Grid.Resources>
    <Style TargetType="TextBlock" BasedOn="{StaticResource
    HeaderTextBlockStyle}">
      <Setter Property="HorizontalAlignment" Value="Center" />
      <Setter Property="VerticalAlignment" Value="Center" />
      <Setter Property="FontWeight" Value="Bold" />
    </Style>
  </Grid.Resources>
  <Grid.RowDefinitions>
    <RowDefinition Height="Auto"></RowDefinition>
    <RowDefinition></RowDefinition>
    <RowDefinition></RowDefinition>
  </Grid.RowDefinitions>
  <TextBlock HorizontalAlignment="Center">NAV BAND
2</TextBlock>
  <Viewbox Grid.Row="1">
    <TextBlock Grid.Row="1"
    Foreground="Red">♥</TextBlock>
  </Viewbox>
  <TextBlock Grid.Row="2"
x:Name="HeartRateDisplay">NO DATA</TextBlock>

  <Button Grid.Row="3" Name="btnCheck" Content="Get Heart Rate"
  HorizontalAlignment="Center" VerticalAlignment="Bottom"
  Margin="10,10,10,10" Click="btnCheck_Click"
  FontWeight="Bold">
  </Button>

</Grid>
```

This XAML defines a UI like the following (♥ is the heart symbol in ASCII):

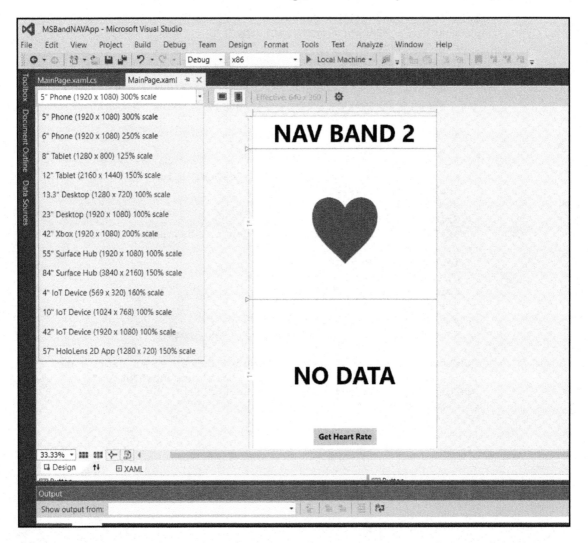

3. In the code-behind, first we need to add a reference to two interfaces in the Band SDK:

```
private IBandClient _bandClient;
private IBandInfo _bandInfo;
```

4. Then, when the page is loaded or when the button is clicked, we can read the
   heart data and transmit them to NAV by calling the REST service by calling the
   GetHeartRate function:

```
public MainPage()
{
   this.InitializeComponent();
   Loaded += OnLoaded;
}

private void OnLoaded(object sender,
Windows.UI.Xaml.RoutedEventArgs e)
{
   GetHeartRate();
}

private void btnCheck_Click(object sender,
Windows.UI.Xaml.RoutedEventArgs e)
{
   GetHeartRate();
}


//Reads the fitness data from the Band
private async void GetHeartRate()
{
    if (_bandClient != null)
    return;

   var bands = await
   BandClientManager.Instance.GetBandsAsync();
   _bandInfo = bands.First();

   _bandClient = await
    BandClientManager.Instance.ConnectAsync(_bandInfo);

    var uc =
   _bandClient.SensorManager.HeartRate.GetCurrentUserConsent();
    bool isConsented = false;
  if (uc == UserConsent.NotSpecified)
    {
       isConsented = await
       _bandClient.SensorManager.HeartRate
       .RequestUserConsentAsync();
    }

  if (isConsented || uc == UserConsent.Granted)
```

```
    {
      _bandClient.SensorManager.HeartRate.ReadingChanged +=
      async
      (obj, ev) =>
      {
        await
        Dispatcher.RunAsync
        (Windows.UI.Core.CoreDispatcherPriority.Normal, () =>
        {
          HeartRateDisplay.Text =
          ev.SensorReading.HeartRate.ToString();
        });
      };
          await _bandClient.SensorManager
          .HeartRate.StartReadingsAsync();

    //Here we can call the NAV Service Layer REST API to pass the
    heart rate data
    }
  }
```

5. In the preceding code, we check for band devices connected via Bluetooth to the machine and we connect to the first one detected:

```
var bands = await BandClientManager.Instance.GetBandsAsync();
_bandInfo = bands.First();
_bandClient = await
BandClientManager.Instance.ConnectAsync(_bandInfo);
```

Then the code checks for the user agreement to send the data and, if the agreement is received (UserConsent.Granted), the heart rate is read asynchronously from the device and displayed on the application UI:

```
_bandClient.SensorManager.HeartRate.ReadingChanged += async
(obj, ev) =>
    {
      await
      Dispatcher.RunAsync
      (Windows.UI.Core.CoreDispatcherPriority.Normal, () =>
       {
          HeartRateDisplay.Text = ev
          .SensorReading.HeartRate.ToString();
       });
    };
    await _bandClient.SensorManager.HeartRate.StartReadingsAsync();
```

Then the data is transmitted to NAV by calling our Web API service layer as described previously (by using `HTTPClient` and creating a `POST` request).

Summary

In this chapter, we have seen how to handle a new integration business case between NAV and mobile clients, where the clients are using Universal Windows applications for managing tasks. You have learned how you can create a REST service layer between NAV and the external client's applications by using ASP.NET Web API 2 and how you can develop a UWP application for the clients.

Regarding the UWP, you have learned also how to handle tasks such as transmitting the location or accessing private data from a fitness device.

After reading this chapter, you should have a complete understanding of how to create a real-world architecture that permits you to expose your NAV business logic to the outside world for handling complex scenarios.

In the next chapter, we'll explore the Microsoft Azure services to discover how you can leverage the power of the cloud to enhance your NAV architecture.

8
Exploring Microsoft Azure and its Services

In the previous chapters, we've analyzed different integration scenarios between Microsoft Dynamics NAV and the external applications. We have learned how to decouple your NAV installation from an external world by creating custom integration layers and by using NAV web services for exposing the business logic.

But what about the cloud? The cloud is actually a great opportunity and you need to start thinking about using cloud services in your projects for handling different tasks that require scalability of resources or services that will be difficult to develop or deploy by yourself.

In this chapter, we'll see an overview of the Microsoft Azure platform and its services. We'll discover what Azure is and what services the platform offers now in all the different areas of the application. The chapter will cover the following topics:

- An overview of the Microsoft Azure platform
- Managing cloud resources on Microsoft Azure
- An overview of the most interesting Microsoft Azure services for a NAV developer/architect

The Microsoft Azure platform

Microsoft Azure is Microsoft's application platform for the public cloud. Microsoft Azure offers mainly IaaS and PaaS services, but also **Software as a service (SaaS)** is covered (Office 365 runs on Azure, Dynamics 365 applications runs on Azure, Azure websites can serve as SaaS offerings as well by permitting you to configure and run applications such as WordPress in a few minutes).

The following screenshot shows the main differences between an on-premise infrastructure and IaaS or PaaS architectures:

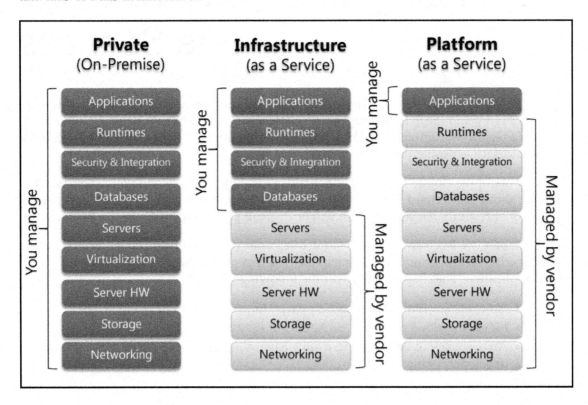

Microsoft Azure is now generally available in 30 regions around the world and the platform is continuously growing (in terms of geographic expansion and the features offered). This is the actual Azure data centers map (with regions covered) provided by Microsoft:

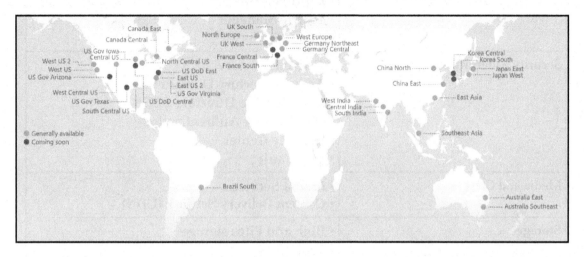

This global network of data centers guarantees high levels of availability and SLAs and data redundancy (locally redundancy in the user's primary region or geo-redundancy in a secondary region).

Microsoft itself provides support for public, private, and hybrid cloud solutions. An hybrid cloud is a mix of private and public cloud services (you can deploy your workloads on your self-hosted data center or on the public cloud). **Microsoft Azure Stack** is an add-on to Windows Server 2016 that allows you to deploy many core Azure services in your own data center.

Azure services can be grouped in the following categories:

Category	Azure App Services
Compute	• **Virtual Machines** • **Cloud Services** • **Azure Container Service** • **Services Fabric** • **Batch** • **Scheduler** • **Remote App** • **Azure Functions**

Networking	• Virtual Network • Load Balancer • Express Route • Traffic Manager • Azure DNS
Security + Identity and Access	• Active Directory • Active Directory Domain Services • Azure Active Directory B2C • Multi-Factor Authentication • Security Center • Key Vault
Media and CDN	• Media Services • Content Delivery Network (CDN)
Storage	• Blob and Files storage • Backup • Import/Export • Site Recovery • StorSimple • Data Lake Store
Web + Mobile	• Web Apps • Mobile Apps • App Service • API Apps • Logic Apps • Search • Mobile Engagement • Notification Hubs
Data	• SQL Database • SQL Data Warehouse • SQL Server Stretch Database • Document DB • Redis Cache • Data Factory

Intelligence + analytics	• HDInsight • Machine Learning • Stream Analytics • Cognitive Services • Data Catalog • Data Lake Analytics • Data Lake Store • Data Factory • Power BI Embedded • Analysis Services • Azure Bot Service
Developer Services	• Visual Studio Team Services • Azure DevTest Labs • Application Insights • API Management • Hockey App
Hybrid Integrations	• Storage Queues • BizTalk Services • Hybrid Connections • Service Bus
Management	• Automation • Portal • Operational Insights • Log Analytics • Azure Monitor • Azure Resource Manager
Internet of Things	• Azure IoT Hub • Azure IoT Suite • Event Hubs • Stream Analytics

Azure provides a web interface called the **Azure Portal** that allows administrators to manage all their Azure resources and services in a centralized way. In Azure terms, a *resource* is a manageable item that you have in the cloud (for example, a virtual machine, a storage account, a database, a blob storage, a web application, and so on).

A typical cloud infrastructure or application is made up of different components (for example, a virtual machine with a storage account and a virtual network) and on Azure you see them as a single entity (a group of resources). **Azure Resource Manager** (**ARM**) permits you to handle your cloud resources as a group.

ARM enables you to do the following things:

- Manage your cloud resources as a group
- Manage your infrastructure through declarative templates (JSON files)
- Define dependencies between resources
- Deploy your cloud solution always in a consistent state
- Apply role-based access control to all services in a resource group
- Tag resources for a better logical organization

When defining a resource group on Azure, there are important aspects to consider:

- All resources in the same resource group should share the same life cycle (deployment and update must be done together)
- Resources can be moved between different resource groups and a resource group can contain resources that come from different regions
- Each resource can only exist in one resource group
- Resources between resource groups can interact

A quick view of the Azure Portal can be found at `https://portal.azure.com`.

Let's take a quick tour to Azure Portal by performing the following steps:

1. When you open the portal, you have immediate access to a dashboard (where you can control many data regarding your Azure subscription and your cloud resources) and to the hub menu (the left panel) where you can access to a core set of Azure features.

2. You can customize the main dashboard and all its tiles as you want. On the default Azure Portal **Dashboard**, there are the tiles that you can see here:

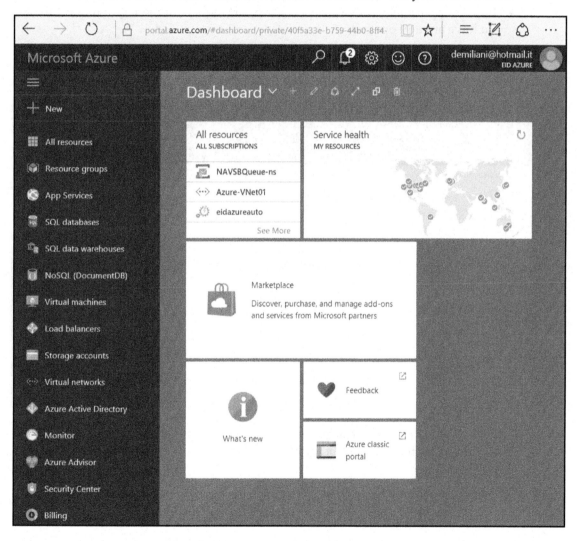

Here are the tiles as shown in the preceding image:

- **All resources**: Here you can see a list of all your cloud resources

- **Service health**: Here you can see the health of the regions around the world and by clicking on a point you can see the details

- **Marketplace**: Here you can search for cloud resources and applications and add them to your subscription

- **Help + support**: Here you can open a support request or manage a request that you have already opened

3. By clicking on the **Resource groups** option in the left panel, you can see all your resource groups defined in your subscription with their geographical location:

4. If you click on the **All resources**option, you can see the details of all the cloud resources you have in your account:

5. You can simply create a new resource group just by clicking on the **Resource groups** option and select **Add**:

6. Then in the opened panel, in **Resource group name** provide a resource group name and in **Subscription** select the desired Azure subscription and select the location in **Resource group location**:

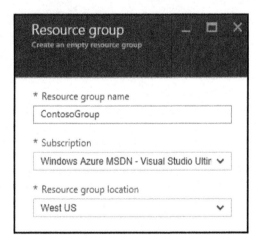

7. The Azure Portal permits you also to monitor your cloud resources. You can select your resource and go to the **Monitoring** section to see a graphical representation of your resource activities. The graphs are relevant to the type of resource you have selected (here, for example, is a storage account resource):

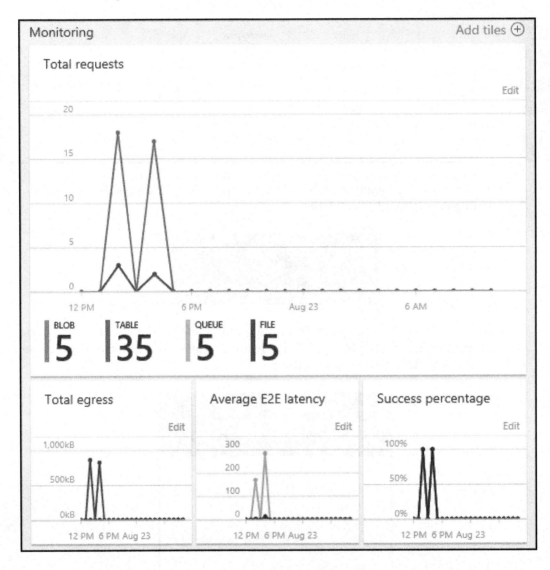

In the next sections, we'll see a brief overview of some Azure services that could be interesting when deploying a Microsoft Dynamics NAV enterprise solution.

Azure Virtual Machines

Azure Virtual Machines is the most famous IaaS service offered by the Azure platform. This service supports the deployment of Windows or Linux virtual machines in an Azure data center and gives you the ability to immediately deploy a VM and centrally manage it (software installation, configuration, maintenance, and so on). When creating a virtual machine, you can select the type of VM that better suits your needs (OS, CPU cores, memory, storage, and so on) and you can create a new VM by choosing a template from an image gallery. A virtual machine can be created on the region that you want.

You can also upload your own Virtual Machine (VHD file) to Microsoft Azure and use it directly or as a template to choose for creating new VMs. Before you upload the **Virtual Hard Disk (VHD)** to Azure, it needs to be generalized by using the Sysprep.exe tool.

Azure VMs are classified as follows:

- **General Purpose (A0-4, A, D series)**: This is ideal for testing and development, for small to medium databases, and low to medium traffic web servers
- **Compute Optimized (F series)**: This is ideal for medium traffic web servers, application servers, network appliances, and batch processes
- **Memory Optimized (D11-15, G series)**: This is ideal for relational database servers, in-memory analytics, and medium to large caches
- **GPU (N series)**: This is ideal for intensive graphic and video operations and is available with single or multiple GPUs
- **High Performance Compute (H, A8-11 series)**: This is the most powerful available VM, ideal for high performance applications

To every cloud service containing one or more Azure VM, a free Dynamics virtual IP address is automatically assigned. You can then have reserved IP addresses or public IP addresses by paying the appropriate IP address offering.

Azure Virtual Machines has an OS disk and a Data disk (VHDs). These disks use Azure Blob storage for storing data and they have geo-redundancy and high availability (you can choose from a Standard to a Premium storage account with high performance SSD drives):

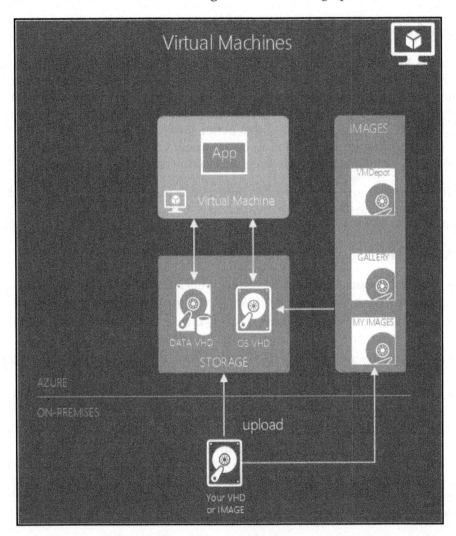

Azure Virtual Machines also includes a temporary disk (not persisted to Azure Storage). It's important to remember that the data on this disk is deleted when you stop or deallocate the VM or in the event of a failure in the physical host (so, do not store sensitive data here or data that must be persisted!).

Let's try and create a Azure Virtual Machine by performing the following steps:

1. You can create a new Azure Virtual Machine by going to the Azure Portal and in the hub menu navigate to **New** | **Compute** and select from the available VM templates:

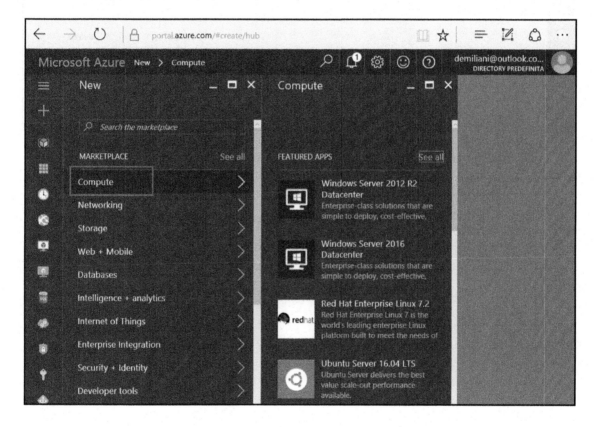

2. You can click on **See all** to discover more templates and search for them. For example, I've searched for `Microsoft Dynamics NAV 2017` and here is the Azure VM template available to create a new pre-configured NAV 2017 environment (suitable for a demo environment):

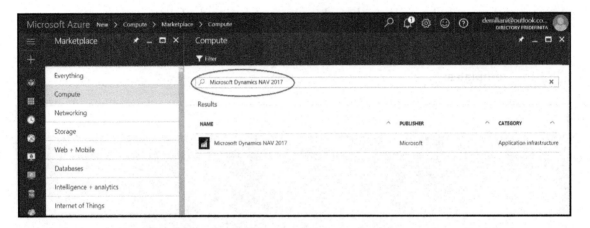

3. When you have selected your VM template, you have to select **Classic** or **Resource Manager** under **Select a deployment model**, I recommend using **Resource Manager**) and click **Create**:

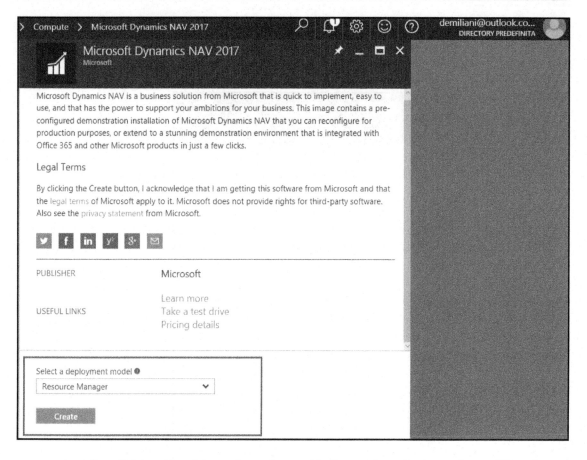

4. After clicking **Create**, you have to specify the settings for your Azure Virtual Machine:

   - **Name**: This is the name of your VM.
   - **VM disk type**: Choose if you want an SSD or an HDD drive (SSD has better performances).
   - **User name**: Enter the username for a local administrator account on the VM.
   - **Password**: Enter the password for a local administrator account on the VM.
   - **Subscription**: Choose your Azure subscription to use.

- **Resource group**: You can create a new resource group or use an existing one. If you choose to create a new **Resource group**, you have to give it a name and select a data center location (region):

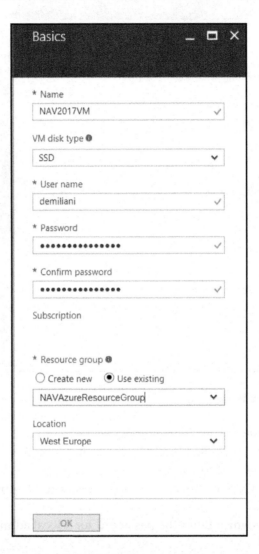

5. In the next panel, you can select the size of your Azure Virtual Machine (what type of physical resources you need) and in the **Settings** pane, you can change the storage and network options.

6. When the virtual machine is created, you can see it by clicking the **Virtual machines** menu in the left hub:

7. By selecting the virtual machine, you can click on the **Connect** menu and download a **Remote Desktop Protocol** (**RDP**) file that permits you to access the VM (you need to enter the previously defined credentials).
8. When you have finished using your VM, remember to click on **Stop** to prevent having charges when you're not using it (this will deallocate the VM).

Azure App Service

Azure App Service is a PaaS service that permits you to create web and mobile apps for any platform and device. You can deploy and run your application in a total cloud environment that is VM and you can scale resources up and out as you want (manually or automatically).

Azure App Service offers these types of resources:

- **Web Apps**: This is used for hosting web applications and web services
- **Mobile Apps**: This is used for hosting mobile app backends
- **API Apps**: This is used for hosting RESTful APIs
- **Logic Apps**: This is used for automating business processes across the cloud

We'll talk more about how you can use Azure App Service in a NAV enterprise architecture in the next chapter.

Azure Cloud Services

Azure Cloud Services are PaaS services offered by Azure and designed to support applications running on the cloud that are scalable, reliable, and cheap to operate. Like the previously described Azure App Service, Azure Cloud Services are hosted on VMs.

The main differences between the two is that Azure App Service is a *managed platform* (there is no need to take care of the VM for your cloud service) while Azure Cloud Services allow developers to access the underlying VM and manage the application container (RDP access to servers, custom MSI installations, ability to execute custom tasks on the VM, and so on).

Azure Cloud Services provide two different VM options:

- **Web Roles**: This runs a variant of Windows Server with your app deployed to IIS
- **Worker Roles**: This runs a variant of Windows Server without IIS

A **Cloud Service** application is a combination of the two options:

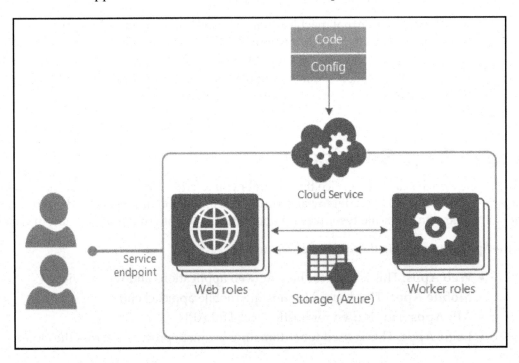

Cloud Services are useful when you need to deploy services that have to support massive scale out and when you need control over the platform.

 Remember that this is a PaaS service, so you don't create virtual machines but instead you provide configuration files for managing resources (web roles and worker roles).

Azure Batch Services

An **Azure Batch Service** is a PaaS service provided by Azure and used for batch processing. This service is useful when you need to run compute-intensive and large-scale parallel applications and processes in the cloud or when you need to process large volumes of data.

You can run batches on demand or via a scheduler and all these tasks are executed on a managed collection of virtual machines. The batch workloads are split into multiple tasks that works in parallel on many servers:

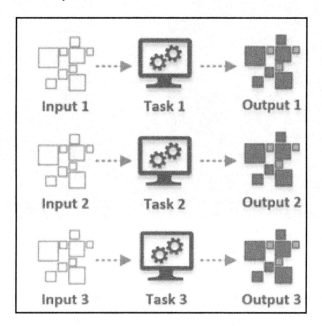

Let's learn how to create an Azure Batch service by performing the following steps:

1. To create a new batch service, from the Azure Portal navigate to **New** | **Compute** | **Batch Service**:

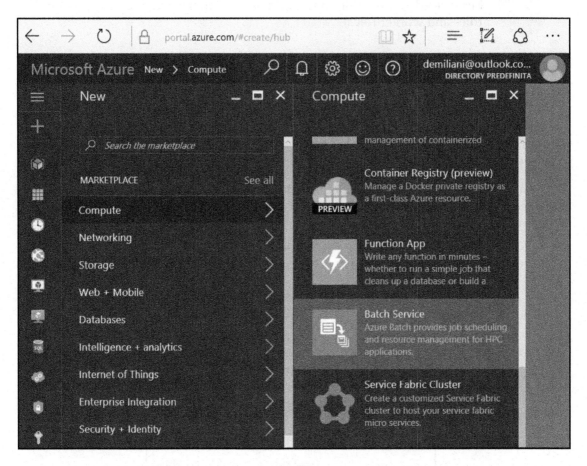

2. In the **New Batch account** panel, you have to provide these parameters:
   - **Account name**: This is the batch account name, unique for the region that you select
   - **Subscription**: This is the Azure subscription where you create the batch account

- **Resource group**: This selects an existing resource group or creates a new one
- **Location**: This selects the desired Azure region
- **Storage account**: You can optionally select a storage account to associate to the **New Batch account**.

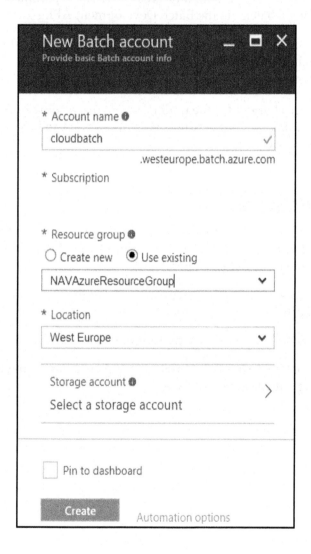

3. Next, click **Create** to create the Batch account.

   When the Batch account is created, Azure provides you with a Batch account URL in the `https://<account_name>.<region>.batch.azure.com` format.

   Azure also provides you with an Access Key. These parameters must be used when creating a batch via the Batch Development API.

4. To develop a Batch-enabled application, I recommend you to check and use the **Azure Batch library for .NET** available on GitHub at `https://github.com/Azure/azure-batch-samples`.

Batch Accounts are charged for the underlying Azure resources that the batch solution consumes. Depending on your Azure subscription, you can have different quotas and limits for the Batch account.

Azure Scheduler

Azure Scheduler is a cloud service that permits you to describe, schedule, and run tasks in the cloud automatically. Azure Scheduler does not host workloads or run any code but it schedules jobs (the code is hosted elsewhere).

Azure Scheduler is useful for handling recurring tasks in the cloud and you can manage tasks via the Azure Portal or programmatically by using .NET, PowerShell, or REST APIs.

Let's see how Azure Schedular works by performing the following steps:

1. To create a job in **Azure Scheduler** via the **Azure Portal**, navigate to **New** | **Monitoring + management** | **Scheduler**:

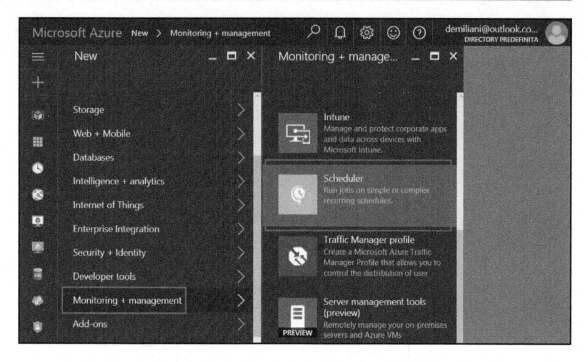

2. Then click **Create**.
3. Now in the **Scheduler Job** window, you can create a job by entering the job name, on which Azure subscription the job must be created, and on which **Job Collection** it must be added (you can create a new one if one doesn't exist).

3. When the job is created, in the **Action settings** window you can define the scheduler action. Here you can select three **Action** types (**Http**, **Https**, and **Storage Queue**) and for the selected **Action** type you can select the desired method:

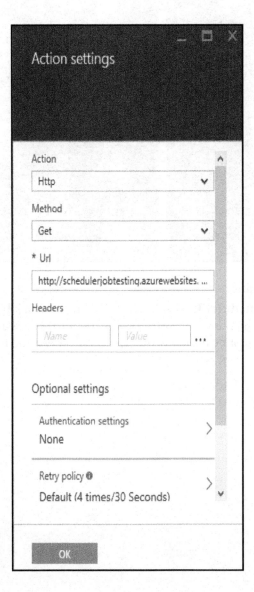

Here we have created a job that makes a GET call to the URL provided (a demo website on Azure).

4. In the final step, we have to provide a job schedule in the **Schedule** window. A job can be a one-time job (**Recurrence** as **Once**) or a recurrent job (**Recurrence** as **Recurring**). If you select **Recurring** you can define the desired schedule:

5. By clicking the **OK** button, the job will be deployed to the Azure cloud and from the Azure Portal you can manage it and check its status.

Azure Scheduler could be useful when your NAV solution requires scheduled tasks to be performed (for example, notifications and so on) and you need to have a distributed environment.

Azure Virtual Network

Azure Virtual Network is a cloud service that permits you to define your own virtual network on the cloud (full control of IP addresses, DNS, routing, security, and so on). This is a useful cloud service for connecting your on-premises network to your own network in the cloud and so using cloud resources (for example, virtual machines) exactly like a computer in your network.

A virtual network can be created directly by going to the Azure Portal and navigating to **New** | **Networking** | **Virtual network**:

If you plan to use Azure VM or some Azure services in your NAV solution architecture, this is a service that is often required (especially for joining the VM to your on-premise resources).

Azure Active Directory

Azure Active Directory (**AD**) is a cloud-based directory and identity management service that permits you to have authentication, **Single Sign-On** (**SSO**), and security on your SaaS applications (Office 365 uses Azure AD).

Azure Active Directory can also be integrated with an existing on-premise **Windows Server Active Directory** and this scenario permits you to have a single way of authentication between on-premises and cloud applications:

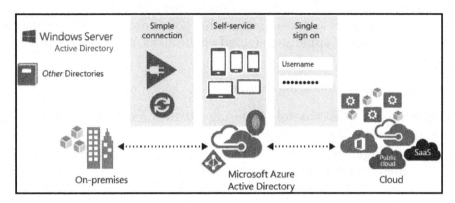

Azure AD is multi-tenanted and geo-distributed, so it guarantees high availability.

In a NAV architecture implementation, you could use and set up this service for certain business requirements, such as showing Power BI reports from Power BI.com, directly on Microsoft Dynamics NAV. NAV 2017 has a wizard to perform this task by navigating to **Departments | Administration | Application Setup | General | Assisted Setup**:

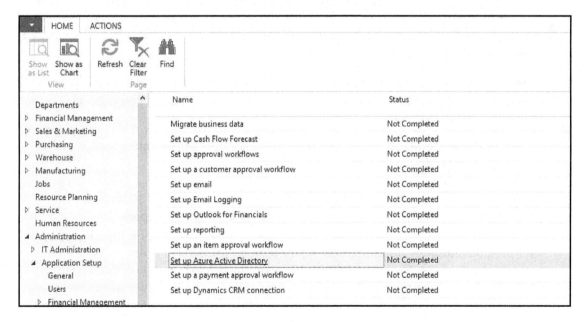

Azure Storage

Microsoft Azure Storage is a cloud storage solution that provides scalability, durability, and availability to your data on the cloud. Azure Storage supports different types of clients and programming languages and it guarantees that your stored data will be available from any location and any type of application (cloud applications, on-premises applications, and mobile devices).

Azure Storage provides the following services:

- **Blob Storage**: This is useful for storing unstructured data such as documents, media files, backup files, log files, and so on.
- **Table Storage**: This is a NoSQL key-attribute data store, useful for storing structured data. It's really fast and cost-effective (lower than a traditional SQL database for the same amount of data). In this storage, you can store any number of tables with any number of entities per table.
- **Queue Storage**: This is a messaging solution for asynchronous communications between applications (queues). A queue can contain any number of messages and a message may be up to 64 KB in size.
- **File Storage**: This provides cloud-based SMB file shares totally similar to the on-premises shares. Applications running on the Azure cloud can access data in the file storage via traditional filesystem I/O APIs. It's important to remember that mounting a file share is only possible for applications running in Azure, while an on-premises application may only access the file share via the REST API exposed by the file storage service.

Azure Storage provides data replication. Your data is copied within the same data center or between different data centers (it depends on which replication option you choose). You can have the following data replication options:

- **Locally Redundant**: This option replicates your data three times within a single data center in a single region.
- **Zone Redundant**: This option replicates your data three times across two to three facilities, either within a single region or across two regions. This option guarantees that your data will be durable within a single region.
- **Geo-Redundant**: This option replicates your data three times within the primary region and three times in a secondary region hundreds of miles away from the primary region (if accidentally a failure on the primary region occurs, Azure Storage will fail over to the secondary region). This option guarantees that your data will be durable in two different regions.

- **Read-Access Geo-Redundant**: This option replicates your data to a secondary region and also provides read access to your data in the secondary region. *This is the default option when you create a storage account.*

Let's create a Azure storage account by performing the following steps:

1. To create a **Storage Account**, go to the **Azure Portal** and from the left menu navigate to **New** | **Storage** | **Storage account**:

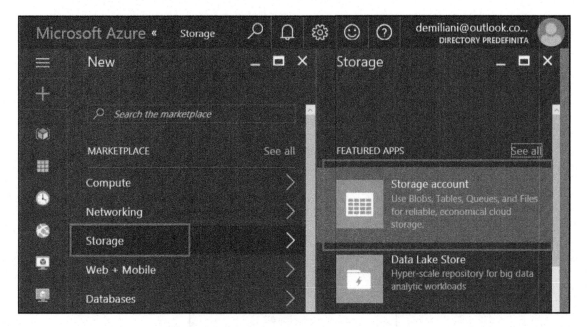

2. In the **Createstorage account** panel, you have to provide the following:
   - **Name**: This is the name for your storage account.
   - **Deployment model**: This could be **Resource Manager** (recommended) or **Classic**.
   - **Account kind**: This is the type of storage account to create. It could be **General purpose** (default) or **Blob storage**.
   - **Performance**: If your storage account type is **General purpose**, you can select the **Standard** (default) or **Premium** performance tier. If the storage account type is Blob storage, you can select from the **Hot** (default) or **Cool** access tiers.
   - **Replication**: This is the previously described data replication option.

- **Storage service encryption**: This is enabled if you want Azure to encrypt data when you store it and decrypt data when you access it.
- **Subscription**: This is the Azure subscription where the storage account will be created.
- **Resource group**: You can select an existing **Azure Resource Group** or create a new one.
- **Location**: This is the location of your storage account (region).

3. Click **Create** to create your storage account.

   When you create a storage account, Azure also generates two 512-bit storage **Access keys**. These keys are used for authentication when you access the storage account:

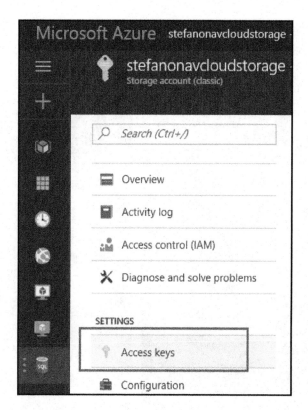

Azure Logic Apps

Azure Logic Apps is a service that permits you to implement scalable integrations and workflows in the cloud by using a visual designer for modeling the process (triggers and actions).

Let's take a look at the following steps to access the benefits of the Azure Logic Apps service:

1. You can start creating an Azure Logic App from the Azure Portal by navigating to **New** | **Web + Mobile** | **Logic App**:

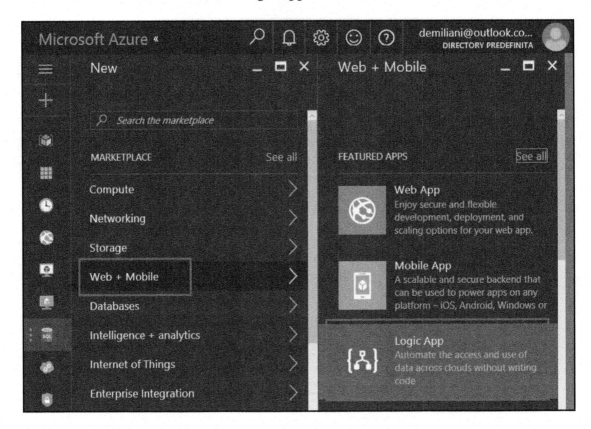

2. In the **Create logic app** window, enter the name of your logic app in **Name**, select the Azure **Subscription** to use, select (or create) the **Resource group** and the **Location** (region), and click **Create**:

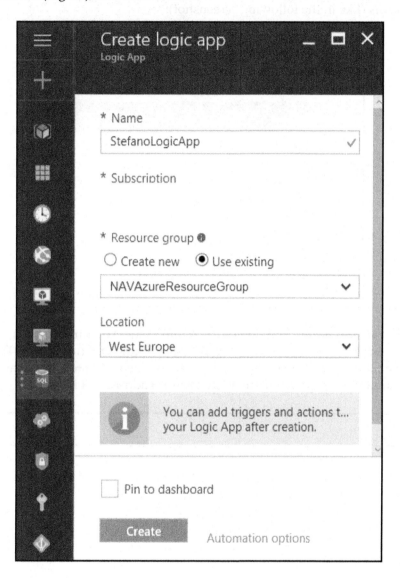

3. Now you can create a logic app by choosing from an existing template, or from a **Blank Logic App**. After that, in **Logic App Designer**, you have to create a **trigger** (the event that starts your logic app) and then you have to add **conditions** and **actions** (like in the following screenshot):

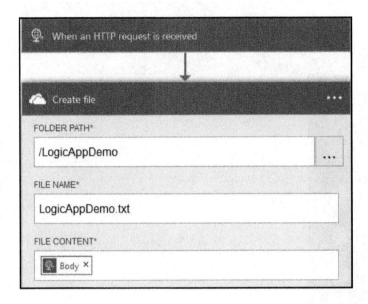

4. You can also design and deploy an Azure Logic App directly from Visual Studio and the Azure SDK. To do so, open Visual Studio and navigate to **Tools** | **Extensions and Updates**. Here, from the online templates, search and select the **Azure Logic Apps Tools for Visual Studio** add-in and install it:

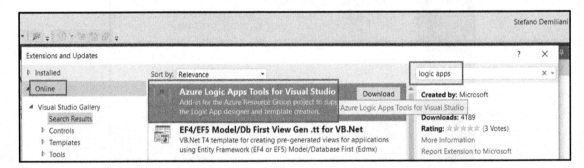

5. Now navigate to **New** | **Project...** | **Cloud** | **Azure Resource Group**:

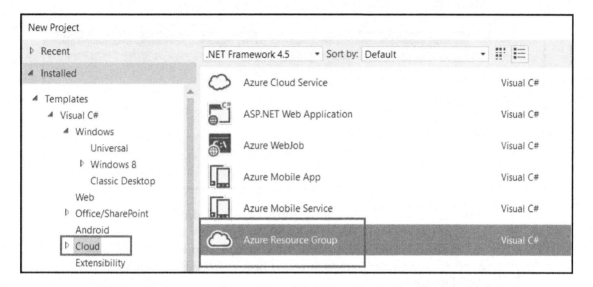

6. Then select the **Logic App** template. Now you have a blank logic app project:

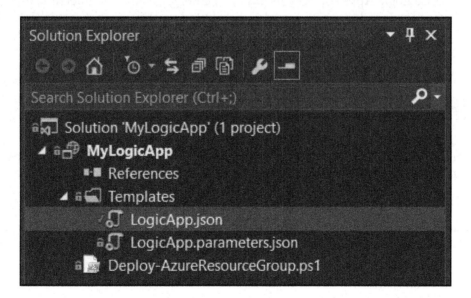

7. Now you can open **Logic App Designer** in Visual Studio and start creating your workflow:

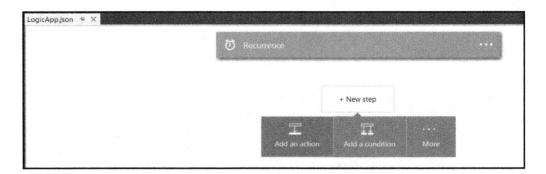

When fnished, you can deploy your Logic App directly from Visual Studio by right-clicking the project in **Solution Explorer** and navigating to **Deploy** | **New Deployment.** In the **Deploy to Resource Group** window, select your **Azure subscription** and the **Resource Group** and click **Deploy**.

Azure Logic Apps could be useful in an enterprise NAV architecture, especially when you need to create complex distributed workflows that require integrations between different systems (in a Logic App, you can make HTTP requests, call services, and create custom actions).

Azure SQL Database

Azure SQL Database is a cloud relational database service based on the Microsoft SQL Server engine that provides scalability, performance, and mission-critical capabilities. Azure SQL supports all the existing tools, libraries, and APIs available for the on-premise option.

Azure SQL is available with the following service tiers (all with 99.99 percent SLAs):

- **Basic**: This is useful for small databases or with small transactions.
- **Standard**: This is the recommended option for standard production-ready cloud applications. *This is the minimum tier required for a Dynamics NAV production environment.*
- **Premium**: This is useful when you have a high transactional application and you require the maximum database performances. For intense workloads, this is the recommended tier to choose.

The interesting fact is that you can start from a small service tier and then scale in or out manually or programmatically at any time without downtime.

There are applications where usage patterns (resources consumed) could be unpredictable and extremely variable during time. For these types of applications, Azure SQL provides **elastic pools**. By using elastic pools, instead of paying for a single database performance, you allocate performance to a pool and pay for the entire pool's performances. All the databases in the pool can automatically scale up and down but without exceeding the limits of the pool (this guarantees predictable costs).

The measure of a database's ability to handle resource demands is expressed in **Database Transaction Units (DTUs)** for a single database and in Elastic DTUs for elastic databases.

Let's create an Azure SQL database by performing the following steps:

1. You can create an Azure SQL database directly from the Azure Portal by navigating to **New** | **Databases** | **SQL Database**:

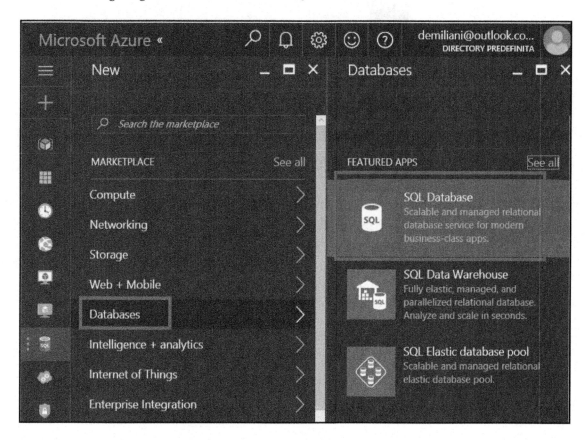

2. Here you can provide all the database parameters (server name, admin login and password, Azure subscription, resource group, location, pricing tier, and collation) and you can select to start with a **Blank database**, a **Sample (AdventureWorksLT)**, or from an existing SQL Server **Backup**):

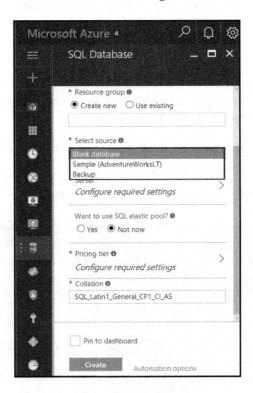

3. To access your database, remember to create a server-level firewall rule in the **Firewall** setting for your Azure SQL instance. After that, you can connect to your Azure SQL database:

If you use Azure SQL for storing your Microsoft Dynamics NAV database on the cloud, remember to create the Microsoft Dynamics NAV service tier on an Azure VM in the same region (data center) of your Azure SQL database. Don't make the error of placing the NAV service tier on your local on-premise server (performances will be poor, this is absolutely to be avoided).

4. When moving a customer's Microsoft Dynamics NAV database to the cloud on Azure SQL, there are certain criteria that you have to provide:
   - Your database must contain only SQL users (no Windows logins or system logins)
   - Your database must have only one filegroup (the primary filegroup)

5. Regarding the last point, normally a customer's database on an on-premise SQL server has more than one filegroup, so you need to re-create the database locally with only a single filegroup and then place this new database to Azure SQL.

6. The second approach that you could use to perform this operation is to open SQL Server Management Studio, select your database, right-click on it, and navigate to **Tasks** | **Export Data-tier Application…**:

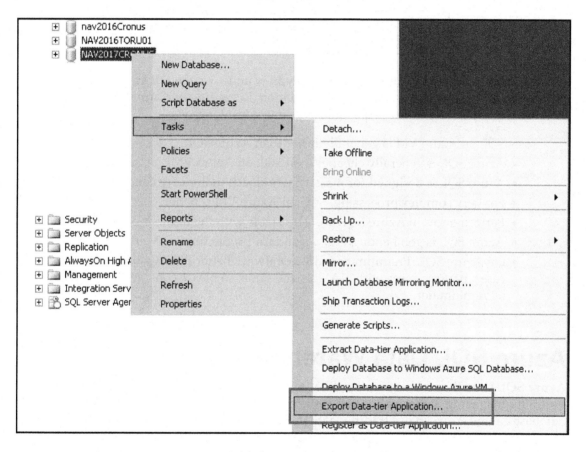

This operation will create a `BACPAC` file on your server with the content of your NAV database.

7. Now you can connect to your Azure SQL instance (always with SQL Server Management Studio), right-click on **Databases**, and select **Import Data-tier Application...**:

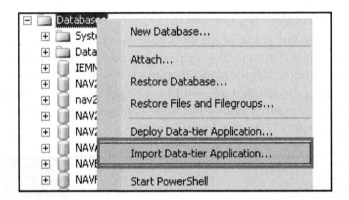

Azure SQL is a very interesting option if you want to use the **DB as a Service** approach for your Microsoft Dynamics NAV installation. Regarding performance, these are the *real-world* conclusions that you could take into consideration:

- SQL on Azure VM is generally faster than Azure SQL.
- Azure SQL is generally cheaper than SQL on Azure VM.
- Azure SQL is designed for massive workloads with many concurrent users.
- For very complex processing, SQL on Azure VM is better.
- Performances in Azure SQL are very stable with the number of users increasing.
- Azure SQL is good enough for a standard production NAV environment.
- On Azure SQL, Premium tiers are not always better than Standard. In many cases, performances with NAV are the same, so please consider if you really need a Premium tier.

Azure SQL Data Warehouse

Azure SQL Data Warehouse is a cloud-based, massively parallel processing database useful for managing data warehouses on the cloud based on the SQL Server relational database engine. You can use traditional SQL Server tools to manage your data warehouse (T-SQL, Analysis Services, Integration Services, Reporting Services, and so on).

Azure SQL Data Warehouse separates storage and compute (you pay for performances and storage when you need them) and all resources are managed centrally in the Azure Portal. Data is stored in an Azure Premium locally redundant storage and SQL Data Warehouse automatically backs up your active (un-paused) databases at regular intervals using **Azure Storage Snapshots** (data protection is guaranteed).

You can create an Azure SQL Data Warehouse simply by going to the Azure Portal and navigating to **New** | **Databases** | **SQL Data Warehouse**:

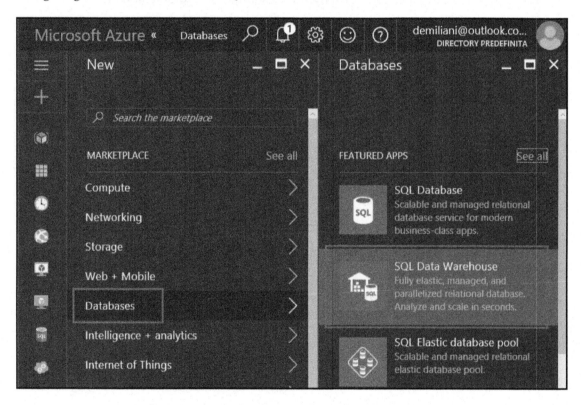

If you plan to integrate a Data Warehouse in your NAV solution architecture (for BI analysis, consolidating data from different systems, and so on), this is an interesting option that you can take into consideration.

Azure Analysis Services

Azure Analysis Services provides the analytical engine of the Microsoft SQL Server Enterprise Edition to the cloud. This is an interesting new Azure service for performing data modeling and analysis on the cloud by using the same tools you use for the on-premises version of SQL Server. If your NAV architecture includes **On-premises** data (from different sources) and **Cloud** data, with Azure Analysis Services you can combine data from both sources in order to provide a hybrid BI solution for your customer:

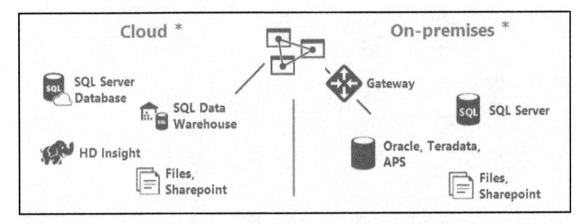

Let's take a look at the following two simple steps to create an Azure Analysis Services server from the Azure Portal:

1. An Azure Analysis Services server can be created from the Azure Portal by navigating to **New** | **Intelligence + analytics** | **Analysis Services (preview)**:

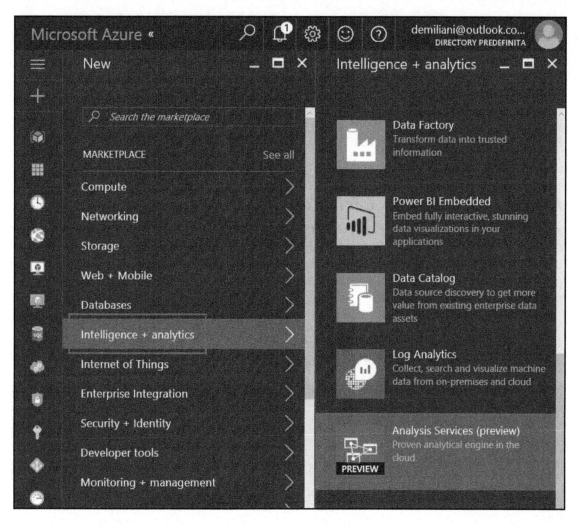

2. When the Azure Analysis Services server is created, you can deploy a data model to the cloud. If your data model involves on-premises data sources, you need to install an **On-premises data gateway** locally.

Azure Service Bus

Azure Service Bus is an Azure service that provides cloud-enabled communication with enterprise messaging and relayed communication that permits you to connect on-premises solutions with the cloud.

We'll go into more details about Azure Service Bus in `Chapter 10`, *Implementing a Message Based Architecture with Azure Service Bus and NAV.*

Azure Machine Learning

Azure Machine Learning is a cloud based predictive analytics service that permits you to create and deploy predictive models based on your data. The service provides a library of data prediction algorithms that you can use and your predictive model can then be published as a web service and used on your applications (for example, you can use a predictive model from NAV).

You can use a pre-built set of analytics solutions by accessing the **Cortana Intelligence Gallery** or you can create your new prediction model by using an interactive Azure workplace called **Azure Machine Learning Studio**:

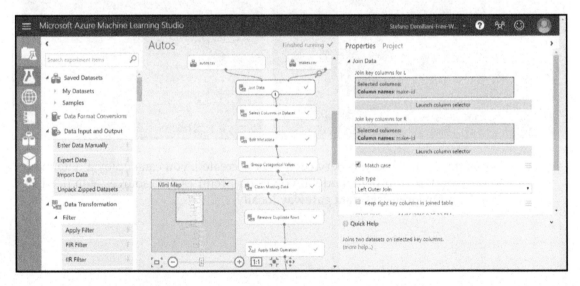

Machine Learning is a quite complex world. You can start exploring the features at
`https://azure.microsoft.com/en-us/services/machine-learning`.

With Microsoft Dynamics NAV 2017, the Sales and Inventory Forecast extension gives you insights about potential sales and an overview of expected stock-outs. This extension uses Cortana Intelligence to predict future sales based on your sales history to help you avoid inventory shortage. In order to use this extension, you have to set up an Azure Machine Learning instance and add the API URI and API Key to the Sales and Inventory Forecast setup in NAV.

Azure Internet of Things (IoT) suite

Azure IoT suite is a set of pre-configured services that permits you to have a full enterprise solution for the following aspects:

- Collecting data from different devices
- Storing and querying large amounts of data
- Analyzing real-time data streams
- Integrating devices with back-office systems

These pre-configured sets of services are base implementations of common IoT patterns that can be totally customizable and adaptable to your needs and they permit you to implement an IoT solution with reduced time.

The Azure IoT suite is generally composed of these services:

- **Azure IoT Hub**: This is a service that provides device-to-cloud and cloud-to-device messaging capabilities
- **Azure Storage** and **DocumentDB**: These provide data storage capabilities for the solution (Blob storage is used to store device telemetry, **DocumentDB** is used to store device metadata and enable the device management capabilities)
- **Stream Analytics**: This is a service that provides in-motion data analysis and message processing
- **Azure Web Apps** and **Microsoft Power BI**: These services are used for data visualization

A typical IoT solution has the following schema:

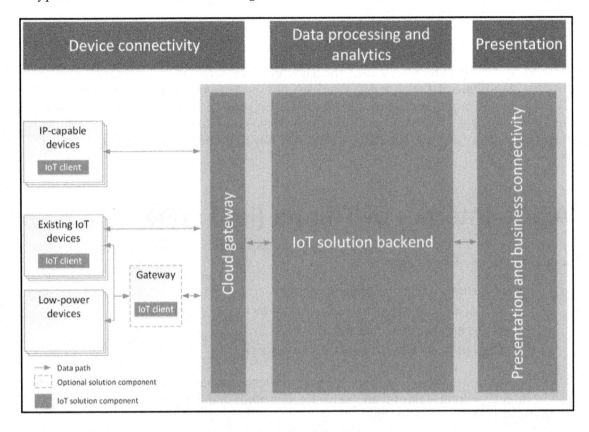

Provisioning of the Azure IoT suite can be started from `https://www.azureiotsuite.com/`.

When provisioned, you can manage your connected devices directly from the Azure Portal:

Every device has an ID, a key, and a connection string. You can use these values to set up your device interaction with the IoT suite:

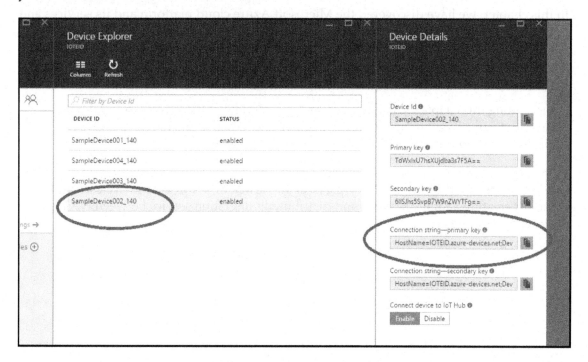

The Azure IoT suite could be interesting in conjunction with Microsoft Dynamics NAV for implementing solutions where physical devices must be monitored in real time and data must be collected to NAV for processing (for example, sectors such as manufacturing, automotive, and so on).

Summary

In this chapter, we have discovered the Microsoft Azure cloud platform and its services and we have seen an overview for many cloud services that could be useful to know about when implementing an enterprise ERP solution based on Microsoft Dynamics NAV. We have seen how you can activate and manage your Azure subscription and how you can manage every cloud service (resources) you want to activate.

After reading this chapter, you have a complete overview of the services offered by Microsoft Azure. To get more in-depth information on each of the previously described Azure services, you can start by visiting `https://docs.microsoft.com/en-us/azure/`.

In the next chapter, we'll see a real-world usage of some of the previously described Azure services in Microsoft Dynamics NAV projects. In particular, we'll see how we can use the cloud for creating a totally scalable and distributed integration service between NAV and external applications.

Working with NAV and Azure App Service

9

In the previous chapter, you have learned how to implement a solution architecture with Microsoft Dynamics NAV as the ERP (master of the business logic), and an external interface layer that acts as a *connector* between the ERP and the external applications.

The solutions described in the previous chapters require that you host the interface layer you developed on your own servers. Here, we want to show how you could extend your solutions by using the cloud.

In this chapter, you'll learn the following topics:

- Enhancing your interface layer by using the cloud
- Working with Azure App Service

The business scenario

In Chapter 5, *Integrating NAV Web Services and External Applications*, and Chapter 7, *Programming Universal Windows Apps with NAV and Devices*, we had an in-depth overview on how to implement a real-world ERP solution that involves many technical aspects such as:

- Microsoft Dynamics NAV as the ERP in the corporate LAN
- The ERP must be the master of the business logic
- External applications need to interact with NAV in a standardized way
- The communication protocols between NAV and external applications must be HTTP compliant (with XML and JSON as response protocols)

To satisfy the requirements, we have learned how to develop and deploy an **interface layer** that acts as a *middle tier* between Microsoft Dynamics NAV and external applications:

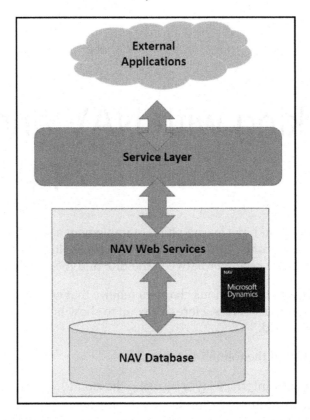

The previously described solutions require that you host the interface layer on your own, and you need to manage deployment, scaling, authorisation, and so on.

Now imagine a requirement where many Microsoft Dynamics NAV instances (physically located in different places around the world) have to interact with an external application. A typical scenario could be the headquarters of a big enterprise company that has a business application (called HQAPP) that needs to collect data about item shipments from the ERP of the subsidiary companies around the world (Microsoft Dynamics NAV):

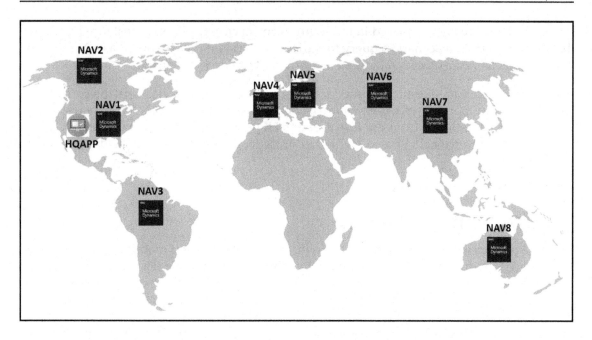

The cloud could help us to efficiently handle this scenario. Why not place the interface layer in the Azure cloud and use the scalability features that Azure offers? The **Azure App Service** could be the solution for this.

We can implement an architecture like the following schema:

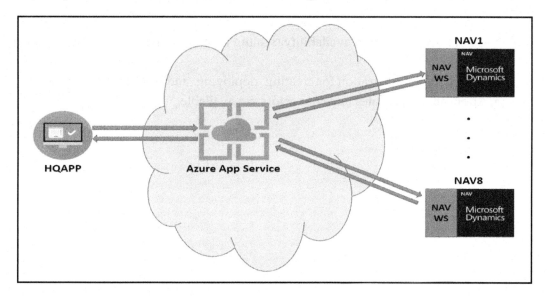

Here, the interface layer is placed in the Azure App Service. Every NAV instance has the business logic (in our scenario a query to retrieve the desired data) exposed as a NAV Web Service. The NAV instance can have an Azure VPN in place for security.

HQAPP performs a request to the interface layer in Azure App Service with the correct parameters. The cloud service then redirects the request to the correct NAV instance and retrieves the data, that in turns are forwarded to HQAPP. Azure App Service can be scaled (manually or automatically) based on the resources requested to perform the data retrieval process.

Azure App Service

Azure App Service is a **PaaS** service for building scalable web and mobile apps, and is able to interact with on-premises or on-cloud data. **Platform as a service** (**PaaS**) is a cloud computing model that delivers applications over the Internet. With Azure App Service you can deploy your application to the cloud, and you can quickly scale your application to handle high traffic loads, and manage traffic and application availability without interacting with the underlying infrastructure. This is the main difference between this and Azure VM, in which you can run a web application on the cloud, but in an **Infrastructure as a Service (IaaS)** environment (you control the infrastructure such as the OS, configuration, installed services, and so on).

Some key features of Azure App Service are as follows:

- Support for many languages and frameworks
- Global scale with high availability (scaling up and out manually or automatically)
- Security
- Visual Studio integration for creating, deploying, and debugging applications
- Application templates and connectors are available

Azure App Service offers different types of resources for running a workload:

- **Web App**: This is used for hosting websites and web applications
- **Mobile App**: This is used for hosting mobile app backends
- **API App**: This is used for hosting RESTful APIs
- **Logic Apps**: This is used for automating business processes across the cloud

Azure App Service has different service plans that you can scale from depending on your requirements in terms of resources:

- **Free**: This is ideal for testing and development, there are no custom domains or SSL, and you can deploy up to 10 apps.
- **Shared**: This is a fixed per-hour charge. Ideal for testing and development, it supports custom domains and SSL, and you can deploy up to 100 apps.
- **Basic**: This is a per-hour charge based on the number of instances. It runs on a dedicated instance. Ideal for low traffic requirements, and you can deploy an unlimited number of apps. It supports only a single SSL certificate per plan (not ideal if you need to connect to an Azure VPN or use deployment slots).
- **Standard**: This is a per-hour charge based on the number of instances. It has full SSL support, up to 10 instances with auto-scaling, automated backups, up to five deployment slots, and is ideal for production environments.
- **Premium**: This is a per-hour charge based on the number of instances. It has up to 50 instances with auto-scaling, up to 20 deployment slots, different daily backups, and a dedicated App Service Environment. It is ideal for enterprise scale and integration.

Regarding the application deployment, Azure App Service supports the concept of the **Deployment Slot** (only on Standard and Premium tiers). Deployment slot is a feature that permits you to have a separate instance of an application that runs on the same VM, but it is isolated from the other deployment slots and production slots active in the App Service.

Let's see how we can create a deployment slot by performing the following few steps:

1. You can create a deployment slot via the Azure portal by selecting your App Service resource and navigating to **Deployment slots** | **Add Slot**:

Always remember that all deployment slots share the same VM instance and the same server resources.

When created, you'll have a URL that refers to the **Deployment slots** instance.

During the development and testing of applications, you can also swap deployment slots. This *swap* operation performs a copy of the currently deployed application code and settings of one deployment slot, and swaps all these things to the new deployment slot.

2. To swap deployment slots, in the Azure Portal simply click on the **Swap** button in the command bar of a deployment slot:

3. In the **Swap** window, select the **Source** and **Destination** slots for the swap operation, and click on the **OK** button:

You can always monitor your App Service's resource usage via the Azure Portal.

Developing the solution

Our solution is essentially composed of two parts as follows:

- The NAV business logic
- The interface layer (cloud service)

In the NAV instances of the subsidiary companies, we need to retrieve the sales shipment's data for every item:

1. To do so, we need to create a `Query` object that reads `Sales Shipment Header` and `Sales Shipment Line`, and exposes them as web services (OData).

   The `Query` object will be designed as follows:

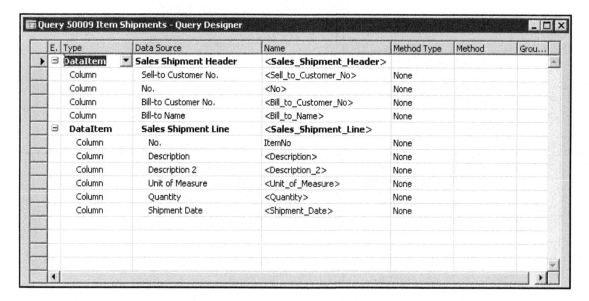

2. For every `Sales Shipment Header` (*table 110*), we retrieve the corresponding `Sales Shipment Lines` (*table 111*) that have `Type = Item`:

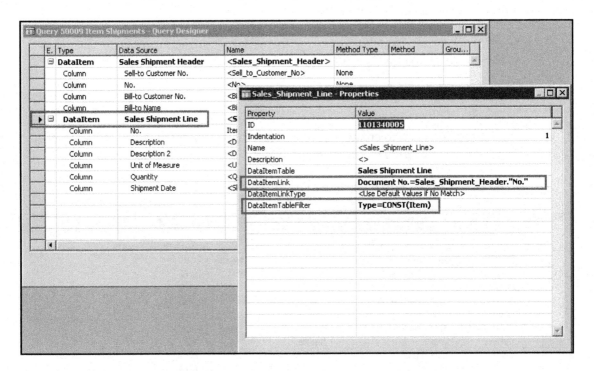

I've changed the name of the `No.` field in `Sales Shipment Line` in the `dataitem` field as `ItemNo` because the default name was used in the `Sales Shipment Header` field as `dataitem`.

3. Compile and save the `Query` object (here I've used `object ID = 50009` and `Name = Item Shipments`).

4. Now we have to publish the `Query` object as a web service in NAV (as described in the first chapters of this book), so open the **Web Services** page and create the following entry:
   - **Object Type**: `Query`
   - **Object ID**: `50009`
   - **Service Name**: `ItemShipments`
   - **Published**: `TRUE`

This is how the screen will appear:

When published, NAV returns the OData service URL.

5. This `Query` object must be published as a web service on every NAV instance in the subsidiary companies.

6. To develop our interface layer, we need firstly to download and install the Azure SDK for Visual Studio from `https://azure.microsoft.com/en-us/downloads/` (if not present). After that, we can create a new Azure Cloud Service project by opening Visual Studio and navigating to **File** | **New** | **Project...**, selecting the **Cloud** templates, and choosing **Azure Cloud Service**:

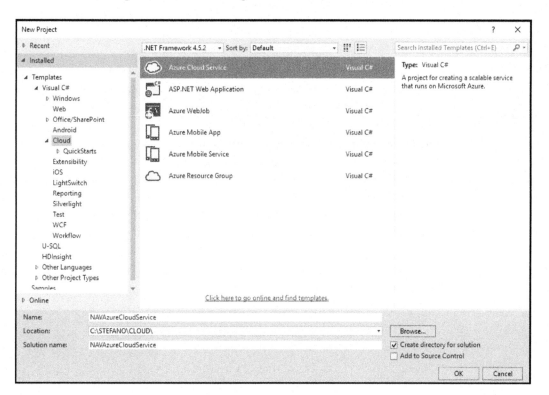

7. Select the project's name (here it is `NAVAzureCloudService`) and click on the **OK** button.

8. After clicking **OK**, Visual Studio asks you to select a service type. Select **WCF Service Web Role**:

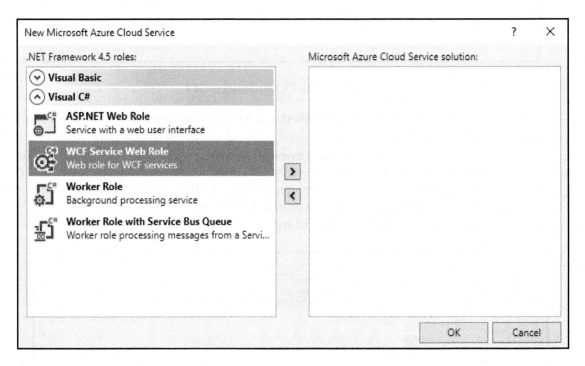

Visual Studio now creates a template for our solution.

9. Now right-click the `NAVAzureCloudService` project and select**New Web Role Project...**:

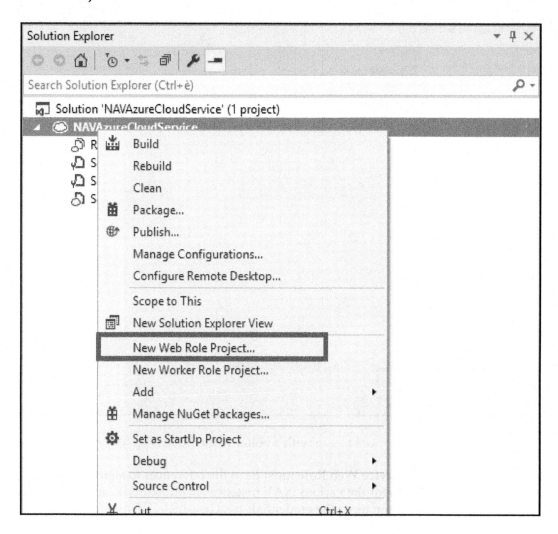

10. In the **Add New .NET Framework 4.5 Role Project** window, select **WCF Service Web Role** and give it a proper name (here it is `WCFServiceWebRoleNAV`):

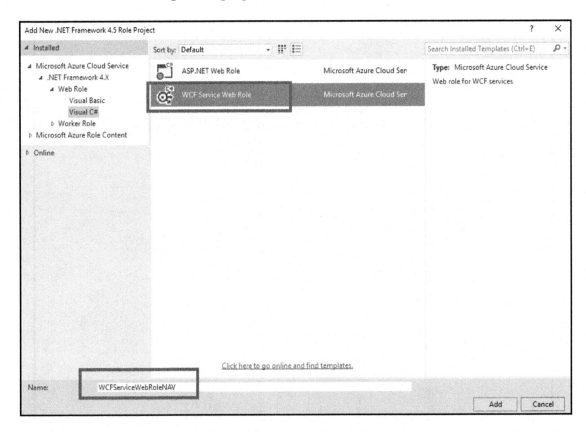

11. Then, rename `Service1.svc` with a better name (here is `NAVService.svc`).

Our **WCF Service Web Role** must have the references to all the NAV web service URLs for the various NAV instances in our scenario and (if we want to use impersonation) the credentials to access the relative NAV instance.

12. You can right-click the `WCFServiceWebRoleNAV` project, select **Properties** and then the **Settings** tab. Here you can add the URL for the various NAV instances and the relative web service credentials. Here is an example for the instance called `NAV1`:

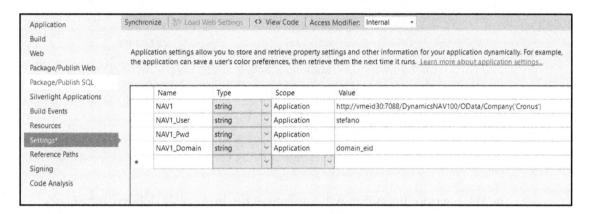

	Name	Type		Scope	Value
	NAV1	string	˅	Application	http://vmeid30:7088/DynamicsNAV100/OData/Company('Cronus')
	NAV1_User	string	˅	Application	stefano
	NAV1_Pwd	string	˅	Application	
	NAV1_Domain	string	˅	Application	domain_eid
*			˅		˅

Application settings (Application, Build, Web, Package/Publish Web, Package/Publish SQL, Silverlight Applications, Build Events, Resources, Settings*, Reference Paths, Signing, Code Analysis) · Synchronize · Load Web Settings · ⟨⟩ View Code · Access Modifier: Internal

Application settings allow you to store and retrieve property settings and other information for your application dynamically. For example, the application can save a user's color preferences, then retrieve them the next time it runs. Learn more about application settings...

The OData URL must be in the `http://servername:port/NAVinstance/OData/Company('company name')` format: By entering these settings, Visual Studio automatically creates an `applicationSettings` section in the `web.config` file for the **WCF Service Web Role** that you can read on code.

Let's start writing our service code.

13. We create a class called `SalesShipment` that defines our data model as follows:

```
public class SalesShipment
    {
        public string No { get; set; }
        public string CustomerNo { get; set; }
        public string ItemNo { get; set; }
        public string Description { get; set; }
        public string Description2 { get; set; }
        public string UoM { get; set; }
        public decimal? Quantity { get; set; }
        public DateTime? ShipmentDate { get; set; }
    }
```

14. As the next step, we have to define our service contract (`interface`). Our service will have a single method to retrieve shipments for a NAV instance and has a shipment date filter. The service contract will be defined as follows:

```
public interface INAVService
    {
        [OperationContract]
        [WebInvoke(Method = "GET", ResponseFormat =
        WebMessageFormat.Xml,
        BodyStyle = WebMessageBodyStyle.Wrapped, UriTemplate =
        "getShipments?instance={NAVInstanceName}&date=
        {shipmentDateFilter}"]
        List<SalesShipment> GetShipments(string
        NAVInstanceName,
        string shipmentDateFilter);
        //Date format parameter: YYYY-MM-DD
    }
```

The WCF service definition will implement the previously defined `interface`:

```
public class NAVService : INAVService
    {
    }
```

The `GetShipments` method is implemented as follows:

```
public List<SalesShipment> GetShipments(string NAVInstanceName,
string shipmentDateFilter)
    {
        try
        {
            DataAccessLayer.DataAccessLayer DAL = new
            DataAccessLayer.DataAccessLayer();
            List<SalesShipment>  list =
            DAL.GetNAVShipments(NAVInstanceName,
            shipmentDateFilter);
            return list;
        }
        catch(Exception ex)
        {
            // You can handle exceptions here...
            throw ex;
        }
    }
```

This method creates an instance of a `DataAccessLayer` class (details later), and calls a method called `GetNAVShipments` by passing `NAVInstanceName` and `shipmentDateFilter`.

15. To call the NAV business logic, we need to have a reference to the NAV OData web service (only to generate a proxy class, as the real service URL will be dynamically called by the code), so right-click your project (`WCFServiceWebRoleNAV`) and navigate to **Add** | **Service Reference...**.

16. In the **Add Service Reference** window, paste the OData URL that comes from NAV and, when the service is discovered, give it a reference name (here it is `NAVODATAWS`):

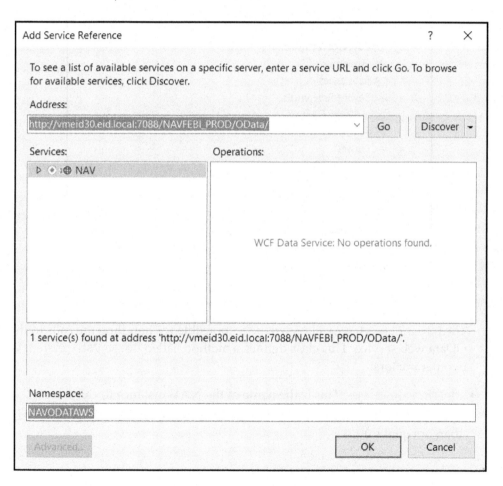

Visual Studio automatically adds a service reference to your project:

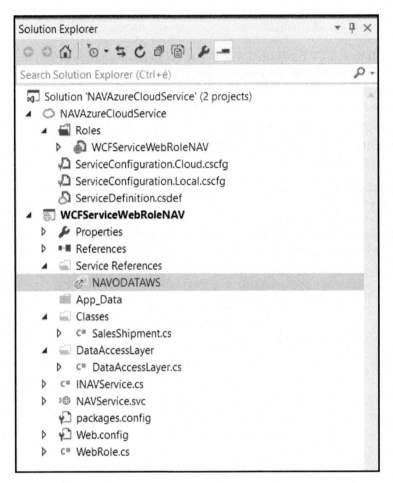

The DataAccessLayer class will be responsible for handling the calls to the NAV OData web service. This class defines a method called GetNAVShipments with two parameters:

- NAVInstanceName: This is the name of the NAV instance to call
- shipmentDateFilter: This is the filter date for the NAV shipment lines (greater than or equal to)

According to NAVInstanceName, the method retrieves from the web.config file
(**appSettings**) the correct NAV OData URL and credentials, calls the NAV query
(by also passing filters), and retrieves the data as a list of SalesShipment records
(our data model).

The DataAccessLayer class is defined as follows:

```
public List<SalesShipment> GetNAVShipments(string
NAVInstanceName, string shipmentDateFilter)
  {
    try
      {
        string URL = Properties.Settings
        .Default[NAVInstanceName].ToString();

        string WS_User = Properties.Settings
        .Default[NAVInstanceName +
        "_User"].ToString();

        string WS_Pwd = Properties.Settings
        .Default[NAVInstanceName +
        "_Pwd"].ToString();

        string WS_Domain = Properties.Settings
        .Default[NAVInstanceName +
        "_Domain"].ToString();

        DataServiceContext context = new
        DataServiceContext(new Uri(URL));

        NAVODATAWS.NAV NAV = new NAVODATAWS.NAV(new Uri(URL));
        NAV.Credentials = new System.Net
        .NetworkCredential(WS_User, WS_Pwd, WS_Domain);

        DataServiceQuery<NAVODATAWS.ItemShipments> q =
        NAV.CreateQuery<NAVODATAWS.ItemShipments>
        ("ItemShipments");

        if (shipmentDateFilter != null)
          {
            string FilterValue = string.Format("Shipment_Date
            ge datetime'{0}'", shipmentDateFilter);
            q = q.AddQueryOption("$filter", FilterValue);
          }

        List<NAVODATAWS.ItemShipments> list =
        q.Execute().ToList();
```

```
            List<SalesShipment> sslist = new List<SalesShipment>
            ();

            foreach (NAVODATAWS.ItemShipments shpt in list)
              {
                 SalesShipment ss = new SalesShipment();
                 ss.No = shpt.No;
                 ss.CustomerNo = shpt.Sell_to_Customer_No;
                 ss.ItemNo = shpt.ItemNo;
                 ss.Description = shpt.Description;
                 ss.Description2 = shpt.Description_2;
                 ss.UoM = shpt.Unit_of_Measure;
                 ss.Quantity = shpt.Quantity;
                 ss.ShipmentDate = shpt.Shipment_Date;
                 sslist.Add(ss);
              }

                 return sslist;
          }
      catch (Exception ex)
            {
                throw ex;
            }
        }
```

The method returns a list of `SalesShipment` objects. It creates an instance of the NAV OData web service, applies the OData filter to the NAV query, reads the results, and loads the list of `SalesShipment` objects.

17. Now you can compile your solution and run it. You can test the solution by launching the project's WCF service URL, which comes from Visual Studio with the right parameters, for example, refer to `http://localhost:64826/NAVService.svc/getShipments?instance=NAV 1 & date=2017-01-01`.

18. You can also test the solution simply by using the Visual Studio **WCF Test Client**:

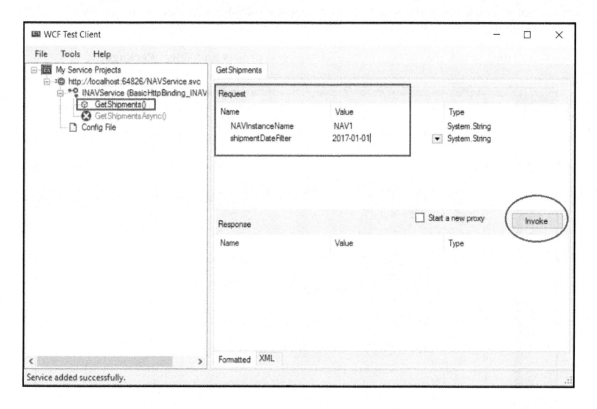

Deployment to Azure App Service

Now that your service is ready, you have to deploy it to the Azure App Service by performing the following steps:

1. Right-click the `NAVAzureCloudService` project and select **Package...**:

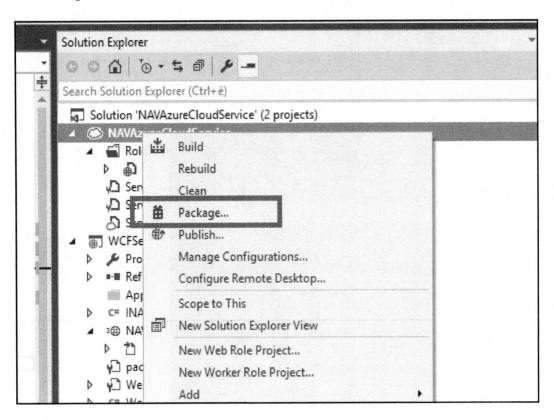

2. In the **Package Azure Application** window, in **Service configuration** select **Cloud** and in **Build configuration** select **Release**, and then click on the **Package** button:

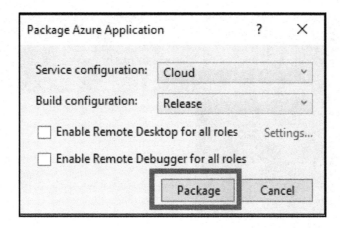

This operation creates two files in the `<YourProjectName>\bin\Release\app.publish` folder:

3. These are the packages that must be deployed to Azure. To do so, you have to log in to the Azure Portal and, from the hub menu on the left, navigate to **Cloud services (classic)** | **Add**:

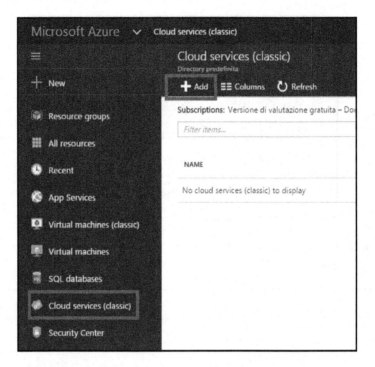

4. In the next window, set your cloud service parameters as follows:
   - **DNS name**: This is the name of your cloud service (yourname.cloudapp.net)
   - **Subscription**: This is the Azure Subscription where the cloud service will be added
   - **Resource group**: This creates a new resource group for your cloud service or you can use an existing one
   - **Location**: This is the Azure location where you wish to add the cloud service

Then click on the **Create** button:

After few seconds, your cloud service will be created and you'll see a confirmation message:

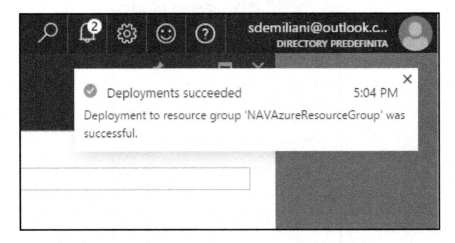

You can see your cloud service in the list of the available cloud services for your subscription:

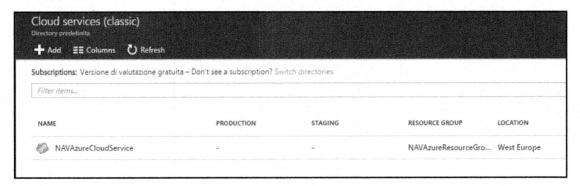

5. Now you have to deploy the previously created cloud packages to the cloud service you just created. On the **Cloud services (classic)** list, click on NAVAzureCloudService, and in the next window select the desired slot (for example, the **Production** slot) and click on **Upload**:

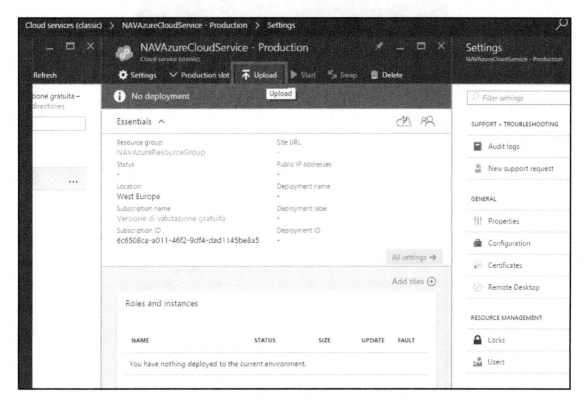

6. In the **Upload a package** window, provide the following parameters:
    - **Storage account**: This is a previously created storage account for your subscription
    - **Deployment label**: This is the name of your deployment
    - **Package**: This selects the .cspkg file previously created for your cloud service

- **Configuration**: This selects the `.cspkg` file previously created for your cloud service configuration:

7. Select **Start deployment** and click on the **OK** button at the bottom to start the process of deployment to Azure.

After few seconds, Azure prompts you with this error message:

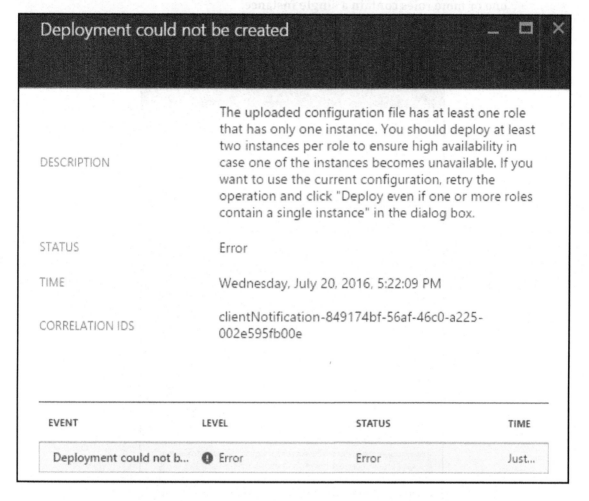

This message occurs because Azure checks for high availability and suggests that you deploy at least two instances per role.

8. To avoid this, in the previous**Upload a package** window, select **Deploy even if one or more roles contain a single instance**:

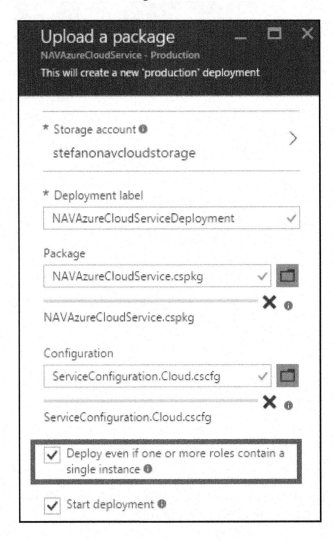

9. Click on the **OK** button and the cloud service deployment on the selected slot will now be performed:

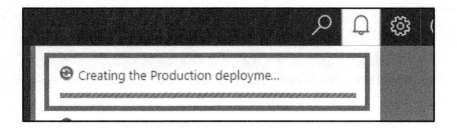

If the deployment finishes successfully, you'll receive a message like the following in the notification area:

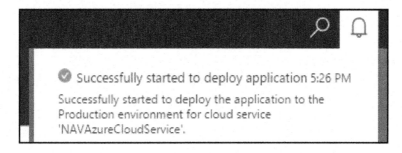

10. Now you can start your cloud service and manage it (swap, scale, and so on) directly from the Azure Portal:

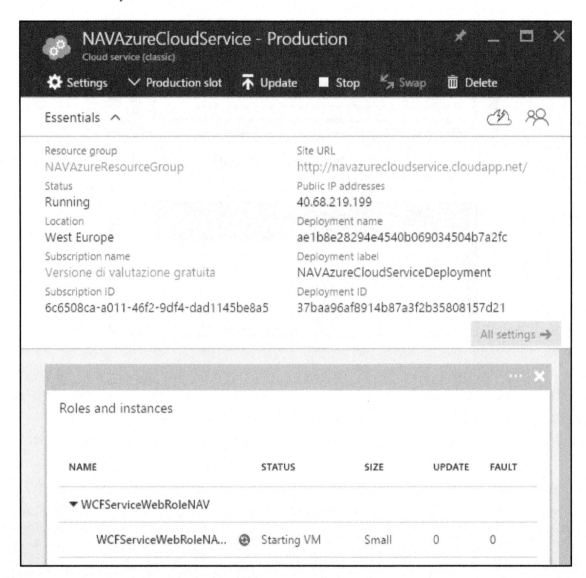

11. When it is running, you can use your deployed service by accessing `http://navazurecloudservice.cloudapp.net/NAVService.svc`:

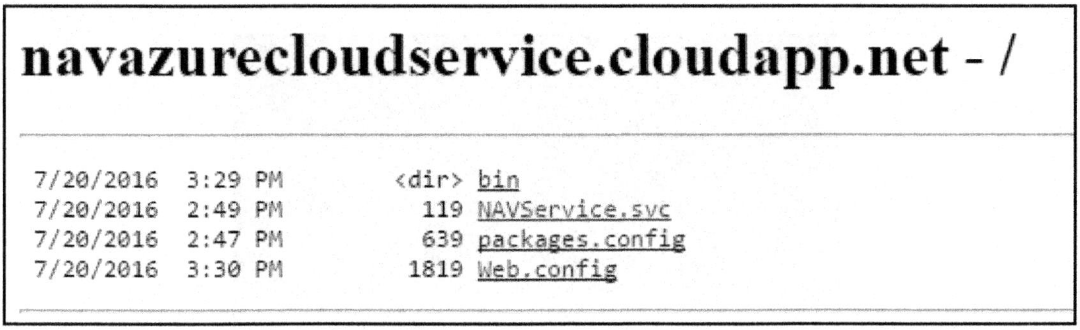

---

navazurecloudservice.cloudapp.net - /

```
7/20/2016  3:29 PM    <dir> bin
7/20/2016  2:49 PM      119 NAVService.svc
7/20/2016  2:47 PM      639 packages.config
7/20/2016  3:30 PM     1819 Web.config
```

This is the URL that the HQAPP in our business scenario has to call to retrieve data from the various NAV instances of the subsidiary companies around the world.

In this way, you have deployed a service to the cloud, you can manage the resources in a central way (via the Azure Portal), and you can easily have different environments by using slots.

12. To scale resources, simply go to the Azure Portal, select your App Service instance, click **All Settings** and then select **Scale Up (App Service Plan)** or **Scale out (App Service Plan)** according to your needs:

Summary

In this chapter, you have learned how to use the cloud to build an enterprise NAV solution architecture. You have learned how to create an integration service between NAV and external clients that has been developed as cloud service, how to deploy it to the Azure cloud, and how to manage the resources associated with the cloud service.

In the next chapter, we'll see a new NAV scenario that we can efficiently handle by using a new Azure cloud service: the **Azure Service Bus**.

10
Implementing a Message-Based Architecture with Azure Service Bus and NAV

In the previous chapter, we learned how to use the Azure App Service to host an integration service for a Microsoft Dynamics NAV enterprise architecture in the cloud.

In this chapter, we'll explore a new business scenario where a new Azure cloud service will be used to implement a wide distributed message-based architecture with NAV. In this chapter, you'll learn about the following topics:

- An overview of Azure Service Bus
- Integrating NAV with Azure Service Bus
- Handling distributed messages to exchange information between ERP instances

The business scenario

In this business scenario, a retail company manages many shop centers around the world. The retail company (here called RC) has Microsoft Dynamics NAV as the main ERP. The shop centers (*SC1 .. SCn*) are geographically distributed in different countries and have different local applications for collecting sales orders. Periodically during the day, the shop centers have to transmit the orders to the retail company for handling:

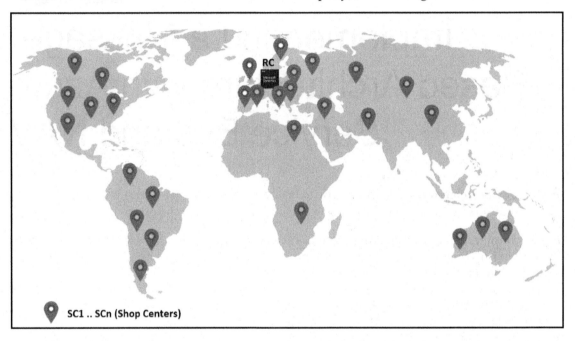

Transmitting orders to the retail company can be very time-consuming (a shop center might collect a large number of orders during the day) and this data transaction must be reliable (we don't want to miss orders).

The transmitted sales orders must be processed one-by-one by the central retail company. The retail company's ERP (Microsoft Dynamics NAV) must be able to receive all orders from the different shop centers and from different countries in a reliable way without impacting on the ERP performance.

How can we handle this scenario?

We have some main aspects that impact on our solution architecture:

- The shop centers are geographically distributed
- The shop centers have different applications for collecting orders, so we need a common interface for data transmission
- The main ERP (Microsoft Dynamics NAV) must not be directly involved in receiving large amounts of data in different periods of the day (we don't want to impact ERP performance)
- Data transmission must be secure
- Orders must be processed as **first-in-first-out** (**FIFO**) in order to guarantee an item's availability

To satisfy these needs, the shop centers must have a common interface exposed to the Internet for transmitting the orders. The orders must not be directly transmitted to the ERP but they must be placed in a queue for handling. The queue will then be processed by the ERP when needed.

The Azure cloud can help us to efficiently solve the problem here. We can implement an interface layer that permits order transmission and hosts this in the cloud as described in the previous chapter. This service will collect orders from the different shop centers and will use the Azure Service Bus cloud service to handle the order processing.

Azure Service Bus is a PaaS service offered by the Azure platform that helps in sharing data between decoupled systems by using messaging and queues. In the next section, we will give an in-depth overview of this service.

In our solution schema, orders are transmitted from the shop centers to our integration service and then stored into an Azure Service Bus queue. Microsoft Dynamics NAV can then call our integration service to handle the orders (when needed) by extracting messages from Azure Service Bus and processing them accordingly. By using Microsoft Azure, we can monitor data transmission and we can scale resources as needed.

This is the schema for the previously described architecture:

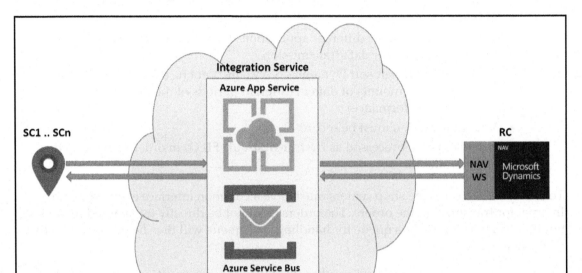

An overview of the Azure Service Bus

Azure Service Bus is a multitenant cloud service for connecting distributed applications by providing different types of communication mechanism. Applications can run on-cloud or they can run on-premise.

When using Azure Service Bus, you create a namespace and then you define the communication rules within that namespace by using different communication mechanisms as follows:

- **Queues**: This is a one-directional communication between apps. The queue stores messages received from applications until another application receives them.
- **Topics**: This is a one-directional communication based on subscriptions.
- **Relays**: This is a bi-directional communication. Here the message is not stored but is directly passed to the destination application.

Queues

When using queues, an application (sender) sends a message to a Service Bus queue and a receiver application reads the message from that queue at a later time (FIFO).

Each message sent to the queue is composed of a set of properties and a message body (binary):

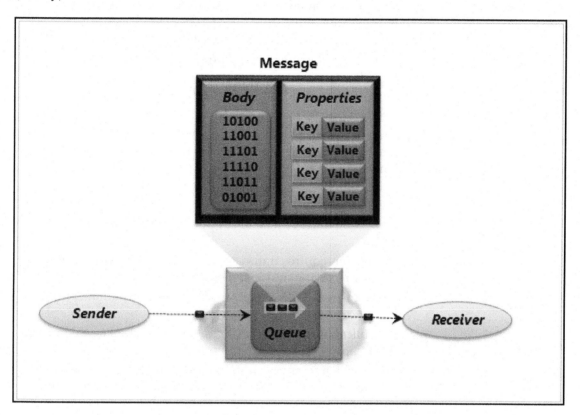

The receiver application can read a message in two different ways as follows:

- It can read and remove the message from the queue and immediately delete it (ReceiveAndDelete mode).
- It can read and remove the message from the queue without immediately deleting it. In this case, the message will be invisible to other receivers and locked. If the receiver processes it correctly, the message is deleted. If the receiver does not process the message correctly, the message is unlocked and it will be available for other apps (PeekLock mode).

Queues are useful when you need a communication between apps that cannot run at the same time or cannot process a message immediately (temporal decoupling).

It's important to note that the Azure platform provides two queuing solutions for managing asynchronous communication between applications: Azure Queues and Azure Service Bus Queues. These are Microsoft's recommendations regarding the two types of queue:

- Azure Queues should be used in the following scenarios:
    - Your application must store over 80 GB of messages in a queue, where the messages have a lifetime shorter than 7 days
    - Your application wants to track progress for processing a message inside of the queue
    - You require server-side logs of all of the transactions executed against your queues
- Service Bus Queues should be used in the following scenarios:
    - Your solution must be able to receive messages without having to poll the queue
    - Your solution requires the queue to provide a guaranteed FIFO ordered delivery
    - Your solution must be able to support automatic duplicate detection
    - Your solution requires transactional behavior and atomicity when sending or receiving multiple messages from a queue
    - The **time-to-live** (TTL) characteristic of the application-specific workload can exceed the 7-day period
    - Your application handles messages that can exceed 64 KB but will not likely approach the 256 KB limit
    - You deal with a requirement to provide a role-based access model to the queues, and different rights/permissions for senders and receivers
    - Your queue size will not grow larger than 80 GB
    - You require full integration with the **Windows Communication Foundation (WCF)** communication stack in the .NET Framework

More information about the different queue types can be found at
`https://docs.microsoft.com/en-us/azure/service-bus-messaging/ser`
`vice-bus-azure-and-service-bus-queues-compared-contrasted.`

Topics

Topics are used to implement a publish-and-subscribe pattern (one-to-many communication). When using topics, a sender application submits a message to a Service Bus topic pretty much as it does to a queue. The difference is that topics enable the receiving applications to create their own subscriptions by using filters (the receiver application will see only messages that match its subscription):

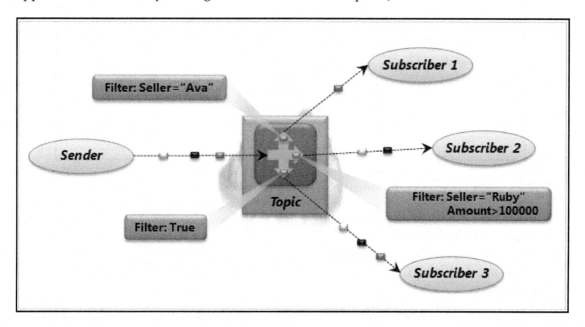

A topic subscription is like a *virtual queue* where every subscriber receives messages according to a filter. In the preceding example, we have a **Sender** application and three subscribers for a topic with a proper filter:

- **Subscriber 1**: It receives only the messages where the message property `Seller` has the value `Ava`
- **Subscriber 2**: It receives only the messages where the message property `Seller` has the value `Ruby` and the property `Amount` has a value greater than `1000`
- **Subscriber 3**: It has the filter set to `TRUE`, so it receives all messages sent to the Service Bus

Relays

Relays permit you to have a synchronous bi-directional communication between applications (while the previously described queue and topics permit only communication from senders to receivers):

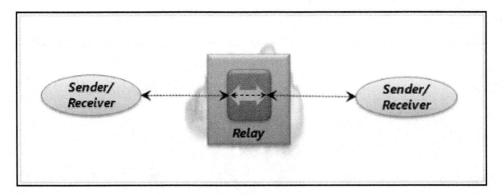

Relays are useful when you require direct communication between applications; for example, when you have a WCF service hosted in your corporate network and you need to expose it to cloud applications without direct access to your corporate LAN. Essentially, the WCF service, configured to use an Azure Service Bus relay, will connect to Azure using a TCP connection. Then other external applications can connect to the Azure Service Bus relay endpoint, and Service Bus relay handles tunneling the communications through the TCP connection.

Azure Service Bus is available in three different tiers (**Basic**, **Standard**, and **Premium**) with different features and costs. You can choose a particular service tier for each Service Bus namespace you want to create and this tier selection applies to all entities created in that namespace.

> For more information about Azure Service Bus pricing, you can refer to
> https://azure.microsoft.com/pricing/details/service-bus/.

Developing the solution

To develop our solution architecture, we have to perform the following main tasks:

1. Configure Azure Service Bus.

2. Create an interface for order transmission from the shop center application to the Azure Service Bus.

3. Create an interface that retrieves orders from Azure Service Bus and saves them into the NAV ERP.

We will cover these steps in detail.

Configuring Azure Service Bus

Let's learn how we can configure Azure Service Bus by performing the following steps:

1. To create an instance of Azure Service Bus, log in to the Azure Portal, navigate to **New** I **Enterprise Integration** I **Service Bus** (or simply search for Service Bus by using the search box):

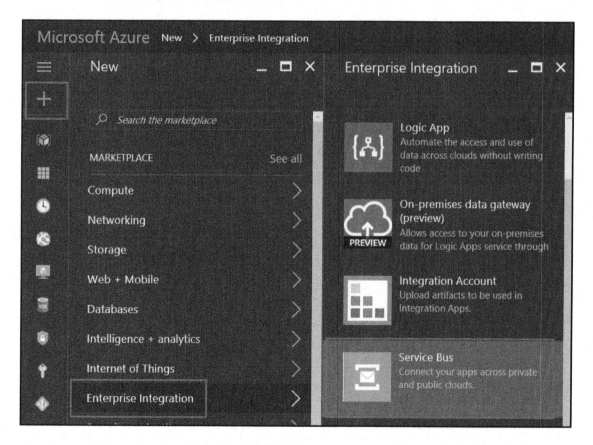

2. In the **Create namespace** window, enter a namespace name (a namespace provides a scoping container for addressing **Service Bus** resources within your application and the name must be unique).

3. After that, select the Azure subscription under **Subscription** and the **Resource group** option (or create a new one), **Pricing tier**, and **Location** where you want to create your Service Bus instance, and click on the **Create** button:

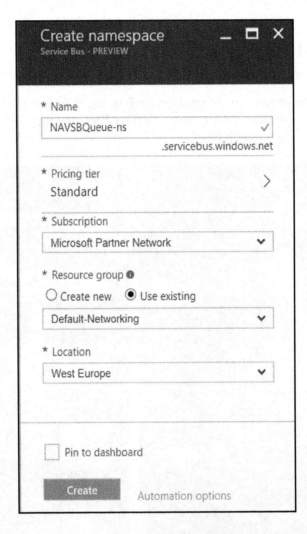

4. When the namespace is provisioned, select the created Service Bus namespace instance, then select **Queues**, and click on the **Queue** tab:

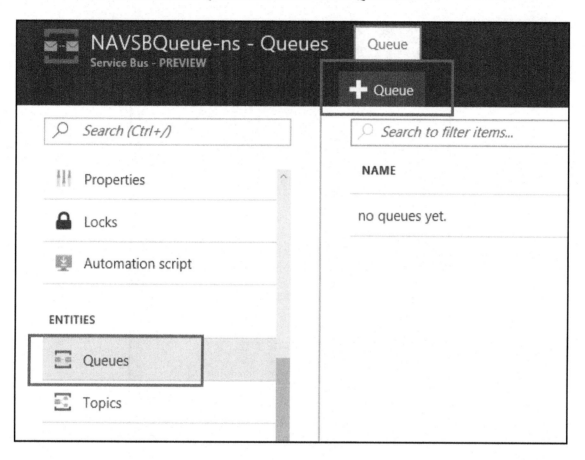

5. In the **Create queue** window, select the name of your Service Bus queue and leave the other parameters as default, then click on the **Create** button:

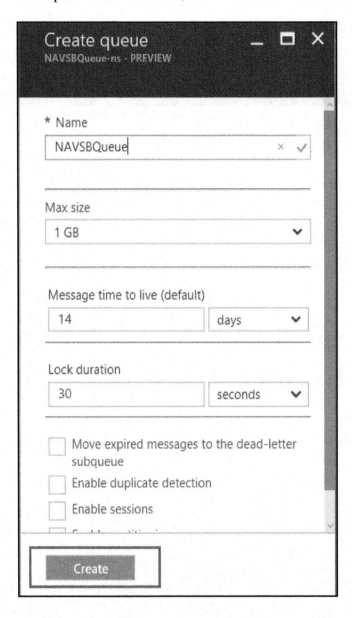

6. When the Service Bus queue is created, you can see its status in the Queue list:

7. By selecting the desired queue, you can monitor messages on it:

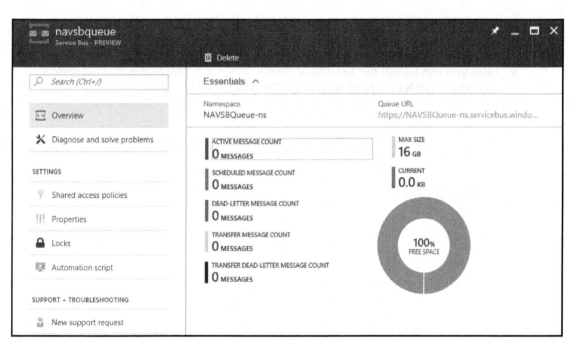

8. To start creating an application that interacts with your new Service Bus queue, you need to have the access key (connection string) to your Service Bus instance. Select your Service Bus namespace, click on **Shared access policies**, and select **RootManageSharedAccessKey**:

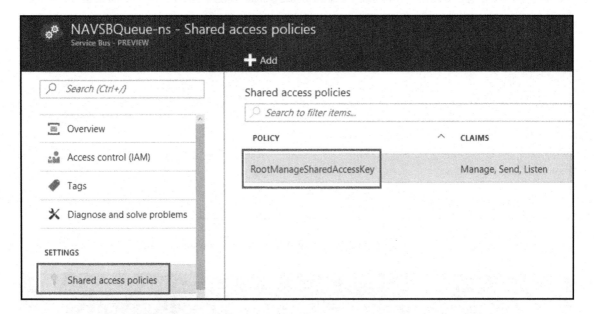

9. Here you can see all the keys to access your Service Bus instance. You need to copy the **CONNECTION STRING -PRIMARY KEY** value:

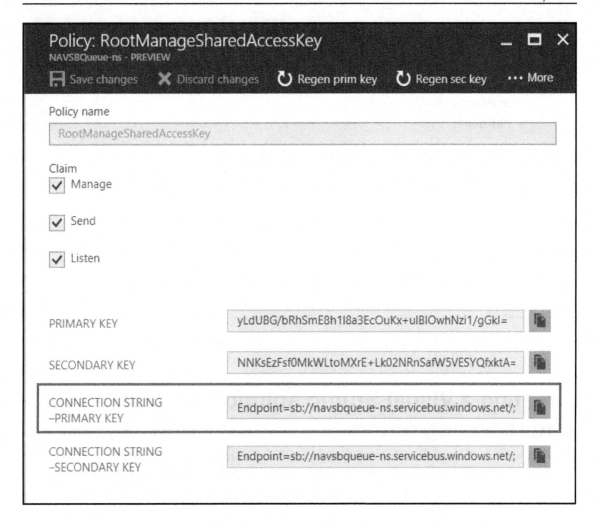

Publishing NAV business logic for sales orders

The headquarters' Microsoft Dynamics NAV instance has to publish the business logic for creating a sales order directly into the ERP itself.

When it comes to publishing the NAV business logic as a web service, we have seen many different practices in the course of this book. Here, we decide to directly publish the **SalesOrder** page as a web service.

Open the NAV **Web Services** page and create this entry:

- **Object Type**: Page
- **Object ID**: 42
- **Service Name**: SalesOrder
- **Published**: TRUE

When published, NAV gives you the SOAP and OData URLs:

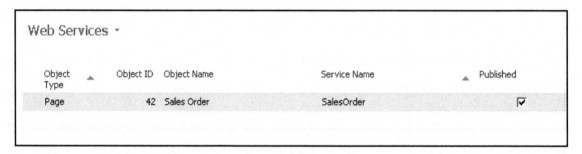

We will use the SOAP URL in our Visual Studio application.

Creating a Visual Studio solution for transmitting and receiving orders

Now that Azure Service Bus is created and published to the cloud and the NAV business logic is published, we can start creating the application code for the following:

- Sending a sales order to the Service Bus queue
- Retrieving a sales order from the Service Bus queue

Here, we create a console application. The console application will have a startup parameter for sending and retrieving orders and it could be scheduled to execute at a predefined interval (with Windows Task Scheduler). Obviously, you could implement something different as described in this book (for example, a web service) but the core code will be the same.

Let's create a Visual Studio solution for transmitting and receiving orders by performing the following steps:

1. Open Visual Studio and navigate to **New** | **Project...** | **Console Application**. Give an appropriate name for your solution and click **OK**:

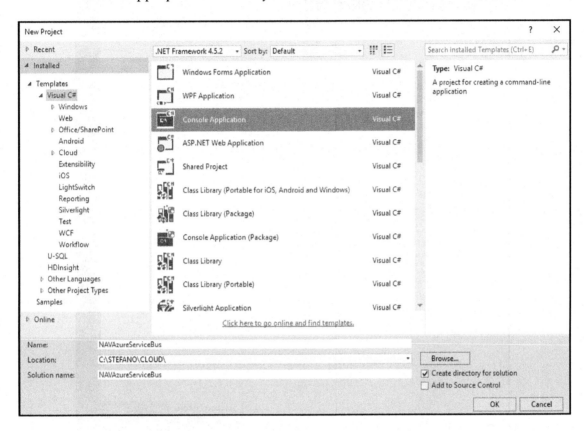

2. To use Azure Service Bus, you need to add the Service Bus package to your project. Right-click on your project and select**Manage NuGet Packages...**:

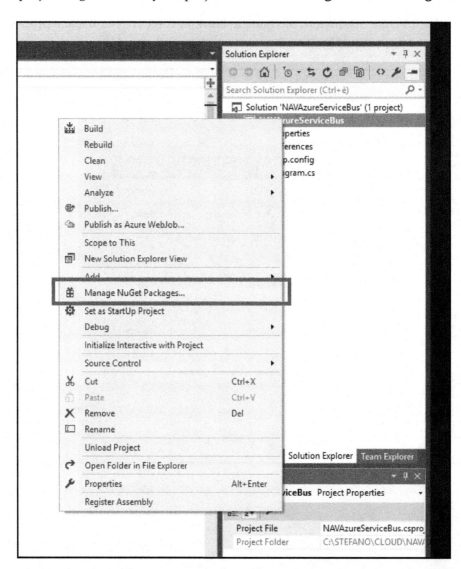

3. In the **Package Manager**, in the search box type `azure service bus`, select the `WindowsAzure.ServiceBus` package, and click **Install**:

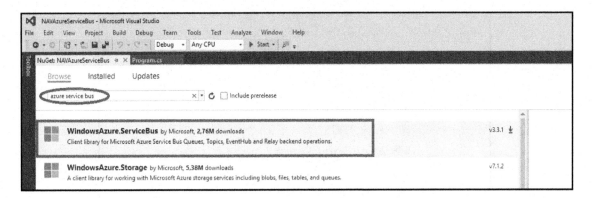

4. Visual Studio will prompt you with an alert message. Click **OK**:

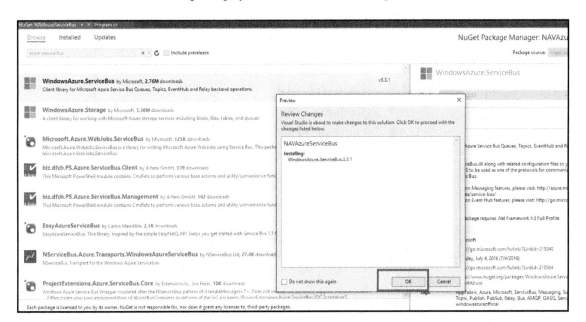

5. Now on your **Solution Explorer**, you'll see a reference to the assembly, `Microsoft.ServiceBus`:

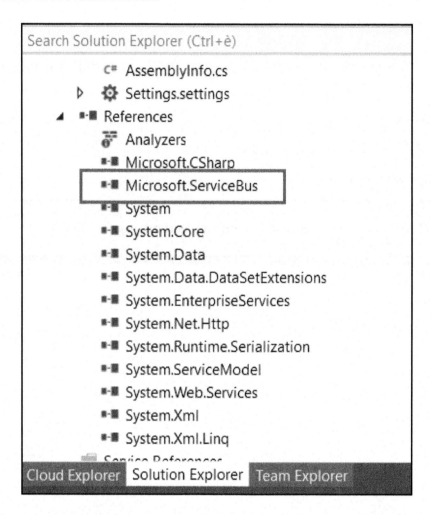

6. In your Visual Studio code, add a reference to
`Microsoft.ServiceBus.Messaging`:

Now we're ready to start coding.

The application that runs on the distributed shop centers has to pull the orders and transmit them to the Azure Service Bus queue.

7. Let's define a class that represents a sales order that coming from the different shop centers:

```
[DataContract]
class ShopSalesOrder
  {
     [DataMember]
     public string OrderNo { get; set; }

     [DataMember]
     public string CustomerNo { get; set; }

     [DataMember]
     public DateTime OrderDate { get; set; }

     [DataMember]
```

```
        public List<ShopSalesOrderLine> Lines { get; set; }
    }

[DataContract]
class ShopSalesOrderLine
    {
        [DataMember]
        public int RowNo { get; set; }

        [DataMember]
        public string ItemNo { get; set; }

        [DataMember]
        public decimal Quantity { get; set; }
    }
```

Here, we have defined a `ShopSalesOrder` class that represents orders that must be transmitted to the Azure Service Bus and then received from NAV. The `ShopSalesOrder` class contains a list of `ShopSalesOrderLine` objects that represents the order lines.

8. Then we define a `ShopAppInterface` class that has a method for retrieving a sales order from a specific shop center application (out of scope here):

```
class ShopAppInterface
    {
        public ShopSalesOrder GetNAVOrder()
        {
            //Retrieves order from the shop center application
            (specific code goes here...
        }
    }
```

9. In our console application (`Program.cs` file), we need to store the Azure Service Bus connection string and the queue name previously retrieved via the Azure Portal. Here, we have used two global variables called `ServiceBusConnectionString` and `QueueName` respectively (you can store these values in the `app.config` file).

Our `Main()` function will be as follows:

```
class Program
    {
    static string ServiceBusConnectionString =
    "Endpoint=sb://navsbqueue-
    ns.servicebus.windows.net/;
    SharedAccessKeyName=RootManageSharedAccessKey;
    SharedAccessKey=GD2cxyENOHyATwzFVAK0bF9AVJjDB+
    n42i6wZFkVhXI=";

        static string QueueName = "NAVSBQueue";
        static void Main(string[] args)
            {
                if (args.Length != 1)
                {
                        Console.WriteLine("-----------------------
                        -------------------");
                        Console.WriteLine(" Parameters:");
                        Console.WriteLine("   S: send orders to
                        Azure
                        Service Bus");
                        Console.WriteLine("   R: receive orders
                        from Azure Service Bus");
                        Console.WriteLine("-----------------------
                        --------------------");
                        return;
                }

            string OperationType = args[0].ToUpper();

            switch(OperationType)
                {
                    case "S":
                    SendOrders();
                    break;
                    case "R":
                    ReceiveOrders();
                    break;
                }

                    Console.ReadLine();
            }
        }
```

10. When the startup parameter is S, the `SendOrders` method is called. This method is implemented as follows:

```
private static void SendOrders()
    {
        Console.WriteLine("\nSending message to Azure Service Bus
        Queue...");
        try
          {
            ShopAppInterface SI = new ShopAppInterface();
            ShopSalesOrder order = SI.GetNAVOrder();

            var client =
            QueueClient.CreateFromConnectionString
            (ServiceBusConnectionString, QueueName);

            BrokeredMessage message = new BrokeredMessage(order,
            new
            DataContractSerializer(typeof(ShopSalesOrder)));

            client.Send(message);
          }
        catch(Exception ex)
          {
            //Handle exception here...
          }
    }
```

11. In this method, we create an instance of the `ShopAppInterface` class and we call the `GetNAVOrder` method for retrieving a sales order to transmit.

12. Then, we create an instance of the Azure Service Bus queue (by using a connection string and queue name). We create `BrokeredMessage` by passing the `ShopSalesOrder` object to be transmitted in the message (a `BrokeredMessage` object represents the unit of communication between Service Bus clients), and we send the message to the Service Bus queue.

When the console application startup parameter is R, the `ReceiveOrders` method is called. This method is defined as follows:

```
private static void ReceiveOrders()
    {
        Console.WriteLine("\nReceiving message from Azure Service
        Bus Queue...");
        try
          {
            var client =
```

```
QueueClient.CreateFromConnectionString
(ServiceBusConnectionString, QueueName);
while (true)
    {
    try
        {
        //receive messages from Queue
        BrokeredMessage message =
        Client.Receive(TimeSpan.FromSeconds(5));
        if (message != null)
            { //Retrieves the order object
        Console.WriteLine(string.Format("Message
        received: Id = {0} " message.MessageId));
        ShopSalesOrder orderReceived =
        message.GetBody<ShopSalesOrder>(new
        DataContractSerializer(typeof
        (ShopSalesOrder)));

        //Send the order to NAV
        NAVInterface NAV = new NAVInterface();
        NAV.CreateNAVSalesOrder(orderReceived);

                //Further custom message
                 processing could
                 go here...
                 message.Complete();
            }
          else
            {
            //No more messages in the queue
            break;
            }
        }
        catch (MessagingException e)
          {
            if (!e.IsTransient)
             {
                Console.WriteLine(e.Message);
                throw;
             }
            else
             {
                HandleTransientErrors(e);
             }
          }
      }
    }
catch(Exception ex)
```

```
        {
            //Handle exception here...
        }
    }
```

13. Here, a reference to the Azure Service Bus queue is created. Then, in an infinite loop, we call the `Receive` method of the `QueueClient` class to receive a message from the queue (a `BrokeredMessage` object).

14. When a message is returned, its body content is deserialized by calling the `GetBody` method and passing the specified object type:

```
ShopSalesOrder orderReceived = message.GetBody<ShopSalesOrder>
(new DataContractSerializer(typeof(ShopSalesOrder)));
```

15. Now that a `ShopSalesOrder` object is retrieved from the Service Bus queue, an instance of the `NAVInterface` class is created and the `CreateNAVSalesOrder` method is called by passing the retrieved `ShopSalesOrder` object (the implementation is detailed later).

    If the `CreateNAVSalesOrder` method is processed correctly (the order is created in NAV), the `Complete()` method of the `BrokeredMessage` class is called. This method completes the receive operation of a message and indicates that this message should be marked as processed and deleted from the queue.

    When all messages are retrieved from the Azure Service Bus queue, the program exits from the loop and the process is completed.

16. To save the retrieved order object from Azure Service Bus to NAV, we need to add a reference to the NAV web service previously published (the **SalesOrder** page).

17. Right-click on your project, navigate to **Add | Service References**, click on **Advanced**, and select **Add Web Reference**. In the **Add Web Reference** window, paste the SOAP URL retrieved from NAV, give it an appropriate name, and click **Add Reference**:

Our `NAVInterface` class will be defined as follows:

```
class NAVInterface
    {
        public void CreateNAVSalesOrder(ShopSalesOrder
        ExternalOrder)
```

```
{
    try
    {
        //Here we have to call our NAV web service for
        creating a Sales Order
        //Web Service instantiation
        SalesOrder_Service ws = new
        SalesOrder_Service();
        ws.Url = Properties.Settings.Default.NAVWSURL;
        ws.UseDefaultCredentials = true;

        //Create the Sales Header
        SalesOrder order = new SalesOrder();
        ws.Create(ref order);

        //Here the Sales Order is created and we have
        the order no.
        //Update the Sales Header with details
        order.Sell_to_Customer_No =
        ExternalOrder.CustomerNo;
        order.Order_Date = ExternalOrder.OrderDate;

        int _rows = 0;
        if (ExternalOrder.Lines != null)
            {
                _rows = ExternalOrder.Lines.Count();
            }

        if (_rows > 0)
            {
                //Create the Sales Lines array and
                initialize the lines
                order.SalesLines = new
                Sales_Order_Line[_rows];
                for (int i = 0; i < _rows; i++)
                  {
                      order.SalesLines[i] = new
                      Sales_Order_Line();
                  }
            }

      ws.Update(ref order);

        //Loads the data into the Lines
        if (_rows > 0)
            {
                int rowindex = 0;
                foreach(ShopSalesOrderLine _shopOrderLine
```

```
in ExternalOrder.Lines)
    {
        Sales_Order_Line line =
        order.SalesLines[rowindex];
        line.Type =
        NAVSalesOrderWS.Type.Item;
        line.No = _shopOrderLine.ItemNo;
        line.Quantity =
        _shopOrderLine.Quantity;
        rowindex++;
    }

    //Update the order lines with all the
    informations
    ws.Update(ref order);
}
    Console.WriteLine("Order {0} created
    successfully.", order.No);
}
catch(Exception)
    {
        //Handle exceptions here...
    }
}


}
```

18. Here, we create an instance of the NAV web service. Then we create the Sales Order Header and Lines according to the object passed in as input to our method (the external order that comes from the Service Bus queue). At the end of this method, the sales order is created in NAV with all the details that come from the Service Bus.

Testing the application

We can now run our project with Visual Studio and set the startup parameters to test the application on sending an order to the Azure Service Bus queue and on retrieving the order from the queue and saving it on NAV.

If we start the console application with s as the startup parameter, a message is sent to our Service Bus queue. The body of this message contains the serialized order object.

If you go to the Azure Portal and check the Service Bus queue, you can see that now the **QUEUE LENGTH** is equal to **1**:

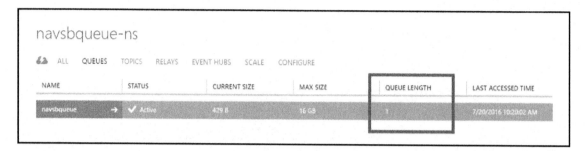

If you send another message to the queue, the **QUEUE LENGTH** increases again by **1** and you can monitor the incoming message's arrival time:

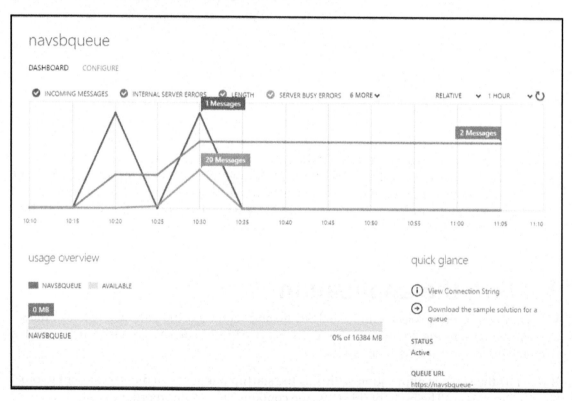

If now you run the application by passing R as the startup parameter (to retrieve a message from the Service Bus queue), the application retrieves the first message to have arrived at the queue, extracts the body, and deserializes it:

```
Console.WriteLine("\nReceiving message from Queue...");

while (true)
{
    try
    {
        //receive messages from Queue
        message = client.Receive(TimeSpan.FromSeconds(5));

        if (message != null)
        {
            Console.WriteLine(string.Format("Message received: Id = {0} ", message.MessageId));
            Classes.NAVOrder orderReceived = message.GetBody<Classes.NAVOrder>(new DataContractSerializer(typeof(Classes.NAVOrder)));
            // Further custom messa      orderReceived {NAVAzureServiceBus.Classes.NAVOrder}
            message.Complete();         CustomerNo  Q  "C0001"
        }                               Lines        Count = 2
        else                            OrderDate    {20/07/2016 11:37:42}
        {                               OrderNo    Q  "OV1"
            //no more messages in the queue
```

The order is now saved on NAV for processing.

Summary

In this chapter, we have seen how we can implement a solution architecture based on messaging that permits you to integrate Microsoft Dynamics NAV with different geographically distributed applications that collect sales orders. Here, we have learned how to configure Azure Service Bus, how to send and retrieve a message from a Service Bus queue, and how to use Azure Service Bus in a business scenario in order to guarantee reliable transactions and FIFO processing of orders.

After reading this book, you should have a complete overview on how you can efficiently handle different business scenario which require integrating Microsoft Dynamics NAV with external applications that can be on your network or geographically distributed. You've learned the following topics:

- Using native Microsoft Dynamics NAV web services tp expose the ERP business logic
- Creating integration layers for decoupling the ERP from the external world
- Creating integration layers that make communication between the ERP and the external applications *open* (XML, JSON, and REST services)
- A positive impact from cloud adoption on your Microsoft Dynamics NAV architecture
- Using cloud services to handle many business scenarios that require distributed applications and extreme scalability

The message I want to leave here is clear: if you know Microsoft Dynamics NAV and the C/AL language, not all tasks that you can have when implementing a NAV solution must necessarily be solved with C/AL! There's a world of technology outside the NAV box. Leave C/AL to handle internal business tasks and start to learn more efficient ways to handle all integrations. Your final solution will benefit a lot from this.

Index